Society of the
Companions of the Holy Cross
Adelynrood • August 1934

The Vocation of Companionship

An Organizational History

of the Society of the Companions of the Holy Cross

from the 1937 death of Founder Emily M. Morgan

through its 100th Anniversary, 1984

Joanna Bowen Gillespie
2006

published for

The Society of the Companions of the Holy Cross
Adelynrood
46 Elm Street
Byfield, MA 01922-2812
ISBN 0-7414-3671-X

Library of Congress Cataloging-in-Publication Data
Gillespie, Joanna Bowen, 1929-
    The vocation of companionship : an organizational history of the Society of the Companions of the Holy Cross from the 1937 death of Founder Emily M. Morgan through its 100th anniversary, 1984 / Joanna Bowen Gillespie.
    Byfield, MA : Society of the Companions of the Holy Cross, 2006.
    Includes bibliographical references and index.
        1. Morgan, Emily M. 2. Society of the Companions of the Holy Cross—History. 3. Episcopalian women—Massachusetts—Societies, etc. 4. Episcopalians—Massachusetts—Societies, etc. 5. Intercessory prayer.

Book design and cover design by Eric Galbreath.

ISBN 0-7414-3671-X

Published by

PUBLISHING.COM

1094 New DeHaven Street, Suite 100
West Conshohocken, PA 19428-2713
Info@buybooksontheweb.com
www.buybooksontheweb.com
Toll-free (877) BUY BOOK
Local Phone (610) 941-9999
Fax (610) 941-9959

Printed in the United States of America.
Printed on recycled Paper.
Published October 2006.

To the ever-renewing procession
of women called to Companionship
who each have a share
in "carrying the Society into the future."

(p. xxx, EMM's benediction)

Contents

Preface xi

Monologue—In Emily Morgan's Own Voice xxi

Chapter 1
The SCHC in Church and National History 1

Chapter 2
1937-1942—EMM's death, and "A time of transition" 27

Chapter 3
Vida Scudder 1861–1954—The Other Founder 47

Chapter 4
SCHC 1941–1954 73

Chapter 5
SCHC 1955–1964 119

Chapter 6
SCHC 1965–1974 171

Chapter 7
1975–1984 SCHC's 100th Birthday 229

Epilogue 269

Author's Notes 273

Sources 281

Index of Names 287

Index of Chronology 288

Index of Topics 289

Familiar, longstanding art objects at Adelynrood: (clockwise from top) detail of Della Robbia virgin and child which hangs at the front stair landing; Della Robbia virgin and child wall ornament; statue of St. Francis in the garden near the chapel.

Preface

I entered SCHC as a Probationer in 1989, almost immediately falling in love with our amazing history. At the time I was beginning to amass materials for the biography of my 18th c. American woman and patriot, *The Life and Times of Martha Laurens Ramsay 1759-1811* (published 2001). The lure of historical detective work was already in my bones; and our Society enjoys a rich archive of historical materials—printed or handwritten, photos, transcribed oral histories. Further, since history is a *highly selective narrative* (dictionary characterization!) what you see here is what caught my eye and heart out of the acres of words, facts and photos. [Other eyes of course might be drawn to other prayers, other events, other Companion papers to cite and excerpt.] My assignment was to discern our organization's evolution after the 1937 death of Founder Emily Malbone Morgan, through its 1974 crisis, up to its 100th birthday. My hope is that my Companions may find the report of my quest interesting and life-giving. It has been for me.

The Society of the Companions of the Holy Cross in 1937

Today the question of our Society's survival may seem unnecessary, even retrogressive. Here I plead for empathy with those first-half-century Companions. The more time I have spent with Emily Morgan's words and person, the more I too understand her elemental magnetism and wisdom; it makes me in the early 21st c. long to see our times through her eyes, pray through a soul as great as hers. No wonder her death raised anxieties among the Companions she left behind: could a Society that had been born of her inspiration and nursed into a real organization continue <u>without</u> her? Could her "creature," (as Companions then described the Society in their admiring thanksgivings) survive? Should it?

We today rejoice that those foremothers were able to keep alive the miraculous Companionly bond of intercessory praying that she envisioned, increasing the organizational underpinnings to accomplish that. Emily Morgan's legacy of willing identification with the poor despite her privileged background still has the power to shock us; the poverty and suffering she lamented and fought is still with us. Her expressions, even in their Victorian diction, haven't lost their power to confront, challenge, and goad us to action. During her time amongst Companions she indeed always had "the last word" but out of awe, respect, and thankfulness, not obligation. That indelible bond of spiritual Companionship ennobles us still. No wonder there was an anxious scramble for the Society's self-definition, identity, and direction in those first years after 1937.

The portrait of this post-EMM Society comes to us through women's voices—prayerful, passionate, sometimes "bookish" about social problems. Companions don't engage in genuine ancestor worship, yet our relationship with her through generations of Sponsors creates a powerful, almost mystical link. It engenders "a way of life," in Companion-in-Charge [hereafter C-in-C] Virginia Huntington's 1957 phrase. I have come to see it as a special "cloud of witnesses" into which one grows; it has become a living component of my own spiritual companionship with God and Jesus.

The Great Depression

I began my serious focus on SCHC with the year of her death, 1937, to assess its impact on her "creature." Although the Great Depression of the 1930s was the backdrop of Emily Morgan's final years, that phrase does not appear (unless I have missed it) in her *Letters* or in the Archive of **Companion Conference** *Annual Reports.* Undoubtedly she was aware of it through her great empathy for the suffering and disadvantaged; perhaps her weakened body and approaching death let it recede in her consciousness.

However, issues of our *Intercession Paper* [hereafter *IP*] indeed reflected the Great Depression from 1927 through the 1930s. During these years, prayers on the Social Justice theme expanded into the largest section of the monthly *IP*—up to 3 1/2 full pages once in 1927, and again several times in 1929. In 1933 an explicit intercession said: *"Don't let our national selfishness prevent the nation's recovery from Depression."* Obviously some Companions were keeping the Society conscious of that tragic loss of jobs, property, and homes, tracking that devastation and our nation's response through legislation and executive order. During this time, Companion prayers may well have been more socially engaged and forward-looking than prayers or sermons in many of our parishes...just as *IP* petitions raised the theme of racial inequity and injustice well before the Civil Rights movement of the 1960s, (see Author's notes re *IP*, p. 267-269) or many of us in our [white] Episcopal churches.

Another historically significant development that Emily Morgan did not address but participated in was the "culture of art," one of the larger societal currents between 1880-1930 attracting educated women. The creation of cultural institutions by "Robber Barons" such as Carnegie, Rockefeller, J. P. Morgan and their ilk, character-ized the upper reaches of the Gilded Age. They were men (and one woman, Isabella Stewart Gardner) who used their vast fortunes in "service" to the nation that had enriched them, as well as to estab-lish themselves as "cultural authorities," historian Peter Williams writes. They built museums, schools, hospitals and art collections. Miss Morgan's modest institution-building remained within the bounds of her New England-ized dedication to her Anglo Catholic leadings; she collected European religious artifacts to brighten and lighten the plainness of "her" dark summer retreat house. Naturally, a substantial proportion of her *objects d'art* depicted women, e.g. various large Della Robbia bas-reliefs of Madonna and Child. These imports of art reproductions made EMM a minor player in the larg-er cultural transformation led by the wealthy institution builders of her era.[1]

Companions' Quest for Authority in Religious Expression

Reading the words of these early Companions has brought into clearer perspective their dependence on two authorities: Em-ily Morgan's charismatic person, as well as her financial support of the Society, and the theological authority of male writers and think-ers. The first hundred years of Companion Papers were replete with quotations from male sources, undergirding and giving authority to the thoughts of these extraordinarily intelligent and committed women. That was the way women's experience in our church was presented and dealt with until the late 20th century. The sources of our Society's written history testify to the coming of age of women writers in the fields of spiritual, religious and theological thought. Discovering this microcosm has been one of the joys of my work on this history.

In my early American history writings, the challenge was [first]

---

1 Peter H. Williams, "The Gospel of Wealth and the Gospel of Art from the Gilded Age to the Depres-sion." *Anglican and Episcopal History* Vol.LXXV#2 June 2006 170-223.

to *find* and then interpret 18th c. women's vocabularies and differing perceptions. In this study, Companions' recorded voices and thoughts are fully 'audible' but the challenge of knowing and entering their worlds remains: what the words meant to them in the times they were prayed or written. For this task, our *IP* prayer agenda record is the indispensable, unique gift of God and Emily Morgan (see Author's Notes, p. 269). Tracing our path through the historical evolution of vocabulary, ideas, and meanings is my challenge and delight. Each intercession cited is indication of many, many others— poems, meditative paragraphs, prayers. The few words creating this chronologically unfolding trail are a taste, informative of "the times" and how Companions understood ourselves in them. This history, refracted through Companion eyes and hearts, translates women's experiences in the real world into spiritual and activist terms.

Index

SCHC is more than our organizational policies, important as they are, more than our social-problem studies or our financial maturing. Rather, the substance of this SCHC organizational account is concrete petitions, words from actual women whose hearts were summoned to this Companionship. Therefore I have cited many, many names. I have created 3 indexes: a name index for looking up a particular Companion; a chronological index identifying major time-periods; and a subject/topical index identifying the focus of various prayers at specific times. I hope these several pathways "in" may lure readers into and through this composite portrait.

Format

Reflecting our contemporary sense of "busy-ness," I made the decision to summarize and excerpt many incredibly important speeches, papers, and thoughts. I hope I have selected the crucial kernels of each. At first I envisioned including a huge appendix of full texts of those cited, along with other supplementary materials. I have had to settle for assembling copies of those Companion presentations listed in the Sources in a labeled folder in the archives. This has meant leaving unmentioned an incredible wealth of talented and inspiring Companion documents, which I deeply regret; I want everyone to know everything. Fortunately, in another several decades a newer Companion will emerge to focus her attention on the same materials, finding different angles to emphasize. The comfort of on-going historical analysis is that it produces multiple angles of vision into the beloved topic.

Key to font, spacing and editorial choice

The office of Companion-in-Charge is abbreviated as C-in-C throughout. Committee names and Theme Committees have been italicized. Published print titles, including SCHC *Annual Reports,* have been italicized. I have capitalized the word Black when it is part of a designation or title, e.g. first Black bishop; in referring to the race of groups of participants, neither white nor black is capitalized. I also refer to both Emily Morgan and Vida Scudder by their initials (EMM, VDS). I have not used honorific titles (Mr. Mrs. Dr. Rev.) except in direct quotations. I have abbreviated the word "century" with a lower case c. Brackets surround my interpolations; parentheses imply background material. **Companion Conferences** and their dates are in **Bold Type**. Occasionally I was unable to resist emphasizing certain ideas with <u>underlining</u>.

Important *IP* <u>Notices</u> are indented.

Lengthy quotes and excerpts from papers or newsletters are indented and set in this format.

All illustrations are property of the SCHC Archive except where otherwise designated.

Consultation

I could not have assembled this wealth of information without the encouraging support and assistance of the Archives Committee, especially Ann S. Lowell [to say nothing of her much-appreciated sighting of typos, commas, and misspellings]. Peg Aldrich, then archivist, loaned me *Annual Reports* to pore over; Mary Steigner tracked down beginnings of financial information and the evolution of committees. Roberta Innan was the first brave Companion to read early drafts of my first chapters and point out the big holes. Many others have read fragments and partial chapters. None can be held accountable for my readings that they find disagreeable or not as they recall. Clare Keller has been a faithful 'inside' advisor, reader, and refiner, in every way clarifying and making my language more readable.

Though the narrative voice is necessarily mine—as are errors of date or fact that have slipped through despite the eagle-eye of Companion readers—my approach to this and any writing project is sponge-like and eclectic. I am grateful to countless Companions who have given me ideas, insights, recollections, phrases. Attaching an idea or interpretation to any one Companion's name commits an injustice against our collectivity. Thanks to the mysterious bond created by our collaborative praying, it is practically impossible to name precise instants when this or that meaning or idea emerged.

Acknowledgements

Beside her vigilance over typos and facts, Ann Lowell helped me select photographs, after discussing the project with Companion Janet Waggoner and others. I give many thanks to C-in-C Joan Melvin (1994-1998) for this assignment—permission to immerse myself in our treasure trove of prayers, conference reports, and administrative records—and to her successor C-in-C. Roberta Walmsley (1998-2002) encouraged me, and Pat Gaukler (2002-2006) helped me finally reach this end point. Heartfelt thanks go to my Tucson, AZ colleagues: page and photomontage designer Eric Galbreath, and copy editor Dixie Nixon. Thanks to Lori Borden, a colleague and fellow parishioner at Christ Church, Bethel, VT, who read every word and eased my prose toward professionalism. Thanks also to the Society Budget Committee for supporting my Xeroxing expenses. Profound thanks for all the Companion encouragement (and horrified disagreement) I have received along this path, and deepest gratitude to my half-century mate who has generously involved himself in the production of this volume. He, David M. Gillespie, is my all-round enabler as well as my resident computer guru.

Author's Background

I was born in 1929 to a high-minded farm family who were also teachers. They idealized education and schooling, and were faithful participants in the (progressive) Mennonite Church in northern Indiana. Graduating from Bluffton College, Bluffton, Ohio in 1951, I married David M. Gillespie, a student at Yale Divinity School. We had met working in the East Harlem Protestant Parish in New York City, summers of 1949 and 1950. Graduate work at the Yale School of Music earned me two degrees, a B.Mus (1953) and M.Mus (1954). David's clergy career took us to Washington DC, upstate New York, Englewood NJ, San Francisco, and Rhode Island; from there we retired to our summer home in Vermont. I had completed a 1973 PhD in sociology of education at NYU and loved teaching at Drew University, Madison N.J. In 1980 my dear friend and colleague Mary Donovan and I launched the Episcopal Women's History Project, which continues to help our church recover from its historical vacuum regarding women's contributions, material and spiritual. Since 1992, my husband and I have enjoyed winters and involvement in a vital urban parish, St. Philips, Tucson, AZ along with summer participation in Christ Church, Bethel, VT.

After knowing about the Society of the Companions of the

Holy Cross from recording the oral histories of a number of Companions for EWHP in 1987, I finally met the Companionship in person, thanks to Companion Maggie Woolverton. My first and home chapter is Providence, sponsored by Sharron Singleton and Frances M. Young. I hold dual membership in the New Hampshire-Vermont and the Arizona Chapters. My fascination with our Companionship and its history continues unslaked.

David and I are the grateful parents of two wonderful adults and their mates, and grandparents of three much-loved budding adults. As joy in my later years becomes more internal, spiritual, and Companionable, the excitement in our lives now comes from our second and third generations, and our two beloved parish congregations. Thanks be to God.

Publications in addition to *The Life and Times of Martha Laurens Ramsay 1759-1811* alluded to earlier include a number of reviews and historical articles. Two essays are included in anthologies about Episcopal women: *Episcopal Women: Gender, Spirituality and Commitment* edited by Catherine Prelinger, (New York: Oxford University Press 1995), and *Deeper Joy*, edited by Frederica Thomsett and Sheryl Kujawa, (NY. Church Publishing House, 2004). My book of interviews, *Women Speak Of God, Congregations And Change* (1995) turned out to be excellent preparation for this overview of SCHC.

Joanna B. Gillespie
June 2006

The young Emily Malbone Morgan

Monologue

In Emily Morgan's Own Voice

In this monologue, Emily M. Morgan's singular voice has been excerpted from the original (unedited) version of her 1921 Annual Letter *to her* Companions. *Companion Mary Cross (and cousin of EMM) who celebrated her 100th birthday in 2006, recalled that even in her early Companion days, this particular letter was considered very significant; she then presented me with her copy of it. It contains one of EMM's many retellings of the Society's origins, her own evolution as the Companion-in-Charge of "her" Society, and reveals her vibrant mind and spirit. She creates a living picture of the early Society in her own vivid voice.*

The words and wit are hers, although phrases have been vastly rearranged and topically organized. The major portion of this letter has been omitted: it ran to 46 small-type 4' x 6' pages. The early Companions had to learn printing (in this pre-copy machine, pre-mimeograph era) because of the expanding number of copies required. Phrases in brackets [ ] are my editorial interpolations intended to be helpful. Apologies if they aren't.

This monologue was originally created to help my Arizona Companion Chapter experience the real Emily M. Morgan who wrote the edited letters they were reading. Companion Laurie Weckel expressed her thanks by asking, "Is this what you'll be sharing with the chapters?" Finally, here is that sharing.

Edited version thanks to Providence, RI Companion Priscilla Martin, September 2002.

I. Emily Malbone Morgan's Youth, Inclinations, Dreams, and Autobiographical Recall

I never imagined myself founding a religious order.

I knew nothing of religious societies in the 1880s; my leading characteristic then was undeviating, hilarious high spirits! I was brought up fairly undisciplined, in a family of boys, animal pets everywhere, spending lots of time on a horse's back. I was free and full of warm impulses: my favorite scriptural image was David dancing before the Lord...The kind of life I yearned for was active work out in the world—not meditating, but out doing! I'd begun my work of Vacation Houses (which at that time were still rare) for workers—women and little children—who were ill or worn out. The privilege of breaking bread daily with so many different children of the world seemed to me like a foretaste of the Kingdom of Heaven.[1]

I've been engaged in fighting against poor conditions in home and factory ever since I turned 20, fighting for some girl's or some woman's life, for children too young for such hard work...[Through offering them vacation weeks], I tried in all too short a time to pour renewed strength into their buckets, little drops of fresh air and good food.

I've always been able to sit down and break bread with people of any race, color, or poverty of outward condition, and to feel perfectly at ease in that happy fellowship...why, I've even slept three or four to a bed, with the working women in Beulahland [one of her

---

1 In 1914, she wrote: "God needs rest centers everywhere in the midst of turmoil, so He can make His purpose known in each place." Original *EMM Letter 1914*, unnumbered.

vacation houses]. I loved the simple life in those summer houses; my enjoyment was usually measured by the number of pounds each person gained there.

So: when we started the Society, I was [still] dreaming large dreams of what I might do for working people. Brought up in a proper Church of England family, my youthful ideas were far too large to consider immersing myself in "church work" with its parochial limitations, or to let myself get caught up in the regular machinery of parish life. I had seriously resolved never to belong to any separate church society or group [e.g. the Woman's Auxiliary or the Altar Guild]. The church itself was a great 'society' quite big enough for me. What I loved was active involvement [outside it] in social-justice work...

Frankly, it's a much harder and more baffling task to be head of a Society like ours...

II. Mandate from Adelyn

But: dear Adelyn wanted a religious society and I loved Adelyn.

Having been moved a distance away from her friends,[2] what Adelyn missed most of all, as she lay on her invalid bed, was her church; if [any kind of support system] was to be started for her, she wanted it to be a Religious Society—one that could give her spiritual companionship. All that her friends knew was that Adelyn had sounded the depths of pain and reached for heights above...so it was to be her society, composed of her friends. Sadly, she died in 1898 before we understood the need for a central house for the Society...When we finally came to naming our Society's house, that gave us a concrete way of perpetuating her name--all dressed up in English church language—by adding the word "rood" or cross, to it: Adelyn's House.

But that didn't come about till...around the early 1900s, after St.

---

2 Adelyn's family had relocated from Hartford CT to near Winsted CT.

Peter's House in Philadelphia was no longer available. [The SCHC had for a few years held annual meetings of the Society there, a place for our work, retreats, and conferences—through the kindness of the rector whose wife was the Associate Companion-in-Charge of that third major chapter. Hartford was first, in 1884, then Boston, and then Philadelphia].

[Thanks to that experience], I became acutely conscious that our Society had to have a physical location—for annual meetings, retreats, conferences, and for withdrawal from the world of employment...Our Society was evolving into a spiritual backdrop for many Companions [assuming the role of a larger spiritual support system], in addition to becoming an inspiration to women already working for righteousness in secular movements such as Working Girls' Societies, and College Settlements...did you know that Companion Vida Scudder gets the credit for starting that latter kind of [social outreach] work?

The social-justice work engaging most early Companions was unjustly receiving lots of flack from good church folk who forgot—or never grasped—the fact that this type of direct outreach started in the 1840s Church of England [in the Oxford Movement, plus English evangelical churches like the Methodists]. Companions were just doing what all serious churchmen were <u>called</u> to do[3]...Our Society was not connected with the church [financially or in terms of administration], yet it consisted of many women who were church leaders and members, all of whom used the Society and the *IP* for intercession about that work. They brought friends to conferences and retreats; we all <u>grew</u> in sympathy with human need and every kind of sorrowing people...We needed [our own] place of retreat to reinvigorate [our] spiritual bonds.

---

3 One of EMM's many expressions of disappointment about the church and uncaring Episcopalians was: "the humbug of a religion professed but not *lived.*" Emphasis in the original unedited *1914 Letter.*

III. Gradual Evolution of the Retreat House

At **Companion Conference in 1898**, we formed a committee to settle on a home for the Society, Margaret Waterman chairing. By a process of elimination, we came to Byfield, MA, in 1901, and a farmhouse at Governor Dummer Academy, where we spent the next thirteen summers. The pastor of the local Congregational Church was very helpful. He even had teas for us at the parsonage and tried to understand our Episcopal ways of expressing ourselves [specifically, Anglican vocabulary like sacristy, eucharist, compline, vestments].

There was some anomaly in a bunch of Episcopal ladies spending their summers in an ancient academy for boys, so by 1911 we'd begun to cast around for a place of our own...We'd looked in Maine, and in [Massachusetts] towns like Northampton, Gloucester, and Essex...We finally found our present place in South Byfield, MA, in 1913.

ADELYNROOD, the house, was planned without an architect, during the winter of 1914. If war had been even a shadow on our consciousness, the house would probably never have been built. Our contractor, Mr. Truman of Portsmouth, was also Senior Warden of St John's Church there. We built our house together...

Companion Deaconess Mary Potter, whose landscape degree thesis was from Cornell, designed the grounds; Amelia Schwarz built the cabin called Serene Meadows [on the grounds below the house, near the flower garden]; another contracted to build New Bemerton [a cottage for long-term residence, of recent times reserved for the C-in-C] and the garage. In 1920 we added electric lights in the chapel, also a pump for our water supply. During WWI, Adelynrood was mostly a rest place for those involved in war work.

After the chapel was built, the Committees on *Church Unity* and *Social Justice* were established and presented conferences. Both our present [physical] plant and the by-laws structure have only been fully in place since 1919.

O my but we were carefree, in those early days: we never worried about supplies...if the food didn't reach, we filled up on apples and pretended we were Franciscans; if the tables were crowded, we took our plates outside and sat on a rock to eat. Some raided the cake box at midnight, to the utter dismay of the House Mother. Many Companions loved to sleep [outside] on top of Sunset Rock. They would drift home at 3 a.m. singing [the hymn] "thru the night of doubt and sorrow"—waking those who were then tempted to empty their water pitchers [out the windows] on them. One night, I remember, one of our Companions from Hull House [in Chicago] flung her mattress out the window in order to sleep on the cool grass. The housemother asked her what on earth she was doing— didn't she want also to fling herself out? Today [regretfully], our House Rules wouldn't allow that kind of highlife.

IV. Living in Community as a Religious Society

We [humans] all have the capacity...to destroy or alienate affection from what we most love and most want to live [survive]. To adapt the psalmist's image, the 'little foxes' that can 'destroy the vines' of an association like ours—[one that requires] living together for even brief periods of time—can best be driven out by two good beasts we should adopt as our Society's pets: BEAR and FORBEAR.

Of course when we take on [the ownership of] property, one has a new viewpoint...yes, it allows us the joy of established physical nearness to the Blessed Sacrament [in the chapel], and the reading of divine offices. But becoming property owners means there isn't any more of the free-hearted joy that belonged to our society's springtime...Reading about St. Francis' own group of brothers tells us that any religious foundation which grows beyond a generation develops cares and responsibilities, and a certain amount of organizational machinery becomes inevitable—the necessity and penalty of growth.

Then too, once we had a permanent center, the size of Companionship grew: we *were* the 'retreat movement' in our early years...Now on top of the ten existing chapters, we've added a Far East Chapter [China missionaries and teachers]. Having incorporated in 1909, we've added an annual June retreat for those outside the SCHC [since the August **Companion Conference** including its Retreat days was too filled with Companions to allow room for others].

Think how long it takes a family to settle in a new place: we're here only four months of the year, and a huge World War has been going on. It's not surprising that we still haven't landed on the best ways of operating our retreat house.

From the beginning, tension has always existed between the Society—which pre-dated Adelynrood—and our new mother house: which should be most important?

Metaphorically speaking, Spring had evolved into Summer when the Society moved to Byfield, 20 years ago, and started Adelynrood...The good news is that [along with summer programs and the increased management responsibilities] many deep friendships have formed from the intimacy of spiritual fellowship...One of the best things our Society has done is to bring together many people who otherwise might never have met, [yet who] now mean so much to each other.

V. Leadership

Much the most baffling task I have to face is being *head* of a Society like ours, with its Companion House and Chapel, and spiritual aims where results are always unseen and can never be measured—where I constantly feel I make imperfect response to opportunity—where there are many slips between ideal and reality, and where my own inner development is not keeping pace with the Society's development...

Some in those early days wanted more a monastic rule, to keep Adelynrood from becoming a mere vacation house. Our safeguard, then as now, is our commitment to prayers and intercession...with my outward-directed ambitions and jollity, I was not very encouraging to the idea of *more* monastic emphasis, and I think most Companions seemed to agree with me. On a more serious note, however, I was also pursued with the fear that we might become a self-contained group of over-pious women living in the country, separated from the great Church to which we belonged. To counter this, I placed great emphasis on the necessity of attending the parish church in Newburyport regularly—on Companions [residing at] Adelynrood going there to attend our corporate communions.

I do feel that the Society will go on quietly unchanged. I'm less confident about Adelynrood—because the one part is a purely spiritual relationship, while the other is expressed in material possessions, close human contacts, and must change its policies as the years pass. Further, I'm always very conscious of the long list of Companions who've never been to Byfield and Adelynrood—there may be as many as two hundred.

VI. To those who think of EMM as conservative and Vida Scudder as radical.

From the very start of the Society we have been interested in social and industrial conditions; it is not [merely] a growth of later years. Some of the more conservative among us should realize these conclusions were reached [by me and other Companions] not by dreams of brotherhood, nor reading radical theories of reconstruction [like the literature of Karl Marx]. No: They were reached by personal contact with inequalities of condition and situations of intolerable misery that couldn't possibly be the will of God.

Those who face the stern reality of actual facts [of inequality] must try to find a possible solution, and [Christian] socialism seems to solve those social problems for some. But inheriting property subjects our social creed to the acid test, it seems to me. Those who have inherited property and yet say they hold such principles [socialistic ideals of sharing everything] must ask themselves if they would gladly give up <u>everything</u> to the cause. If they can say yes, they are real believers [in Christian socialism]. But if they waver, finding themselves unwilling to put into practice the theory they hold, they are calling themselves something that they are not, no matter how sympathetic on many points. I am a waverer, and since I have inherited property, I have fallen from the ranks [of true believers].

VII. EMM as C-in-C

Now it's time to give serious consideration to my successor...a founder can be the most obstreperous thing on earth...in 1924, the Society will be 40 years old. You must contemplate a change in leadership. The Society must have another springtime, especially in relation to Adelynrood. It must appeal to the young through conferences and by other means. The next C–in–C should have a direct purpose and commitment to sharing our Companionship with those younger, to help train them for the life of prayer. Of course, when you think about it, we hardly know the ABCs of praying ourselves— but we can at least tell others there is an alphabet [of praying].

And CHANGE in the Society must be made gently, slowly, and prayerfully, without hurting feelings. Don't let our business meetings lose themselves in the machinery of a new organization so much that we shut out one who loves the Society as much as we, but is slower to see the desirability of necessary changes. Wise reconstruction must be done in the spirit of prayer, recollection and love...

Many faces in our Society now see their lives more in the past than in the future, but we all hold one transcendent dream: to grow more gentle each year, to try to understand everyone and the world's intensity of human need a little better, until we come finally to abiding peace. Let us, as older Companions, resolve not to be hurt. Let us try to remain flexible and not contract mentally; our vision must grow wider as our lives flow onward to that great free and eternal sea.

Do you want the secret of a life of simplicity? I believe it is to sit loosely to all things of time and sense, and to find joy in being released from them...

Of course, that sounds easier on paper than it is in reality.

Final Quote:
From 1932 Annual Letter *(She died in 1937.)*

In 1934, we'll be fifty years old...we're already planning a conference on that half-century, a series of papers that will be compiling the records of our society...I [was the one who] started the Society for Adelyn in my teens, but the word "SOCIETY" means an association of people who each shared in carrying us into the future...The five editions of our *Manual* make us realize what a family tree has sprouted from that little acorn...Occasionally it seems like only yesterday; I still get up in the morning with the high spirits of one who is sixteen, but I no longer can dance a highland fling with that agility... This is preface to pointing out that anyone who has been head of a Society for fifty years better resign and go, while the going is good... I'll stay till you find a successor...But I'm willing to resign without any pension except your love. And remember: my offering to resign is not a mere gesture—I will still always be your Companion.

The **Chapel** at Adelynrood, circa. 1930, first completed in 1916, remained unchanged until the 1960s when the altar became freestanding, the dossal hanging was removed, the sanctuary cleared, choir stalls eliminated, floors restored to their natural wood color, and a simple cross was suspended over a table on the back wall; **Common Room**, circa. 1950—written in Old English lettering on the banner: "Peace be to this House and to All that Dwell in it".

Chapter 1

The SCHC in Church and National History

"Intercession is spiritual defiance of what is, in the name of what God has promised."

Walter Wink, *Engaging the Powers: Discernment and Resistance in a World of Domination*. 1992, Augsburg Fortress Press, 298

Companionship as a Spiritual Vocation in the Gilded Age[1]

When young Emily Morgan and seven Hartford friends set out to establish a women's spiritual support group in 1884, they recapitulated a radical Christian form of organization while engaging in the nineteenth-century resurgence of sacramentalism in the US Episcopal Church. Their deep motive was to give their own lives meaning and focus, along with helping their friend Adelyn Howard. Perhaps half-consciously, they were also subtly defying the form of religiosity prevailing among their social class in Hartford, Connecticut. They were determined to open their eyes and hearts to social realities very different from those of their parents.

Today we can see their religious vocation—to reform themselves, and ultimately perhaps their church—as a spiritual protest against the Victorian post-Civil War "gilded era."[2] It was their quiet

---

1 A version of this chapter was presented as a paper at the Tri-Church History conference in Toronto, Canada 2001 whose theme was *The Americanization of the Anglican Church.*

2 Paul A. Carter, *The Spiritual Crisis of the Gilded Age, 1865-95*, DeKalb: Northern Illinois University Press, 1971, 189-94; Bernard Kent Markwell, *The Anglican Left: Radical Social Reformers in the*

critique of a Christian church totally disengaged from real world problems. These young women's choice of *intercessory prayer* expressed both idealism—"spiritual defiance of what is"—and practicality, living out an actual claim on God's promise about what life could be. They brought educated, dedicated commitment to working out the absolutely central pledge to spiritual growth and praying—with their hands and feet, minds and spirits.

Emily Morgan's Society carried the imprint of "religious order" in its spiritual and organizational DNA. But in none of its founding legends did she actually name its genesis in the Anglo-Catholic renewal movement then crossing the Atlantic from the Church of England. During its first thirty-four years, 'her' Society was an organized prayer association held together by the verbal bond of written intercessory prayers. Additionally, each summer Companions held a gathering that included a day (or more) of spiritual retreat. Companions eventually designed and built their "mother house," Adelynrood, in Byfield, Massachusetts—dedicated in 1914. Thereafter, those Companions who were able spent varying periods of summer community-residence in that retreat house. They kept their Society autonomous—independent of ecclesial management or oversight—avoiding both the language and authority structure of traditional religious orders, e.g. their leader was called Companion-in-Charge instead of Mother Superior.[3] Decisions were made consensually rather than hierarchically, a mode that was rare for churchwomen's organizations in that era.

The singularity of this Society was that it gave an organizational form to women's hunger for an intensely spiritual focus otherwise unavailable in their lives. Such prayer intensity seemed to resonate with Episcopal women in other locations, especially first-generation college-educated daughters whose quest for

---

Church of England and Protestant Episcopal Church 1846-1954. N.Y., Carlson Publishing 1991, Chapters 6, 7 & Conclusion; Vida Scudder, *On Journey,* New York: E. P. Dutton, 1937.

3 Scudder ed., *Letters to her Companions, [hereafter Letters],* 148.

significance needed social *and* prayer activism. The Society of the Companions of the Holy Cross quickly expanded by word of mouth from Hartford to chapters in other cities—a second in Boston, the third in Philadelphia.[4]

The Society's origin also suggests kinship with the then-flourishing women's club movement that emphasized self-education and self-improvement. However, this was to be a "club" with a Rule of Life, a daily discipline, a lifetime vow, and the structure of a Holy Routine (morning prayer, noonday intercessions, and compline) when they were in community. Dedication to intercessory prayer was its charism.[5] From the beginning, Morgan's intention was never as simple as creating another venue for women's "church work." She envisioned an association unabashedly placing a life of prayer in its center, as in traditional monasticism. In that era, young Emily dreamed "large dreams of what [I] might do for working people," uncircumscribed by the church. To her, work with the needy was the true engagement with her own world and times, a corrective to her upper class Victorian rearing.[6]

The post-Civil War period saw a variety of women's associations emerge. Another Episcopal society, called *The Society of the Royal Law,* was initiated in 1880 by Mary Abbot Emery Twing (1843-1901). Her organizational skills and leadership were responsible for helping plant Women's Auxiliary chapters in all the dioceses and missionary districts of the Episcopal Church. Twing's *Society* aimed to promote church work as a career for women, then a radical idea, and to connect Episcopal women with each other—all viewed as potential members of the Women's Auxiliary by virtue of their baptism. This included the actual workers: deaconesses, church school

---

4 EMM *Annual Letter 1921*, 9. The unedited letters, in the SCHC Archive, Adelynrood, Byfield, MA, are unbound. Some quotes here are from the Scudder ed. *Letters to her Companions.* Privately published by the Society of the Companions of the Holy Cross, 1944.

5 Charism was not their term. Rather, "intercession unites most perfectly our love for God and for our neighbor. . . Social intercession is in a peculiar sense the prerogative, duty, and self-expres-. sion of a Catholic democracy" in Vida Scudder, *The Church and The Hour*, New York: E. P. Dutton and Co., 1917.

6 EMM *Annual Letter 1921*, 30.

teachers, even women invalids who could participate via intercessory prayer. Twing's *Society* for strengthening and recruiting more women workers, launched in New York, Boston and Philadelphia, asked women to pledge to follow "the Royal Law"—"do unto others what thou wouldst have them do unto you," and to aim for "special cultivation of the grace of charity." She avoided any suggestion of "sisterhoods" because of the cultural distrust of anything "catholic" or "immigrant." And her organizing efforts then moved toward promoting (through General Convention) the canon for deaconess training and legitimization. Dr. Mary Donovan, historian of Episcopal churchwomen's organizations, concludes that this women's *Society* did not develop into a lasting movement.[7] Typical of the way leaders among women had to proceed in that era, both Mary Abbott Emery Twing and Emily M. Morgan cast their motives for founding Societies in terms of others' need, not their own.

Emily Morgan, known in the 1880s for her high spirits rather than prim religiosity, saw her dear friend, Adelyn Howard, stricken with a degenerative bone disease (possibly tuberculosis of the bone). Adelyn requested spiritual companionship to help her stave off dependence on mind-numbing narcotics. EMM's succinct rationale was: "Adelyn wanted whatever we founded to be a religious society, and I loved Adelyn." In the Boston winter of 1884, Emily and another friend, Harriet Hastings, who "was religious and understood all about religious societies," drew up the first rules and aims "printed afterwards, with little change, in our first wee manual." We "little dream[ed] that there would be four editions of that manual or that it could ever attain its present fat proportions." Looking over a number of books, they selected "our prayer, an ancient collect,[8] and our name, 'Companions of the Cross.'" All this was done more or less innocently, EMM recalled, "at a time when neither of us... re-

---

7 Mary S. Donovan, *A Different Call*, Wilton, CT, Morehouse, 1986, 99-102. See Chapter 7, "Developing Church Work as a Profession for Women, 1870-1889."

8 Elizabeth Goudge, SCHC, *A Diary of Prayer*, New York: Coward McCann, 1966, 203, identified it as being from a Greek orthodox liturgy. A more definite source has not been located, despite serious research efforts.

ally knew much about the cross or what it meant. All we knew was that our dear friend Adelyn had sounded the depths of pain and [longed to] reach... heights above it, and it was her society."[9] This self-effacing trope captured the image that most nineteenth-century churchwomen were expected to embrace. Further, the simple-beginnings pattern was a popular theme in many nineteenth-century American autobiographies.[10]

Most of the early Companions enacted their Christian service-work in college settlements or hospitality houses for factory women, outside the new Society. However they also cultivated a more traditional religious *zeitgeist*, one that emphasized spiritual (rather than physical) mission. Their outreach work was "to spring *from* that prayer life" instead of being a substitute *for* praying, the reigning cultural expectation for churchwomen.[11] "Church work," stereotyped as women's form of praying, was precisely what this Society wanted to reshape. Morgan had experienced her first monastic retreat at age twenty-one with the imported English Society of St. Margaret's, newly established in Louisburg Square, Boston. Though deeply moved, it "scared [her] out of ten years growth;" a convent presumed a kind of piety of which she felt unworthy. After that weekend, her impulse was to "clear the 6'8" fence [surrounding] dear St. Margaret's House at one jump!"[12] The Society envisioned by EMM must combine disciplined religious commitment with the mental and spiritual independence American Episcopal women expected. This created what was and continues to be its organizational anomaly.

In later years, Miss Morgan's annual letters to the Compan-

---

9 EMM *Annual Letter 1921*, 4-5.

10 The first Companions were Harriet Hastings, Mary Johnson, Lena Barber, Annie Goodman, Caroline Fellowes, Harriet Putnam, Hattie and Mary Pratt, Charlotte Tracy, and Elizabeth Prince. SCHC was instituted "on the Feast of Invention of the Cross, a lovely day in May, full of apple blossom scent." EMM *Annual Letter 1921*, 7.

11 James B. Simpson and Edward M. Story, *Stars in His Crown: the History of Community of St. John Baptist,* Seabright, NJ Plowshares Press, 1976, 279, characterizing CSJB vows.

12 John Mason Neale's novel, *Ayton Priory: The Reformed Monastery*, London, 1843 led to his founding the Sisters of St. Margaret, 1855, a branch of which arrived in Boston, 1871. EMM's recollection cited by C-in-C Emilie Hurd's Opening Paper, Conference on Discipleship (1941) 8. SCHC Archive.

ionship rehearsed the legends of the Society's beginnings in sentences of "Johnsonian" complexity, her typical writing style.[13] Today, the idea that a group of progressive-thinking, sophisticated young women would choose monasticism as their generating motive raises many questions. Was there a relationship between Emily's initiative, shaped into a conservative, culturally retrograde organizational form, and the first stirrings of American feminism? The ideal of feminist independence attracted many educated, quasi-professional young women, especially those whose older brothers were their models of achievement. How then are we to account for the empathy with which these young Companions viewed exploited female factory workers, how understand that unusual identification as the rationale for deepening their own religious longings? Morgan herself exemplified the aristocrat's confidence in being able to span "race, color, or poverty of outward condition." She enjoyed "ease [and] happy fellowship" with the factory women her own "vacation house" offered them—a week's rest, feeding, and fresh air. She was proud of devising this personal social-work outreach, of having slept "three and four to a bed with working women" at one of the three houses established with her family inheritance.[14] Further, in this historic period of fierce, principled struggle between high- and low-church Episcopalians, and in the wider Protestant culture viewing anything Roman Catholic as regressive, how could even a modernized form of "religious order" be perceived as innovative by those young women?

---

13 Emily Malbone Morgan descended from Dennis Morgan who settled in New London CT, not Junius Morgan from Springfield, MA, who was progenitor of the famed Episcopal financier J. Pierpont Morgan. The two Morgans were apparently interrelated, her cousin Sophie Brown noting that Emily was born in a Hartford house owned by Junius P. Morgan. Her mother spoke like "a Britisher," was a devout churchwoman and often "otherworldly." Tutored at home and through extensive travel, Emily struggled to express her altruistic impulses as a writer and escape confinement from "the Victorian social life of that day" (6). Cousin Sophie alluded to 18th c. British lexicographer Samuel Johnson to characterize Morgan's phraseology ("Johnsonian"). Scudder, ed. *Letters to her Companions*, 2.

14 *EMM Annual Letter 1931*, 32: "Over 11, 000 wage-earning women and girls have lived with me in these houses; my family's derisive title for me was 'Ursula and the eleven thousand virgins.'" Her first summer vacation house in Hartford, Heartsease, for working girls, opened when she was 21; the next in Saybrook Point, CT, included experimental anti-tuberculosis work for slum children from New York City; in 1883, she opened Beulahland in Blandford, MA, a convalescent house where SCHC also held its first five conferences before moving them to Byfield, MA and eventually building the retreat house. After WWI she built Kingswood in Putnam Elms, CT, all of them further testimony to her institution-building talent.

From earliest Christian history,[15] any women's organized response to God's call had been allowed to emerge only outside the church itself, in unique, spontaneous form, e.g. the Beguine movement in the Middle Ages that gradually evolved into ecclesiastically controlled convents.[16] As the early Companions groped their way toward an organizational structure,[17] their need for a residential center became clear. In 1914, the retreat house they designed and built with union labor was dedicated to honor Companion Adelyn Howard, by adding the English "rood" or cross to her baptismal name.[18] What had come into being as an unhoused association, a prayer companionship, was brought to its next organizational step via the responsibilities of property management. As this hybrid Society continued to expand (there were some seventy Companions by 1890),[19] a process of membership formation became an additional necessity. Called "probation" as in many convents, it remains today. Companion Vida Scudder originated and shepherded that system as Companion-in-Charge of Probationers from 1907-1942, outlasting EMM's tenure as Companion-in-Charge by seventeen years. [A description of that membership-formation process appears in Author's Notes, p. 273.]

Emily Morgan's lifelong self-education acquainted her with many ways of promoting prayer and spiritual awareness in an Episcopal era that mistrusted the very term "spirituality." In her 1932 *Annual Letter*, she reported having joined the *Confraternity of the Spiritual Entente*, a society considerably more ephemeral than the SCHC. Initiated by British mystic Evelyn Underhill, it was to be "a brother-

---

15 See e.g., JoAnn McNamara, *Sisters in Arms*, Cambridge MA: Harvard University Press, 1996.

16 See e.g., Saskia Murk-Jansen, *Brides in the Desert: The Spirituality of the Beguines.* Maryknoll, NY: Orbis Books, 1998.

17 EMM's 1901 letter cites "a new era for the Society, in the establishment of a Companion House" already being called Adelynrood. Summer retreats had before been held at nearby Gov. Dummer Academy. In 1913 Morgan reported purchase of the present property and drawing up plans for the new house. Dec. 31, 1914, was "a great Thanksgiving day for us, for Adelynrood is finished." 1915 was likely the first summer in which Companions lived in the present building.

18 EMM *Annual Letter 1921*,10-11. "We might have become a Church Society for Invalids and Shut Ins—since two of our key figures (Adelyn Howard and Harriet Putnam) were both helpless. . ."

19 Chapters expanded in the following order: Hartford, Boston, Philadelphia, California, Providence, Utica, Chicago, Vermont and New York.

hood without vow, rule or habit; members [may come] from every nation, class, or form of Christian faith; they [were] also free to enroll any new members by a signed card, which they keep." It was to grow "like leaven," invisibly, without external organization. Its only object was to hasten God's kingdom on earth through prayer and each individual's own work. Reporting this to the Companionship, Morgan cited a then-well-known European spiritual mentor, Abbe Huvelin, in support of this ideal of universality: "Christianity has no more dangerous enemy than whatever tends to diminish it or make it narrow."[20]

Throughout her life, Morgan's spirit of independence and family background led her to embrace broad inclusiveness, to the point of tolerance for bobbed hair and rouged cheeks of the flapper generation. Supremely at ease in her own substantial physique, she enjoyed deflating pompous Episcopal clergy. One had expostulated from his lofty New York City pulpit that ready access to *bath* water (being piped in from the new Croton-on-Hudson reservoir) would endanger the morals of the poor, the godliness associated with cleanliness supposedly unnecessary for ordinary workers. In that same letter, EMM reported on the "first major scientific study of religion" (William James' new book *Varieties of Religious Experience*, 1902). That distinguished author addressed why we should or shouldn't pray, EMM wrote, but had little to say about "the reason why we *do* pray, which is simply that we cannot help praying. Man in his inner processes seeks and finds a great Companion... we are all haunted till we find that ideal spectator."[21] Her remarkably clear blue eyes saw little worth in the finer points of doctrine.

The Anglo Catholicism Factor

Emily M. Morgan's initiative emerged from her Anglo-Victorian roots. Genetic confidence helps explain her gift for organiza-

---

20 EMM *Annual Letter 1932*, 5, 37.
21 EMM *Annual Letter 1930*, 23, 30.

tion and her innate leadership, but not her attraction to Anglo-Catholicism. Her adult recollection of the family's private chapel in the Connecticut countryside was "spiritually meager," eucharistically speaking. That small house of worship presented Communion once a month—preceded by "a fortnight's preparation of morning and evening prayers [and] followed by a fortnight's thanksgivings in morning and evening prayers." What Morgan did honor was its production of "earnest, valiant souls." Her patriotism and citizenship were quintessential Victorian Episcopal: strong families schooled in honesty, thrift, clean living and high thinking—true to God, church, marriage vows, and family ties. She maintained that such "basic principles...build a nation's defense against decay and loss of power better than battleships or armies."[22]

Yet on that Anglo-Protestant scaffolding in the 1880s, EMM superimposed a deep inner response to Anglo-Catholic liturgical practice.[23] The first American Episcopal religious orders for women in the 1850s-1860s were literal transplants from English convents. The Rt. Rev. William Croswell Doane, for example, brought the pattern for the Community of St. John Baptist from England. He recognized that convent life was an antidote for "the spiritual loneliness of women in the Church of England," and downplayed "Romanish tendencies" that offended his fellow Episcopalians.[24] The former Lutheran William Augustus Mulhenberg, one of the first proponents of an American sisterhood in 1845, had minimized resemblance to Roman Catholic nunneries by calling it an "association of deaconesses," not nuns. Only the sexton and Bp. Muhlenberg witnessed the "setting aside" (not "receiving her vow")[25] of the first deaconess in the US, thirty-nine year old Anne Ayres.

The women's orders that crossed the Atlantic were given a sus-

22 EMM *Annual Letter 1930-31*, 27.

23 T.J. Jackson Lears, *No Place of Grace: Anti Modernism and the Transformation of American Culture 1880-1920*. University of Chicago Press [1981], 1994, 192.

24 Simpson and Story, *Stars in His Crown*, 10.

25 Sister Mary Hilary, *Ten Decades of Praise, Community of St. Mary 1865-1965*. Racine, Wisconsin, De Koven Foundation, 1965, 4.

picious welcome: only two churches in 1860s New York City employed any type of ceremonial. Candles on the altar were considered advanced ritualism.[26] Bishop Horatio Potter, the Anglo-Catholic churchman who in 1861 received the first vows of women for the Community of St. Mary, was saluted with awe by one of his supporters: "Not since the dissolution of English monasteries in the sixteenth century had an [American] Anglican bishop dared to stand in a parish church and officially constitute a Religious Community, a true monastic body, not [merely] a philanthropic sorority."[27] By contrast, in 1866 twenty-eight US bishops signed a condemnation of Eucharistic vestments, altar lights, incense, and the practice of "reverencing the altar."[28] Sisters in the newly established Community of St. Mary's recorded "a feeling of threat" during the General Conventions of 1877 and 1880. Fr. Huntington had established the male Order of Holy Cross the same year as SCHC. He attributed monastic defensiveness to their isolation within the church. A sense of feeling "foreign" often characterized relationships between the religious and their diocesan bishops.[29] The Rev. Morgan Dix, chaplain of the women's Community of St. John Baptist and reputed to be "a terrible Romanizer," attributed his fellow bishops' "distaste for Catholic worship" to a resistance against "creedal dogma and moral law."[30]

Anglo-Catholic religious orders in England had come into being as a vehicle for ministering to the urban poor, as well as to reinvigorate Anglican esthetics and ritual. Although historically, male religious communities preceded the founding of female religious orders, and contemplative orders preceded the social-service orders, English monasticism reversed that pattern.[31] Sisterhoods, coming

---

26 G.E. DeMille, *The Catholic Movement in the American Episcopal. Church*, (2nd ed), Philadelphia, 1950.

27 Simpson and Story, *Stars In His Crown*, 39.

28 Ibid, 41 n.2.

29 Ibid, 207 n. Through the influence of priests or bishops, many women's religious orders were imported from England after the 1850s. See: *Ten Decades of Praise*, also *The Planting of the Lord* (1995) and Simpson and Story, *Stars in His Crown*.

30 Simpson and Story, *Stars in His Crown*, 38.

31 Thanks to the Rev. Sandra Boyd for references: male communities began with the Society of St. John the Evangelist, the Cowley Fathers, founded by Richard Meux Benson, 1865; see Nigel

first, enjoyed a great deal of autonomy. They founded hospitals, orphanages, schools, and other service agencies, even choosing their own episcopal visitor or clerical overseer. As the church system gradually absorbed this new women's phenomenon, the bishop of a diocese in which they were located often exercised episcopal oversight. Women's more active religious response to poverty than men's may explain women's religious orders appearing before men's. Also, the nineteenth-century religious activism among both Church of England evangelicals and budding Anglo Catholics attracted numbers of "redundant women," the demographic term for the imbalance between men and women that war and societal changes had produced.[32]

To the dismay of their critics, these new religious communities were popular with women. They offered a place to "work as a free person in a community of equals," an escape from the confines of family. Florence Nightingale's biography commented on "the petty grinding tyrannies" attributed to women's convent lives; in her view, these were "nothing as bad as the petty grinding tyranny of a good English family."[33] Emily Morgan's way of stating the Companions' *vocation* addressed similar American concerns demanding women's domestic circumscription, those requiring religious justification for involvement outside the home. Companions are "living in the world and having individual influence, social or otherwise, [also] banded together to meet the problems of our age, first by prayer and then by battle."[34] Traditional religious orders could point out that Companions required only periodic withdrawal into spiritual community, and could enjoy the fruits of criticizing or renounc-

---

Yates, *The Oxford Movement and Anglican Ritualism*, London: Historical Association, 1983, 28. Anglo-Catholic female communities were the first successful activist women's movement; see A. M. Allchin, *The Silent Rebellion: Anglican Religious Communities*, London: SCM Press, 1958, 120. The first women's order founded in 1845 had eighty nuns by 1861, and over two thousand at century's end. Brian Heeney, *The Women's Movement in the Church of England 1850-1930*, Oxford: Clarendon Press, 1988, 63-64; Allchin, 119.

32 Martha Vicinus, *Independent Women: Work and Community for Single Women, 1850-1920*. Chicago: University of Chicago Press, 1985, 47.

33 Cecil Woodham-Smith, *Florence Nightingale*, New York: McGraw Hill 1951, 62.

34 Scudder, ed., *Letters*, 45.

ing the world without totally leaving it. In this modern adaptation, Companions were realistic as well as innovative: external financial support, often from families, helped maintain their retreat house and outreach work.

T. J. Jackson Lears has interpreted late nineteenth century American Protestant adaptation of Roman Catholic images (and the influence of its symbols) as "anti-modernism," a reaction against too-rapid change and chaotic times. By then, Calvinism, still the dominant ethos of the culture at large and the U.S. Episcopal Church specifically, had taken on an "Emersonian gloss" that deepened the appeal of Anglo Catholicism's historical authenticity, its "certainty."[35] The burden of original sin had begun to seem less grim, allowing a hope that human nature itself could generate moral improvement—Lears' "Emersonian optimism." Still, even if prosperous Anglo-American Protestants knew good from evil and could make virtuous choices, the idea persisted that any real accomplishment required divine assistance. And the post-Civil War mood encouraged activism for idealists. Evangelist Charles Finney expressed it thus: "religion is the *work* of man, something for man to do."[36]

In this bristling atmosphere, the Anglo-Catholic esthetic embraced by EMM and her colleagues conveyed both the comfort of historical continuity, and a dignified corrective to the ritual sparseness of much Episcopal worship. Historian Anne Rose observed that radical religious innovations in that era (like Phebe Palmer's holiness movement in the Methodist Church), and conservative reactions (like Millerites predicting the end of the world in 1843) prove that "church" and religion were seen as the vehicle of action for questing women. Within the U.S. Episcopal Church, rediscovering a taste for ancient Catholic liturgy and images, particularly among sophisticated Americans like Emily Morgan, may have seemed a bulwark against too-rapid modernization, or eased the impact of the

---

35 Lears, *No Place of Grace*, 198-203.

36 Anne C. Rose, *Voices of the Market Place, 1830-1860*, New York: Twayne Publishers, 1995, 4.

brash, streamlined twentieth century. For example, Companions found silent meals at Adelynrood, listening to works of medieval St. Catherine of Siena read aloud, an enriching counter-cultural experience. Historian Lears connects this counter-culture with the great 1870s museum-building efforts in the United States and the re-appropriation of historical sacramental practices. While Isabella Stewart Gardner was collecting her trove of European artworks for her Boston museum, Emily Morgan was creating her own institution: preserving and updating liturgical treasures including the retreat form. The two women knew each other and were undoubtedly products of the same New England consciousness; they may even have shared the hope that their respective institutions would deeply influence others, and outlast them into the future.[37]

In 1863, when Emily Morgan was one year old, the storm crested between Episcopal factions of High and Low church. That same year, racial riots in New York City erupted over the Civil War draft that allowed white men to pay others to go in their places. Also in that year, the Rev. Morgan Dix lost an Episcopal election, thanks to his unpopular stand on the issues of racial tolerance and Anglo-Catholicism.[38] In 1870s Episcopal partisanship, evangelicals struck a blow for Protestant orthodoxy by establishing the Reformed Episcopal Church. At first these Low-church enthusiasts claimed the moral high ground of inclusiveness and ecumenism, but conservative fundamentalists later rejected that. Low-churchmen then became militantly exclusive, warring against sacerdotalism.[39] An early attempt to allay Protestant hostility toward nuns in 1880s New York City employed the term "second order," originally synonymous with Lay Sister or Mission Sister. But the underlying resistance to Episcopal women's religious orders, as in England,

---

37 Isabella Stewart Gardner (1840-1924) collected European art works 1870-1890 and opened her museum in 1903, making her a symbol of "enthusiasm for pre-modern emblems of authority." Lears, *No Place of Grace*, 186-188.

38 *Ten Decades of Praise*, 113: Dix's setting aside of Sister Agnes was denigrated by low-church clergy as a "desecration;" it had involved no imposition of hands, no tonsure, no chrism, and historically inadequate vows. A snide comment: "she is only an 'almost' nun, only almost the bride of the Bishop."

39 Carter, *Spiritual Crisis of the Gilded Age*, 177-198.

stemmed from criticism that such women's "societies" promoted female independence from family and church control. They were providing women with an honorable path that helped them evade patriarchal expectations.[40] Morgan and her fellow idealists, never denying family and secular job responsibilities, admired Anglo-Catholicism's historical inclusiveness, and welcomed its worship symbols as spiritually freeing. In their eyes, its Christ was less dependent on words and concepts, and thus more accessible to deprived, downtrodden non-Episcopalians.

Retrieving the cross as a powerful symbol (at that time, derogated as purely "immigrant taste") became a totem of Anglo-American Episcopal sisterhoods. The earlier dominant Protestant Low-Church ethos had banished religious symbols for personal ornamentation or display: a crucifix was too "Romish." That mood had kept the cross off most New England altars before the 1850s. Thus the cross itself, "more than veil, ring, or name," assumed visual and material primacy for Anglican women religious, and for the SCHC. In EMM's chosen name for her *Society*, in its admission liturgy and vows and its official prayer, the membership insignia—a plain copper cross, stamped with the initials SCHC, ensured a theological and organizational identification that even today unifies Companions.[41]

In attempting to live out their vocation while remaining in the daily workaday world, the Companions had to endure contradictory currents. On the one hand, they were expected to maintain the SCHC daily discipline while living, working, and praying at home. If possible, they were to spend a part of each summer in residential community at Adelynrood, their version of withdrawing from the world. Companions' implicit feminism led them to forge an independent religious niche outside yet within the institutional church. One price of that early independence, EMM noted, was being criti-

---

40 The Sisters of St. Mary's heroic work nursing yellow fever victims in Memphis, 1873 and 1878, garnered new appreciation; Sisters were no longer stereotyped "old maids of dour countenance and rimless glasses." *Ten Decades of Praise*, 93, 63.

41 Simpson and Story, *Stars in His Crown*, 25-26.

cized from their own pulpits for associating with unwashed non-Episcopalians. Involvement with society's dregs was denounced by so-called "good church people" who "forgot [or never knew] that this type of outreach work *started* [for Anglicans] within the Church of England." Companions found themselves "preached against," their activities called "irreligious work and wrong humanitarianism" by clergy unable to "grasp" [Morgan's diplomatic verb] the Christian, Benedictine ideal "of making *all* secular work religious."[42]

On the other hand, the Society armed Companions for spiritual combat out in the world with first-hand knowledge of, and experience with, the poor. Companionship promoted *social-justice awareness* rather than overt political reform. The new frontier for Companions was the emergence of settlement houses, reading rooms for workers, and hospitality houses like Emily Morgan's.[43] "We felt the wrongs of the world very keenly, and expressed our feelings strongly," Morgan reflected. "We were a small enough group to understand each other, to make allowance for impetuosity of temperament. [Still] we felt an ardor that cooler people might have [denigrated as] unbaked zeal."[44] Companions' determined acquaintance with the industrial segment of their era called attention to the human damage resulting from slums, factory work conditions, and poverty, helping to arouse the smug, early twentieth century Episcopal Church.[45]

In the larger American context, Emily's Morgan kin, J.P. Morgan, was slowly imposing financial and organizational order on the huge waste and fraud that accompanied the building of the first national transportation and monetary systems. His lifelong dedication as an Episcopal Church loyalist, and his massive wealth provided detrac-

---

42 *EMM Annual Letter 1921*, 11, 12; Markwell, *The Anglican Left*, 229.

43 See Note #14, 6.

44 *EMM Annual Letter 1921*, 22.

45 Lears, No *Place of Grace*, 200, 201. Markwell, *Anglican Left*, credits Anglo Catholicism (and especially Companion Scudder) with "changing the political complexion of the Anglican establishment" (245), opening up the Church to engagement with social reform issues—along with traditional orders like the American men's Order of the Holy Cross, and the imported men's Society of St. John the Evangelist.

tors with a platform for caricature. The human tragedies underlying his economic and business success were incalculable, accused a writer in *Machinists Monthly Journal*: "When J.P. Morgan, patron of bishops and exalted pillar of the church, is at his devotions; when with a gilt-edged prayer book in his hand he wiggles himself into a more comfortable position in his satin-lined pew...does he think of the starving miners suffering through his efforts (and that of his colleagues in the coal trust)? When he reads the [scripture] lessons of charity and good will toward men, does he think of the tyrannous system that reduces wages to the subsistence point, or is he figuring some new combination whereby he can augment his plethoric fortune? When the organ peals forth, does not his conscience supply discord from the wails of those whose lives are sacrificed to the voracious demands of his class?"[46]

Ironically, thanks to a female Morgan, and her colleague Vida Scudder, the radical Christian and professor of medieval literature at Wellesley, Companions were directing *their* moral energies and prayers toward those exploited in the conditions of labor practiced by the male Morgan and his fellow capitalists.

Anglo-Catholic Companions, perceiving their home congregations' "cold, heartless, and highly cultured" distance between themselves and those who were powerless in America, hoped that sacramentalism would be a bridge. They hoped that rediscovery of the transcendent and mystical aspects of church worship could open the hearts of the rich to their low-wage employees. In Lears' analysis, Ralph Adams Cram's Gothic architecture, his "ministry of art," created a theology of sacramentalism that elevated beauty as a gauge of moral worth. Religious esthetic was Cram's concrete protest against the crass materialism of American secularity. The Companions' equivalent response was shaped by the New England fear of luxury, a more Puritan ethos. They idealized high-minded goals of simplicity, ecumenism, and the reconciliation of social

---

46 Jean Strouse, *Morgan: American Financier*, NY: Random House, 1999,324.

classes. The Society was *their* protest against a soul-less world and uncaring church.

During the 1920s the two founding pillars of the SCHC, Morgan and Scudder, gradually evolved their understandings of the Society as a religious order. Morgan reacted against the image of "a group living outwardly separate from the world, concerned exclusively with... religious matters, and wearing a garb" as undemocratic and hierarchical. Scudder agreed that the SCHC was not that kind of order, "except in terms of obedience to our organization in [a] democratic fashion, and to our principles. So far as ordinary appearances go, we do not look a bit like an Order." Yet in the larger conception, we are indeed "a group living under definite vows, strengthened by a corporate life, aiming at specialization of spiritual purpose...and keeping in constant mind...the Counsels of Perfection." The SCHC possessed "all the profounder notes" of an Order, "implying a special quality in one's union with the world."[47]

The Americanization of Church of England Practices

The quality of American individualism, bedrock to EMM's vision of the Society's structure, was the prime factor that had to be incorporated even by traditional orders of Episcopal nuns. The Community of St. Mary, transplanted from England and Scotland, vowed its sisters to corporate communal life, prayer, and work, but also to "retaining *the cardinal quality inherent in individuals*." It abjured the demand of complete self-surrender to the community.[48] Actually, recognizing individualism as a cultural given was the ultimate Americanization of Episcopalians in general, Anglo Catholic and Low Church alike. Many inheritors of, or converts to, a Church of

---

47 *Papers of the 29th Annual Companion Conference*, August 18-25, 1925, "The Life of the S.C.H.C.," 8-9. Adelynrood Archive, Byfield, MA. "The trouble with Religious Orders for many spiritually minded American women is its limits on their corporate freedom...because of medieval models. Surely there is room for a corporate life more spontaneous, flexible in form, motivated by special religious aspiration, and with no claims on control of outward life, still being organic, united, consecrated...Perhaps the closest model would be the Third Orders of the Middle Ages." (12-13), Vida Scudder, *House of Holiness* (pamphlet), reprinted 1964 from *On Journey*.

48 *Ten Decades of Praise*, 12.

England identity, not just visionaries like Emily Morgan, felt free to employ their church's inherited beliefs and practices as a means of expressing *their* personal callings.[49] The exuberant late-nineteenth century American mood seemed to encourage a view of their religion as instrumental, rather than as "received" inherited tradition and practice.

The Society's spiritual mode, sacramentalism, gave Companions the emotional and theological support for expressing individualism outside class and family assumptions. Companions wanted their form of Judeo-Christian theology to make an impact on their world, to give meaning and purpose to their own female lives. In their comfortable homes they had grown up imbibing optimism; they intuitively modernized a version of saintliness for their activism amid the world's suffering. Their post-Civil War world was evolving in two directions: toward greater democratization (more enfranchisement of people and groups)—and toward a countervailing cohesion of structure in professional organizations (such as the American Bar Association, the American Medical Association). The scent of Roman Catholic cloisters played only an unacknowledged role in their religious imagery. Companions could channel their idealism into external, social goals, e.g. support for labor unions and the co-operative movement, because the popular religiosity of the times focused on improvement in the here-and-now, not in the next life. This activist trend might have been labeled secular if it had not been generated by *spiritual* energy.[50] Still, the reigning expectation for proper middle-class women was that they content themselves with background work in their churches, or at most, the servant role of deaconess.

From the testimony of the Society's own "holy writ,"[51] Morgan's

---

49 Rose, *Voices of the Market Place*, 2.

50 Markwell, *The Anglican Left*, 164, cites Vida Scudder's writings. The cohesion of authority encouraged occupational professionalization, from medical associations to undertakers and barbers. See Daniel Boorstin, *The American Experience*, Vol. 2, New York: Random House, 1965; Rose, *Voices of the Market Place*, 23, 28-29.

51 Elisabeth H. Clarkson, C-in-C Annual Message, 1989, Archive. Morgan always used "the Society" rather than the acronym SCHC.

"religious order" was conceived and born of, for, and by women, without benefit of male midwifery, sponsorship, or theological authorization. Though Society records carry an always respectful tone toward their church as source and resource, careful thanks to those clergy invited to conduct retreats and celebrate Holy Communion at Adelynrood underline the Society's independence, along with its social and political politesse.[52] A more overt feminism may be seen in the Companions' determined focus on women: women were its members and most often the specified recipients of Companions' social outreach and intercessions. Women Companions themselves expected to embody revitalization of the American Episcopal Church via this previously untried spiritual path. In a sense, SCHC at Adelynrood was its own church, where women could conduct their own prayer services, write their own prayers, and discuss painful social issues without deferring to any male authority.

In addition to operating outside any church oversight or authorization, Companions made womanly distaste for institutional politics another organizational bedrock. In the early 1930s, Emily Morgan "looked down the table at Adelynrood and saw people from some thirty dioceses in the east, south, and west." These Companions represented "churchmanship high, low, and broad, but all *catholic* according to their understanding of the word [emphasis mine]." In her own vivid image, she added, "[it was] like a feminine fragment of a General Convention without a House of Bishops." EMM had determined, from "when we were all young, [that we would] never...identify with any [church] party and...remain non-partisan, [lest] we break ourselves against the rock of controversy and injure our...usefulness to the larger number." Valuing the Americanism of inclusion over doctrinal stringency, Morgan proclaimed an "open mind toward all that will deepen and enrich our spiritual life, but—as a great Englishman said in the realm of politics—not to get

---

52 "There have been many clergy associated with [our] different chapters who have given kindly of their service, time, and sympathy, and to all of them, for all that they have done, we can never be sufficiently grateful." *EMM Annual Letter 1920*, 10.

too far ahead of our constituency." Alluding to her own theological bias, she cautioned: "We must have great sympathy with the slower approach toward more frequent sacramental opportunities [than] many [of our Companions]." Such restraint might "show as much reverence toward [the sacraments] as more ardent appropriation of them." The "highest objective" of our Society [must be] "to try recapturing for the Church, and for the world, personal *holiness*, which we can only do by cultivating it ourselves [emphasis added]."[53] Always careful to balance her class privilege with awareness of its accompanying burdens and obligations, her form of spiritual high-mindedness was to avoid partisanship. To her, this justified, even sanctified, the Companionship's semi-monastic stance vis-à-vis the larger church.

Another Americanization was the assumption that Companions must be *useful* in something beyond themselves, their church, and the Companionship. They must have an external, social-action component of intercession, commitment to the cross and the Christ. Those first young women were determined to have lives different from that of their parents, the overstuffed Victorian Sunday tables symbolizing their distaste. Companion dismay must be channeled into action along with prayer, to address the huge inequities they saw. Morgan called herself "a good deal of a socialist" in the early 1900s, "because I was in touch with factory conditions [through her own houses for working girls]...At times, [we] were almost overwhelmed, when illness came, [by] the narrow margin between work and hunger." She was clear about Companions' physical well being in contrast with poorly paid laborers. "From the start of the Society, we have been interested in social and industrial conditions, [an emphasis that] is not a [product] of later years."[54] Such radical involvement was made palatable for the "more conservative among

53 EMM *Annual Letter, 1930-31*. Cultivation of personal holiness includes "the widest freedom [from churchmanship disagreements]... deepening spiritual life is our common aim, external expressions or lack of them are simply differing interpretations of the music of some great composer's motif and theme"(33-36).

54 Referring to Vida Scudder's visibility in scholarly, political, and church circles.

us" because their empathy was evoked by "personal contact," rather than via the ideology of "social reconstructionists" like Marx and Engels. "The intolerable misery" Companions saw at first hand "surely [could] not [be] in accordance with the will of God."[55]

A more subtle Americanism was Morgan's appeal to history for authenticity and justification. Her deep New England roots—Connecticut forbears who in pre-revolutionary times tried to import an English bishop for the colony, and childhood in the oldest Episcopal Church then preserved in the Diocese of Connecticut—grounded all her action in the authority of precedent. She had instinctively reached backward for a medieval-sounding name and the Society's prayer, along with elements of a "religious order." "Fervent thanksgivings that it never occurred to either of us [Harriet Hastings or me] to *compose* a prayer for our society," Emily recalled, "that we went instead to ageless primitive sources for the selection. That winter afternoon... Harriet and I thought of the countless generations of Christians who may have said it [the official Companion prayer], and to glimpse the full meaning of its central phrase, 'His [Christ's] Life-giving Death.' "[56]

Morgan's resistance to church partisanship also stemmed from her family history. "Lands confiscated at the time of the Commonwealth" belonged to "my mother's people, who fled because Puritans made it hot for those true to King and Church [of England]"—in other words, they had been Loyalists. Then, as American settlers, they had "struggled to maintain the Church's order and worship here in New England" during the Revolutionary War, when Tory loyalties could result in the public ritual of being tarred and feathered. Adelynrood must not be confined to one group, but embrace all "different schools of thought that the Church permits." In 1934, when the Society was fifty years old, Morgan confessed a modest gratification that

---

55 EMM *Annual Letter 1921*, 27-28-29.

56 EMM *Annual Letter 1921*, 6. "Unlike typical human associations that touch mostly surfaces, our companionship [was] based on the spirit [embodied in our Companion Prayer]...As we say it daily, it feels as if we were guided specially in our choice, though at the time we hardly even sought Divine Guidance. Such is the sufficiency of youth in itself."

the liturgical practices of a vested choir, early Communion Services, and Saints Day observances had become "ordinary:" they had all been considered "too advanced" during the Companions' first half-century. EMM had even heard a radio preacher use the words "Holy Eucharist," a "sign of progress, in phraseology at least." Tolerance about churchmanship was integral to awakening the responsibility of the privileged for the "have-nots." The real barrier, she believed, was resistance by the rich and powerful to "sharing even a fraction of their privilege," just as overly-rigid attitudes toward ritual, for or against, were the true enemy of inner spiritual depth.[57]

Yet one more Episcopal Americanization was distaste for fanaticism. Morgan was always concerned lest the Society turn into "a self-contained group of over-pious women living in the country in summers at Adelynrood (the retreat house)." As Companion-in-Charge she tamped down potential zealotry by encouraging connections between Adelynrood and the Episcopal parish in nearby West Newburyport, MA. On the other hand, of course, "there were always some Companions who wished for more monastic rule" during their summer retreats, who worried lest Adelynrood lose its charism and become a "mere vacation house." Her response to that was to institute a nine-day cycle of spiritual unity, a ritual in which Companions located everywhere could join.[58]

The unique element of "Americanization" in the Society of the Companions of the Holy Cross was the expressed in and through its organizational form, its view that intercessory prayer was "spiritual defiance of what is, in the name of what God promises."[59] No equivalent for women emerged in the Church of England. There, a long-established system of social rank allowed well-born ladies to champion particular causes or crusades. But

---

57 *EMM Annual Letter 1930-31*, 32-33.

58 The chaplain of CSJB said sisterhoods must be "in harmony with church order, not interfering with regular church services or holy days though they may have their own special days of observance." Simpson, *Stars in his Crown*, 18.

59 Walter Wink, *Engaging the Powers: Discernment and Resistance in a World of Domination. Augsburg Fortress Press*, 1992, 298.

in the United States, no structure existed that could enable well-educated, outgoing young women to engage their minds and hearts in religious dedication and social outreach. EMM's Society and its awakened consciousness, religious and societal, gave intelligent churchwomen a critical perspective on their world's, and their church's, shortcomings without requiring them to totally renounce either the world or their church.[60]

Meanwhile, perhaps the Society's longest-lived Americanism was Morgan's employment of print as *the tangible medium of community* within a non-residential "religious order." Print was the form of corporate activism for Companions. From 1885 through the present, the *Intercession Papers* provided a concrete medium of corporate prayer. The archive of these monthly prayer agendas offers an invaluable map of the Society's spiritual, theological, and emotional trail. It is also a unique historical artifact that fleshes out and humanizes standard administrative records.

Always careful not to claim too much, Emily M. Morgan's 1921 *Annual Letter* encapsulated the Society's thirty seven years of existence in this single modest sentence: "We have prevented some disbelief in prayer, and discouraged some loneliness on the part of Companions, [through establishing] many lasting friendships."[61] During the ensuing 20th century, public welfare agencies increasingly directed primary programs of relief to the poor. Companions and religious orders in general turned toward the world's spiritual impoverishment, through the ministry of retreats, workshops, and conferences. In this way, the small Society initiated by a young Emily Morgan played its part in recalling the Episcopal Church to its "bridge" role between Protestantism and Roman Catholicism. An Americanized organizational hybrid, the SCHC has led women into profound engagement with scriptures, meditation, silence, societal critique, and the bond of spiritual community—above and beyond

---

60 I thank colleague Rima Schultz, Chicago, IL, Episcopal historian, for this insight.

61 *EMM Annual Letter 1921*, 44.

anything available in their parish churches or other aspects of their complex modern lives.

Emily Morgan's penetrating blue eyes and short, upright stature were the embodiment of a Companion-in-Charge right to the time of her death in 1937. She was primary articulator of the Society's ideals and aims, the much loved spiritual and emotional tone-setter. She was also the chief channel of print communication binding the wider community of Companions together through her *Annual Letters to Companions*. These combined inspiration, theology, exhortation, organization maintenance, "Far and Near" news, items about Companions' travels, illnesses, and special topics of her and other Companions' concern. During her lifetime all organizational strands were funneled through her. [A *Newsletter* for the scattered membership was officially established in 1947, ten years after her death—though irregular brief pamphlets of news items about Companions and the Society had appeared from time to time.][62] Her worldwide knowledge of writers, thinkers, activists and other international "movements of the spirit" magnified the scope of her leadership.[63] And personal magnetism was a prime factor in her benevolent, all-encompassing authority. Emily M. Morgan possessed "an Elizabethan gusto—and a strong sense of humor" that lightened her words and ways, a 1960s C-in-C recalled.[64]

EMM's final written communication departed from her usual state-of-the-Companionship tone. Rather, in her opening talk at the **1936 Companion Conference** [her last, read for her since her health prevented attending in person], she reviewed the progress of the Episcopal Church's "social actions" over the past fifty years, and the part SCHC had played in opening Episcopal perceptions (lay and clerical) to the world's crying needs, including for spiritual retreats.

---

62 Emilie W. Hurd, EMM's appointed successor, reported that the IP only began to be printed when SCHC was 20 years old. Before that the IP was often issued in longhand. *1912 Annual Letter.*

63 See footnote #11, EMM reference to E. Underhill's group. She was the rare Episcopalian of the 1930s who knew about, and spoke respectfully of, the Sufi mystics of Islam. *Letters*, 1931, 53.

64 1962 Companion Conference, Opening Paper, Virginia Huntington C-in-C: "The Meaning & Purpose of the Society of the Companions of the Holy Cross," *Annual Report*, 3-5.

To her, this proved that "Companions had done *something* besides talk," the accusation of which she was most fearful. She also commended open-mindedness toward future transitions, lest ignoring them stunt the Society's growth in new directions—her perpetual concern that Companions not "lose touch with their own times." Her concluding flourish gave the Society a virtual shove into the future: "Old ways may NOT be the best ways now."[65] As will be evident in this historical trajectory, that mandate was difficult to honor. Its gradual attenuation in favor of individualized psychological focus helped ignite a crisis in 1974.

---

65 Ibid.

Emily Malbone Morgan, circa. 1930, pauses in the Portal at Adelynrood; and at her home in Connecticut.

EMM died 1937.

Chapter 2

1937-1942
"A Time of Transition"

Message from the Executive Board

Emily Malbone Morgan,
our beloved Companion-in-Charge
Entered into Life Eternal, Sat. Feb.17, 1937

For many weeks of her illness we carried her on the wings of our love and prayer, realizing only slowly that God was calling her home. On Tuesday morning at 8:30, those of us near gathered in the familiar rooms at the Hotel Victoria to say our prayers with her for the last time. And at 2:30 in the beautiful Hartford Cathedral church of her own people and youth, her last service was held with Bishop Brewster, the Dean, and clergy from NY and her little church in Brooklyn, CT officiating.

Boston, March 6, 1937.

INTERCESSION PAPER
May 1937

(Front Page Announcement)

A SERVICE OF THANKS-GIVING was held March 10 and March 11 in the Boston & Philadelphia chapters, for Emily Malbone Morgan and for the SCHC, her Chief Creation over which she watched with loving wisdom for fifty years. [1]

separately interpaginated in the
*41st Companion Conference and
Annual Report (1937)*

The Impact of EMILY M. MORGAN'S Death

In May 1937, a unique Thanksgiving Paper with the special prayers honoring EMM expanded the usual monthly *IP*. These were read at the above-announced Service of Thanksgiving in both the Boston and Philadelphia Chapters on March 10 and 11, respectively. Because of their specificity, they are here excerpted at length but are not verbatim:

First was a thanksgiving for her gifts as leader, "for the spirit of joy in

---

1 Chapters were urged to establish a corporate communion of thanksgiving honoring her birthday in December.

her, her zest in living and her welcome to every good offered by life, sustained through endurance of all handicaps and pain...

For her sympathy, swift, patient, and boundless, which reached in healing love to all within her ken;

For her dignity and gracious bearing, for her sense of fun, for her laughter, for her sanity, for her simplicity;

For her ripe wisdom in common things, and for her habitation in the high places where man draws near to God;

For the secret of her heart, the devotion to Christ Crucified, which led her to entitle the Society she formed and led, the Companionship of the Holy Cross;

For her noble achievements, being lifted out of "private-mindedness" and given a "public soul to work for thy Kingdom;" for the centers of hospitality she formed to help working women;

For the hidden support, temporal and spiritual, she gave to countless souls in need; for her chief creation, the SCHC, over which she watched with loving wisdom during more than 50 years...We thank thee for the labors and joys of these mortal years, for our sense of mysteries which lie beyond our dust, and for the eye of faith...[2]

This was followed by usual thanksgivings submitted from individual Companions grouped under the usual *IP* themes. The second theme, *The Church and its Mission*, included thanksgivings for the "wonderful blessing of frequent Communions," for the Holy Cross Mission in Liberia, and interest in Episcopal "work among Negroes" through studying their needs. Under the third theme, *Reunion of Christendom*, there were thanksgivings for the upcoming Conferences on Faith and Order, and Church Unity, to be held in summer, and for the "unity of spirit given us over the years in the life of our C-in-C Emily M. Morgan." One petition named a conviction that while the "roads must be many, the end of our earthly pilgrimage is to see the face of Jesus Christ in the land of the eternally living." There was a special thanksgiving for all constructive forces of cooperation between religious groups—the Fellowship of Reconciliation, the

---

2 In the Scudder edition of EMM's *Letters*, the Thanksgiving Memorial is reprinted in full, 310-314.

National Conference of Jews and Christians, the Kingdom of God Movement, the Oxford Group Movement, "any quiet prayer movements which link people without display." The fourth topic, *Social Justice*, offered thanksgivings for intimations that the Nazi regime in Germany could be losing force, that US Steel Corporation avoided a strike by recognizing the CIO, and that every state now protected children from exploitation either by direct law or by requiring school attendance. The fifth topic, *Growth in the Spiritual Life*, gave thanks for being allowed to share the sufferings and the Cross of our Blessed Lord. The sixth theme, *The Nations*, offered thanks that there was increased yearning for international peace, for the Town Meeting of the Air (on radio), and for commentators who emphasize good news. Under the seventh theme, *Individual Needs*, thanksgivings were offered for the safe birth of a much desired baby, for Sara's health improvement, and for a small share in the love and prayers of our dear Emily Morgan for many years.

At the end of this special *Intercession Paper*,[3] a quote appeared from SCHC by-laws about the role of the Assistant Companion-in-Charge—whose office it was to "aid the C-in-C in such ways as she may desire, and in case of her disability or decease, shall act in her place until the election." The by-laws had been updated in 1934, and Miss Morgan had then been elected C-in-C for a term of three years on August 27, 1936. The quote explained that the *IP* was publishing this information since few Companions had copies of the by-laws. "Accordingly, Mrs. John Hurd, formerly Asst. C-in-C, automatically succeeded Miss Morgan on her [Morgan's] decease, and is acting in her place according to Article V, Sec.3 of the by-laws...which by-laws explain why the forthcoming ballot contains no nominations for C-in-C and Asst. C-in-C."

In her first address to **Companion Conference 1937**, the summer after EMM's death, Emilie Hurd named the Society's dominant mood as "anxiety." Companions could not help feeling uncer-

---

3 *IP* Thanksgiving Paper (pamphlet), May 1937, 14-15.

tain about "the meaning of our Companionship in these years of change."[4] In that year's *Annual Report,* there was little talk about the Companion vocation or intercession. For the first time in the Society's fifty-three years, the organization's very roots seemed vulnerable. The structure that had somehow grown in EMM's charismatic presence—Companions living their own individual lives yet spiritually united—was suddenly seen as both bane and blessing. Tension between the Society's vaunted aspirations and its administrative machinery would inevitably emerge in "years of change." Meanwhile, Emilie Hurd considered hers a caretaker regime, a holding action until the next Companion-in-Charge, duly elected, could take over in 1941.

EMM's forty-three years of leading, and in herself symbolizing the Society, had personified great-souled inclusiveness in an era of American Protestant partisanship and competitiveness.[5] Yet a practical-Yankee understanding about property counterbalanced her theological expansiveness. Her leadership genius had insured the Society's identity within the Episcopal Church while quietly maintaining its formal independence. ["She saved us from pious-ity," a 1950s Companion quipped.] At a succeeding **Companion Conference**, Hurd cited another of Miss Morgan's complex restatements of Society form and purpose that did not so much clarify as reiterate the dual emphases. "The only way for us to be monastic at Adelynrood, and not [merely] a counterfeit of the religious [who live] in sisterhoods, is to have the same individual liberty as always, [but] for each Companion to strengthen her own life in meditation, prayer, intercession, and the loyalty of silence."[6]

The early twentieth-century decades witnessed a shift in the

---

4 *Annual Report* 1937, E. Hurd, Opening Paper, 2. She was appointed during EMM's last few years,

5 Alice Bartlett, "Picture of Miss Morgan as She Appeared to her Contemporaries," SCHC Companion Conference, (separately printed) 1957, 4: "All branches of [churchmanship in] the Episcopal Church held her allegiance; Morgan's trope about churchmanship and theology was "Broad and Hazy, Low and Lazy, High and Crazy."

6 Quoted by E Hurd, Opening Paper, 1940 Companion Conf., theme "Simplicity of Life," 8. The silence referred to secrecy about belonging to the Society, an unspoken norm cultivated during EMM's life.

literate Anglo-Episcopal culture of Companions, an alteration in popular ideals. Abstract words like "glory, honor, courage" had been used "to lure men to World War I." Ernest Hemingway captured post-war disillusionment with that grandiose ethos in a spare, "hardboiled" tone that functioned to exclude idealists like spiritually awakened Companions.[7] The entire vocabulary and vocation of compassion that Morgan, Scudder, and Companions sought to embody and promote was viewed as extraneous in the brisk, "real" [business and economic] world. The only women's influence to count journalistically was political—the vote. Secular-reform feminists in the 1930s were struggling for voting equality. In contrast, most Companions worked behind the scenes; women who wanted to be taken seriously were told to "write about important stuff," not domestic issues like health, children's welfare, and schools. That standard of significance tended to dismiss the work of Companions and other religious do-gooders as secondary, irrelevant.

Hurd's somber opening sentence in August 1937 exuded tentativeness: "These are years of transition, dear Companions. Are those my words, or are they yours that we all constantly say to each other?" Or were they indeed Emily Morgan's own words, read for her at her final **Companion Conference in 1936**?

Hurd's introductory remarks reflected the community's unease about the future. "We've been moving toward this...hour of strange loneliness," this first "meeting in our Common Room without our Founder" for months. In no way could this particular gathering of the Society be "like any other year that has ever been in the past, or can be in the future"—due to our "ever-deepening sense of [the] hour to which we have at last come." The only way Companions can live into and through this earth-shattering transition is by "keeping our eyes steadfast on the cross, each step dedicated to the life we now face together without her, our beloved C-in-C." Everyone pres-

---

7   Claudia Pierrepont Roth, Essay, *New Yorker* Feb. 8, 02, 67-73 for "hardboiled" lingo and detectives as emergent new literary heroes.

ent was acknowledging the "ordeal of taking our places here, [and] facing the moment when we begin without the visible presence of her who was the embodiment of it all, great leader, great soul, great spiritual genius, great lover, to some our Lady Abbess, to all our friend, our first and great Companion, our incomparable C-in-C."

Here, Hurd offered a new and figurative interpretation of the phrase "life-giving death," from the official Companion prayer. In March, the month after EMM's death, a Companion had written Hurd that, in her mind's eye she saw clearly "the Lady Abbess in her scarlet stockings, sitting in the big chair, a wicked twinkle in her eye." Miss Morgan's twinkle would be great comfort just now, Hurd sighed. Without it, Companions must rely on the schooling in healthy community life via "the art of conversation" that EMM had created, her insistence on civil, informed discussion of difficult social problems amid and despite conflicting viewpoints. Hurd also invoked Miss Scudder's maxim that Jesus was never interested "in spiritual experience for its own sake, nor as an end in itself... [only for] what [one] did with it, what use was made of it." Hurd further recalled that, earlier this same painful summer, Gerald Heard, the famed Quaker mystic and retreat leader, had buoyed Companions with his assurance of the Society's survival: "In a small, like-minded group...trained in meditation [as this one is]...[resides] power essential to curing conflict—in self, society, and humanity." That was his motto for "waging active Peace." A Morgan-less future, however, confronted Companions with not just spiritual affinity but with the physical and financial realities of property stewardship.

Finances had to be faced in a new earnestness. The 1934 deficit had been $2,300; in 1935, $2,500; in 1936, $1,980. Repairs continued to depend on the uncertainty of special gifts. A fund honoring EMM was to be established: the Finance Committee undertook a $10,000 memorial to her. (As of Nov. 2, 1937, however, only $4,415 had actually been received.) Hurd knew first-hand the unvarnished truth about Companions' financial dependence: "I worked closely with Miss Morgan; there was always a deficit that she made up each year, [which] now we must."

During the remainder of 1937, *IP* petitions prayed for missionaries in Liberia, the Church Army [the Church of England's version of the Salvation Army], the Conference of Christians and Jews whose goal was "turning the minds of men from hatred to a better mind, especially toward Jews and Negroes," the Oxford Group movement in the Church of England and the US [sometimes known as Buchmanites, after the man who devised its creed of spiritual "absolutes"— Absolute Honesty, Absolute Purity, Absolute Unselfishness and Absolute Love]. There were also prayers for defeating Nazi Germany's misuse of power, and a change in US law that would eliminate child labor, among many other domestic and personal petitions.

The ritual incorporation of EMM's words and vision at Companionship gatherings, the SCHC's own liturgy, began at the **1938 Companion Conference.** C-in-C Hurd pronounced EMM's Annual Letters, which constantly reiterated SCHC meaning and purpose, as their "foundation stone." [A more recent C-in-C, Nan Clarkson, 1985-1990, called the 1944 edition of *EMM Letters* and the *SCHC Manual* our "founding canon, our own holy writ."] Hurd cited Miss Morgan's distinction between SCHC and other intercessory societies in the Church: they could ignore those aspects of injustice that were uncomfortable to face, but these were central to Companions. Morgan's coded statement—"their [other intercessory groups'] conference papers [were] far less complex than ours"—hinted at the Society's more demanding aspiration. Companions not only admitted these social problems but also studied them. Hurd also noted EMM's confrontation of another issue: some thirty years earlier, a few men had expressed interest in "joining our Society." One priest had dared comment that Companions' prayers were, by and large, "too feminine." Hurd evoked "the gleam in [EMM's] eye, the spice in her tone" at this historical hubris. Miss Morgan had utterly dismissed the idea that "men's petitions" might strengthen either the Society or the Intercession Papers.

During her active regime, EMM had singled out the distinctive factor that separated SCHC from other "ordinary" societies of intercession. It was <u>companionship</u>, in both spiritual and human terms. Intercession was indeed the major "binding link" for the SCHC, but that was sustained and maintained by another equally basic component: women's spiritual companionship, invisible power that knew no need for men's contribution. EMM's leadership, Hurd reminded them, had firmly established a second practice unusual among Victorian women: active discussion of real-world issues (about which they might well disagree), grounded in factual information. Companions were expected to be articulate and informed about labor unions, not merely proper tea-drinking. Morgan's euphemism for the Society's study of problems and internal debate was "the need of larger intelligence attained by thorough discussion of both sides." Companions must never be "muzzled on subjects of public interest." To her, intercession gave women permission, even the obligation, to inform themselves appropriately and thoroughly on any moral issue without limitation.

At **Companion Conference, August 16, 1938,** Companions sang the hymn of the Holy Cross "to include those Companions not physically present with us: missionaries in England, China, Japan, the Philippines, and heaven." And C-in-C Hurd invoked "the sense of the presence of our great founder who first set us on the Way of the Cross Companionship. In every **Companion Conference** she always speaks the last word still."[8] Hurd concluded that evocation of Miss Morgan by stating the Society's ideal in her own words: Companionship must recognize "no boundaries to the breadth or scope of intercessions in the *IP*." It must be independent of any conscious or unconscious deference to "the prevailing schools of theology and discourse." Hurd cautioned that the only unacceptable petition was one "dictatorial to God," one that lectured other Companions under the guise of addressing God.[9] [In subsequent years, *IP* petitions would sometimes overstep this norm.]

8 Companion Conference 1938, Opening address.
9 1939 *Annual Report*, Companion Conference, 8-9.

At the first SCHC *Business Meeting* not presided over by Miss Morgan, some sixty Companions listened to C-in-C Hurd on two subjects that elicited an organizational sigh of relief: Adelynrood's water supply was finally connected with the Byfield town water system. And the chapel roof could finally be re-shingled, thanks to the gift of "four [monetary] nest-eggs," including one from Congregational Church women who had worshipped there that spring. Both concerns had burdened Miss Morgan for years. However her death reduced the membership of both Endowment and Finance Committees. And the Boston winter headquarters maintained during EMM's last years constituted a drain of $50 rent for the two rooms, plus a fee for the landlady who managed the Society files and archives during the off-season. Further, "our Probationer and Miss Morgan's companion these past six years, Sarah Locke, must now use her own car" for SCHC errands.[10]

In the Society's first confrontation with financial reality, someone proposed a new class of Companion membership—Associates—as a new source of funds. The decision was "no change for now," a bellwether of the Society's post-Morgan mindset. Their vow of Christian Unity might require them to admit women from other denominations, which they were unready to consider. Concluding her report on "our material fabric," Hurd pointed out Companions' responsibility to schedule time in the Chapel. "Regularly praying intercessions there, and the offices of Prime and Compline" must not be the work of just a few Companions but of all. "I plead for the structure of our spiritual home with the same earnestness as...for [our] material structure. Miss Morgan always named <u>holiness</u> that which we must care about, above all."[11]

Programmatically, the Companionship was in much better shape, being filled with women experienced in administering—planning programs, organizing conferences—from other parts of their

---

10 *Annual Report,* 1938, 3-4.

11 Ibid. 17, 18,8.

lives. A workshop on co-ops and the cooperative movement, sounding then much like the Aims and Prophetic Ministries Committee established in 1998, urged Companions to promote the new idea of "credit unions" at home.[12]

Interestingly, despite the new C-in-C's financial alarm bell, the topics of money and fiscal responsibility continue to be invisible outside the actual business-meeting report. Even as the Society's spiritual horizons expanded to praying about huge national issues–peace, ethnic diversity, labor-management injustice—talk about the money required for the Companionship's continuation remained naïve, light-hearted. If the Companionship had been composed of more working-class white women or more than a handful of American Negro women, their high-minded ignoring of financial concerns would more likely have been challenged.[13] As it was, many Companions were used to letting expenditures be a concern of church leaders or their husbands. They were not experienced in financing their own organizational memberships and commitments.

How did far-flung Companions assimilate EMM's death in terms of SCHC's continuation? During 1938, the *IP* published five thanksgivings for the life of EMM, along with a prayer that Al Capone's detention in prison could be "cleansing and educational for the nation." A petition for the Church League for Industrial Democracy acknowledged Companion Vida Scudder's importance within the larger church as well as the Society. Prayers for the "just settlement of labor troubles" and "ever deepening thanks for life of founder EMM and our Beloved Society which is her Foundation and the perpetuation of her spirit and ideals" accompanied concern for the ominous war machine building in Japan. There were thanksgivings for the "witness of all religious orders of women... their superiors and leaders." In September, a Companion rejoiced that the "Scottsboro

12 Ibid. 56-58.

13 Claudia Pierrepont Roth, Essay, *New Yorker* Feb. 8, 02,: 1939 establishment of the Endowment Fund.

boys [poor black illiterate laborers wrongly accused and imprisoned for rape] were nearly all freed, in keeping with our beloved founder's ideals." It seemed easier to pray for the ills in the outside world than to think about SCHC finances.

The following year, Hurd's **Companion Conference** Opening Paper (August 15, 1939) began with the ritual evocation of Miss Morgan. Hurd recalled the view from Miss Morgan's hospital window, and EMM's vision of "our Lord walking there, coming toward me in the trees and among the people;" the dying woman had loved to imagine her "little-girl self holding fast to God's hand in childlike faith." At six years of age, little Emily had prayed not just for the heathen, but also for those things that appeal to a child, like "dogs, and any man wearing brass buttons." Morgan's serene faith easily leapt "from brass buttons to the infinite realms of the eternal," Hurd reflected. EMM's "spontaneity, her unerring historic sense, and utter naturalness were and are part of our foundation." This Morgan vignette, appropriate to the Conference theme "Living Trees, Living Vine, Living Water," came in Hurd's second year as C-in-C.[14]

At the **1940 Companion Conference** on Simplicity of Life, Hurd's Opening Paper paid tribute to EMM for having made the ideal of simplicity "almost synonymous with reality." This, she noted, was the more remarkable considering Morgan's monied heritage (always there but unstated). Thanks to her, Companions had been enabled to see, via the literary eyes of Tolstoy and St. Francis [heroes of historic Christianity not likely to be cited in mainstream Episcopal sermons, at that point] that industrial societies could not help producing "people starv[ed] for the Bread of Life." For Miss Morgan, simplicity had also been the ideal that freed Companions from slavery to social rituals and fashion.

EMM's simplicity was both practical and spiritual. Hurd recalled

14 EMM's ability to draw from ancient liturgies—Coptic, Armenian, Nestorian, Greek [included in our Companion Prayer]. Our Office Book was adapted by Margaret Waterman and Florence Converse from an original by the Mirfield Fathers. During the Great War, every intercession service was prefaced with the Navy hymn. Companion Conference Report, 1939.

a favorite Companion story involving "Joanna Charles, our old Companion (1906-1915), our old saint, our cook in white cap and apron sitting in her chair by the fire." When a Companion confessed a fear of dying, Joanna, "her black face serene and happy," had replied, "why should I be afraid of dying? Me and God ain't had no trouble." Companions idealized that genuine and artless theological simplicity. Hurd concluded by reporting that specific memorials of EMM, written by EMM's cousins Carolyn and Sophie Brown, would be presented at a future conference [they would finally appear in 1955] to document the origins of some of Miss Morgan's innovations and traditions. "Whisper lunches," for instance, were a custom EMM had instigated not "out of piety so much as to reduce the voice of the American Lady," whose volume often rose to "a social screech."[15]

During the **1940** summer, Emilie Hurd tendered her resignation and called for the election of a Companion-in-Charge according to the new bylaws. She summarized her three post-Morgan years. "I've bridged, so far as in me lay, the difficult period following EMM's death." In those three years enough Companions had carried on to establish some confidence about the Society's survival. "You've seen my loyalty to her personally, and to the ideals and aims of her Foundation [original vision]...Although I've been a Companion for thirty-two years, I'm now seventy and too old for the development and leadership of the Society." At the business meeting, she reported thankfully that, in 1939, Adelynrood had closed its season without a deficit. Even so, without "special gifts," finances remained "perilous." The hot water system in the house had had to be repaired: "our sister Water in those pipes [is] neither serviceable, nor precious, nor clean" [referring to a stanza in the Hymn of St. Francis, said daily and antiphonally from the Adelynrood porches during summer residence]. And Companions should know that the numbers attending the various summer conferences, "our financial salvation" (then as today), must increase.

---

15 Miss Morgan's words in *Adelyn's Story*, being republished, E. Hurd's personal thank offering paying for it. E. Hurd, 1940 Opening Paper, 11; Joanna [Charles], 14, from 1906-1915, identified in 1954 Paradise Chapter list; history of whisper lunch, 37.

1940 *IP* petitions included a November thanksgiving for the existence of the NAACP, and a prayer that the crime of lynching be outlawed. A large Episcopal missionary group of some fifteen Companions flourished at several stations in China, bringing this huge international outreach to the forefront of SCHC consciousness and prayers. During that year, petitions honoring EMM appeared in February ["our beloved founder's death three years earlier"], and September ["for the life and personality of our Founder, for the depth of her spirituality and breadth of her humanity"].[16]

Discipleship was the **Companion Conference** theme in **1941**, and of Hurd's Paper, "the fifth year I've opened our Conference, and the last for me." Preoccupied with the war building in Europe and the Far East as she wrote, "we move forward not knowing whither paths will lead us." Companions were already in the habit of plumbing Miss Morgan's writings for guidance as if they were Biblical parables, for "memories, energy, and the courage to face our financial and world challenges." Issues of self-definition remained paramount. "Are we as a Society a democracy? Yes, I say, but I have heard No in these last weeks. It's a good thing the election is at hand." [Any actual internal disagreements were already being smoothed over in the printed *Annual Reports,* an internal Society pattern that persisted up to the crisis of 1974 and beyond].

Hurd's polite administrative note observed that since Miss Morgan's death, the Society Council had been reluctant to "take its own power and use it... to recognize its value to the Society, and vice versa." This was the most organizationally analytic statement in her preserved record. She listed topics urgently requiring wide discussion and action: the need for a permanent Arts Committee for Adelynrood; the subject of rotation and length of terms in the offices of Committee chairmen, in the Society as well as Adelynrood; the office of C-in-C and its eventual re-interpretation; and potential new divisions of responsibility within administrative roles. Should

---

16 Chinese missionary historian (and Companion) Cynthia McLean's observation. Hurd 1940 paper 13, 16, 15.

the Society's **Annual Meeting** adopt the Quaker method of deci-sion-making? Twentieth-century women's penchant for efficiency obviated that proposal. The time required for "the pauses of silence waiting for the Spirit's leading" would not accommodate "the many points of business in a Society of nearly 500 persons." That only one-fifth of that number was likely to be present at any actual busi-ness meeting was lamented but already taken for granted.[17]

Then Hurd spelled out the first-ever election procedure, "sim-ple, solemn, and under the conscious guidance of the Holy Spirit." August 21, 1941 was to be the date Holy Communion would be cel-ebrated "with special intention for the election." [The phrase "spe-cial intention" was a High Church expression meaning "dedicated" or consecrated to a specific event.] After noonday intercessions and lunch, all Companions present in Adelynrood would gather in the chapel to say Veni Creator,[18] "again with special intention for the election." All would then sit in complete silence for fifteen min-utes. Only the actual electors, the Council and the Executive Board, would proceed to the library; the others, continuing in silence, re-mained in the chapel until the election itself was completed and the Companion Prayer had been prayed. Mrs. Hurd, presiding, read prayers for guidance in this "solemn hour." Eighteen names had been sent to the electors, but the sole nominee was Elizabeth Cook. Nine spoke in seconding her. "When sureness was made triply sure, it was voted that the Secretary cast one ballot" for the one-year term, completing what would have been Hurd's fourth year, Oct. 1, 1941-Oct. 1, 1942. When everyone was once again present in the chapel, all would "make our act of Thanksgiving together, say the Te Deum, and lift the name of the new C-in-C for His Blessing." That evening, "this fifth summer of our crisis being ended," the three-

---

17 Hurd, Opening Paper 1941 Comp Conf., 13-14; 16.

18 This is the only hymn specifically prescribed (since the 11th century) in the *Book of Common Prayer*, having a long and distinguished history for use in the ordination ritual. Its origin is uncer-tain but clearly medieval; it was sung with special bells, incense and lights. Its significance may have been that it was offered as a "witness" to persecutors while Christians were being martyred, according to the *1940 Hymnal Companion*, 79, 194. Its role in this ceremony was to acknowledge SCHC's total dependence on and participation in the leading of the Holy Spirit, as well as God's authorship of the whole of creation.

day silent retreat [then an integral part of the combined **Companion Conference-Annual Meeting** schedule] would begin. Confident that the Society had "bridged the years [following Miss Morgan's death] with love and faith, a new era is dawning. Adelynrood faces the Sunrise," Hurd concluded.[19] House property-management and the larger Society were being conflated; blurring spiritual concerns with community euphoria disposed of money concerns.

At the **Business Meeting** that August, Hurd had pleaded for conserving water usage, and again that a permanent committee be established for decisions on furnishings, maintenance, and décor. She also read an affirming note from Companion Alice V. V. Brown who had spent her first entire summer as a volunteer in residence at Adelynrood. Despite the warning that a "whole summer's worth of community life" might be disenchanting, Brown reported exactly the opposite: "The rhythm of life [here], the chapel offices, the prayers, the charged atmosphere, have kept my heart at peace." She endorsed an elderly Companion who, when asked what Adelynrood meant to her, had said: "You'll laugh... To me it is the Gate of Heaven."[20]

The years of transition were underway, Emily Malbone Morgan's elemental magnetism only spiritually present. Companions instinctively began to coalesce around the tangible physical customs of this "monument" that was her Society. By prolonging patterns she established, they hoped to perpetuate her vision and presence. An implicit worship of custom—"we've always done it this way"—automatically became a shield from the conflicts inherent in their two-pronged vocation.

In the first years following EMM's death, Companions unwittingly recapitulated the organizational dynamics cycle characterizing most contemporary organizations, religious or secular. The birth of any organization required a catalyst like EMM whose vision

---

19 Companion Conference Opening Paper, Hurd 1941, 16.

20 In the *Annual Report* 1941, 94, the process was described more fully.

could inspire others—in this case, educated, socially-attuned Christian women craving a deep religious center within their Episcopal identity. They also sought a profound commitment engaging their moral energies and creativity. As the Companionship of such women expanded into a multi-chapter organization, its own narrative evolved—customs, routines, traditions. The Society's philosophical platform took shape through EMM's team leadership with Vida Scudder, who joined the SCHC in 1889. Their dialogues of definition and purpose became an unfolding articulation of the Society's meaning and way of life.

The need for a system of membership formation benefited from EMM's gift as organizer and VDS's as spiritual director. While Scudder set benchmarks for assimilating newcomers and a vocation honoring "the Way of the Cross," Morgan's wide-souled prayer focus remained indelible. Her innate administrative skill regularized the Society's structural procedures except financially, where she persisted in quietly paying off outstanding bills. Drawing on the historical imperative of her New England roots, EMM established an archive of the Society's records, prayers, and retreats. She attracted outside groups to rent Adelynrood facilities, established patterns of communication [her annual printed letters being the primary channel of internal community news], managed connections with outside organizations [today called public relations], and of course maintained a personal fiscal commitment for Adelynrood and the larger Society that bypassed the Society's own bookkeeping. As Companion-in-Charge during the Society's founding era, Morgan's many rehearsings of the Society's founding legend helped weave new Companions into the Society's internal culture.[21]

After the death of a charismatic founder, any organization is challenged by the tendency of organizational currents to draw energy toward the edges, away from the center. At the same time, Companionship custom at Adelynrood was settling into routine.

---

21 Arlin J. Rothauge, *The Life Cycle in Congregations: A Natural Process*, Alban Institute. 1996,

A "natural aristocracy of firsts"—founding members, established customs—shaped the Society ethos into something of a "good ol' girls club," atmospherically if not literally. Organizational legalisms that preserved the central structure inevitably produced a negative mirror image: new ideas and new people could be seen and feared as intrusive. Increasingly, dynamics that were habit-conscious and rule-bound began to dominate the summers at Adelynrood, the physical center of the Society. EMM's idealized inclusiveness warped toward practices that became the cultural property of an "in group." Outsiders and newcomers could be given the impression that true "insider" status in the Companionship would be accessible only after a very long time.[22]

During the four years of her final illness and death (1933-37), the Founder's organizational momentum gradually diminished even while loyally carried on by her chosen successor, Emilie W. Hurd. A desire to memorialize the accumulated traditions of EMM's "creature" (the SCHC), keeping everything just the way she liked it, became an assumed mandate. At the same time, her spiritual legacy, the Society's prayer bond, remained ever new. The prayer Companionship itself, carried by Companions in various careers over the globe, was constantly discovering new mental and spiritual horizons. Through the monthly *Intercession Papers* and the annual Summer Conferences [before the late 1950s, women had fewer opportunities elsewhere to discuss public, complex topics], far-flung Companions raised topics that broadened Companion horizons. These were the product of the modernization generated during World War II: a flow of international refugees, outreach through foreign missions, and the post-war consumer-goods revolution as wartime industries were freed from military production. Contrastingly, at the Society's center, the in-house structure was allowed to congeal around the laudable goal of "preserving" that which had been established (viewed as ordained) by EMM. One of the vehicles forcing Companions to con-

---

22 Categories adapted from Martin F. Saarinen, *Life Cycle of a Congregation*, Alban Institute [1986] reprinted 1998,

front the meaning of their "spiritual unity" was the sacred location of the Society's corporate physical life, their retreat house.

An example of solidifying may be found in the language of the Temporary Committee on Furnishings & Decoration (at Adelyn- rood) in the *1941 Annual Report.* It stated that any decisions, al- ways before deferred to Miss Morgan's final word, were of course experimental. "Dealing with visible objects" put the Committee in the position of honoring the "claims of sentiment. Certain spots we have left untouched, as, for example, the corner around Miss Mor- gan's marble portrait [bust] and the desk in the Common Room with its memorials and the apple-blossom picture-memorial to Adelyn Howard." Determined to keep the House uncluttered while aim- ing to reconcile many tastes, the Committee "tried to keep in mind a due reverence for tradition, but also a firm memory of our first leader's inventiveness and flexibility, [a person who was always] looking forward" to change. Nevertheless, conservation became the prevailing legacy. "Sometimes the inward life of Adelynrood seems to [feel like] the only important thing... But then the outward beauty of the place becomes almost sacramental... the desire to make the house a shrine of beauty is urgent."[23] The Founder's openness was being allowed to slip under the surface.

EMM's organizational dream was to meld aspects of convent life with a commitment to prophetic action, reflecting her own spacious spirituality. Her early religious habits, Calvinist Episcopal immersion in *Book of Common Prayer* language, seemed to face backward toward high-church sacramentalism. Yet she clearly modernized the historic "sisterhood pattern," aware that twenti- eth-century Companions would be "greatly cumbered" by "petty ob- servances lifted from twelfth-century religious-order rituals."[24] Her interesting hybrid Society would undergo an uneasy fifteen years before it again felt solidly grounded.

---

23 1941 *Annual Report*, 47-49, SCHC Archive.

24 *EMM Annual Letter* 1920, 187.

Vida Scudder on Wellesley
faculty, 1931; advanced in years
at Adelynrood; October 2, 1999 Living Church article by Steele W.
Martin entitled "Social Justice and Spirituality," describing VDS as "an
active socialist, involved with the settlement house movement, working
conditions of women and children, and issues of class and affluence."

Chapter 3

Vida Scudder
1861–1954
The Other Founder

"The noble leadership of the
Society in its formative years"

C-in-C Elizabeth Cook, Companion Conference
1944 Annual Report, 2-3

At this point, a focus on Vida Dutton Scudder (1861-1954) will fill in the image of a 'second founding pillar' of the SCHC.[1] Today VDS is considered nearly a co-founder, even if she entered the Society five years after EMM initiated it. Undoubtedly reflecting their social class backgrounds, neither founder wrote or said much about the financial underpinnings of their Society. The building and management of the retreat house, Adelynrood, ultimately forced them toward more complex administration, e.g. more committees and financial records than either they or the membership at large had anticipated. For that matter, Episcopal Church women historically were better at programmatic response and organizing to raise money or meet human crises than at financial management.

EMM envisioned a community of women who chose <u>praying</u> as their vocation, their most important "work." Interestingly, how such work was to be supported or financed was never verbalized. VDS contextualized that vocation in deep and rich historical patterns,

---

1 Biographical information in Teresa Corcoran, *Vida Dutton Scudder*, Boston: G.K.Hall & Co, 1982.

and helped shape its focus on contemporary issues. In teamwork with EMM, VDS developed the formative role of Companion-in-Charge of Probationers, the membership process, and filled it for almost a half-century, 1889-1943. She had the foresight to ensure that annual Companion Conference themes would be drawn from and explore the stated SCHC aims from the *Manual* (see Chrisman, *To Bind Together*, 1984[2]). And within the Society, Scudder helped develop the "retreat" experience as an essential step in forming Companionship. The individual Companion of course always brought her own Christian experience and practices to the Society, but developing the community bond required shared commitment to study, action, and prayer.

Outside the Society, Vida Scudder's name became an icon of social justice agency, and she herself a personification of the Social Gospel, as labeled by Bernard Markwell, historian of social reform in the English and American (Episcopal) churches.[3] Her radical causes included fairness to industrial workers, support of and advocacy for labor unions, and peace activism during WWI. As early as 1894, she opposed racial prejudice in the Anglo bias of immigration laws. Perhaps because 20th century readers find political protest more magnetic than institution building, Scudder's foundational leadership attracts more non-Companion interest than Emily Morgan's structural genius. Within the 1890s American Episcopal Church, Scudder symbolized "profound spiritual reaction" that led her, in her publications and lectures, to adjure educated, religiously awakened women "to break out of the frustration [and unthinking limitations surrounding them], the sheer dullness of urban industrial culture."[4] Her biographer, Sister Theresa Corcoran, designated VDS a revolutionary Christian and churchwoman, always on the cutting edge of social problems. Emily Morgan, similarly dissatisfied with her church, invested her mature energies in building the Society, its own variety of radicalism in their times.

---

2   Cited in Scudder's editorial notes, *EMM Letters*, 145.

3   Markwell op.cit, *Anglican Left*, 119-131.

4   John Higham, *Writing American History*, Indiana University Press, 1977, 133; Corcoran, 41.

Always determined to capture the pain of *the real* in her words, VDS embodied spiritual defiance of the seemingly immutable cultural and social arrangements in her world. As early as 1887, she penned words critical of upper-class women who were at ease in their privileges. She reflected the new college woman's admiration of self-direction and purpose. She was not an early supporter of women's suffrage, though she expected college graduates to be useful in society. She saw her role as awakening women-in-general to awareness of the societal injustice all around them; in this, her soul united with Morgan's. Scudder's vision broadened women's religious horizons by encouraging them to take their own moral purposes seriously. She believed that women needed to lead, to cultivate and claim their own spiritual authority. For her, as for EMM, *gritty reality* was the only antidote to the pastel-colored, enclosed, ornamental life that elite women were supposed to lead.[5]

The sudden death of a Wellesley classmate, Clara French, seemed to propel VDS toward the spiritual community of the Society of the Companions of the Holy Cross, its charism stringent enough to meet her needs.[6] Sponsored by Companion Florence Humphries, VDS embraced SCHC even though the role of religion in her life was unclear; her faith was still "provisional," she recalled. But rejecting what the Church represented "would seem more false than accepting it." She realized that heart-felt certitude about God would come "by living, not by thinking." Already deeply oriented toward women and suspecting serenely that marriage was not for her, she lamented the world's ignorance in segregating women and not crediting their contributions: "Except for the novel, which is essentially a social document, [there are] few women in the front rank" of achievement, she lamented.[7]

Fittingly, her lifelong target was the complacent Christianity

---

5 Corcoran, *op.cit*, descriptive phrases, I, 21.

6 Ibid. 86-93. The SCHC rule served as a prod about social issues, 41. Scudder, ed, *EMM Letters*, 196-97.

7 *On Journey*, 119; about marriage, 99; pro-woman focus, 65. She cited a poem by Helen Cone that expressed her impatience with the current preoccupation over sexual orientation. 211-12.

that made a mockery of religion, and churches "the bitterest farce of civilization." She and EMM agreed in that, and supported "the feminine subculture within the Progressive [political] Movement," though it would later be decried as a prettied-up Currier and Ives image of Victorian womanhood. VDS, who had secretly dreamt of enrolling in Harvard disguised as a boy, wanted women who would confront the suffering world with or without male support, despite a "cold, uncaring and unchristian" church. In 1919, Scudder's unusual participation in the General Convention of the national Episcopal Church let her see its male leadership as "totally preoccupied with the *mechanism* of legislation." That, she disdained as "administrative Christianity"—more concerned with crafting resolutions than with confronting moral and spiritual issues. Her dismay at these supposed men-of-God almost "drove her to the Quakers," she recalled. Surely parish churches and congregations, the only organizations with a legitimate claim to the label *Christian*, would rather involve themselves in bold action for Christ's vision of righteousness than in protecting their institution and agreeable relations among fellow clergy![8]

This chapter focuses on the avenues through which Scudder's influence became integral to Companionship. Her authorial voice and radical critique of mainline religion was well known in early twentieth-century reform circles outside the Society. Naturally, some of that larger "star" quality reflected back into the Society, inspiring generations of Companions. But here Vida Scudder's public persona will be background to Vida Scudder, Companion.[9]

Biography and Formative Influences

VDS was born in India in 1861, the first child of Congrega-

---

8 Ibid. *Letters*, 53; Scudder, *On Journey*.

9 For example, *The Witness*, Dec.1986, 23, listed her in a *Litany of Contemporary Episcopal Saints* (by the Rev. Sanford Cutler), reminding us constantly that justice and peace are linked, and that both are deeply rooted in our peculiar Anglican tradition." A recent article in *The Living Church* Oct. 2, 1999, 12, in the series *Shapers of the Church in the 20*ᵗʰ *c.*, was titled "Social Justice and Spirituality: Vida Scudder." By the Rev. Steele W. Martin, husband of Companion Priscilla Martin.

tional missionaries from Boston, and her father drowned when she was only a year old. Her mother returned to her maternal family in Boston, giving Vida the private schooling that nurtured her daughter's precocious intelligence. After graduating from Girls Latin School, Boston in 1878, she attended Smith College. Three years of post-graduate travel in Europe with her mother exposed young Vida to English poets like George MacDonald, theologians such as John Woolman (the notable Quaker spokesman), and radical critics of their own upper-class mentality, like John Ruskin. Once admitted into the new association of Companions, VDS quickly became an invaluable friend to and co-worker with EMM, their dialogues quintessential to the Society's self-understanding. A descendant of the E. P. Dutton family of Boston publishers, her scholarly and authorial gifts bloomed. Her published legacy comprised an extensive list, from *The Grotesque in Gothic Art* in 1887 to her last in 1952, the autobiography *My Quest For Reality.* [Her biographer Corcoran has compiled a complete chronology and bibliography.][10]

After being confirmed at Boston's Trinity Church in 1875, by the famed preacher Phillips Brooks, she was torn between her equal needs for contemplation and public action. "I must *live* if I am to interpret life. I cannot shut myself away [in libraries] and study medieval legends of the Holy Grail while men today are perishing for the Bread of Life."[11] Trying to fend off the dread "specter of unreality," in 1886-1887 VDS earned her master's degree from Smith College and joined the Salvation Army—both a protest against a stifling "plethora of privilege" [her phrase, quoted by Corcoran]. Considered a "fearless thinker and spellbinding speaker," VDS struggled to combine the social-justice activism demanded by her conscience with her calling to scholarship, writing, retreat, silence, and prayer. Like many privileged, brilliant, and vigorous white-Anglo-Saxon women in the early 1900s, she was determined to be *real,* to escape the superficiality that haunted educated women. With no professions

10 Corcoran, vi-ix.

11 Ibid 1.

yet open to such talented Protestant females, her constant goal was to connect with the reality of the world's miseries. Being appointed to the Wellesley College faculty was a first step. As a teacher of Medieval Literature, she could share her deep fascination with saints Francis and Catherine of Siena, and social critics like Ruskin. Teaching gave her a stage from which she could persuade others to open their eyes to social-class injustice.

VDS was the rare professional Episcopal woman of her time who had such a public platform. The same year she joined Wellesley (1887), she launched one of the early college settlement houses [sponsored and maintained by college women] in Boston, Dennison House, one of several precursors of professional social work with urban immigrants. [In the 1960s, as the women's history field began to appear in American colleges, VDS was named one of its early heroes: in William O'Neill's *Everyone Was Brave* (1969) and Jessie Bernard's *Academic Women* (1964)]. Scudder also published novels: *A Listener in Babel,* 1901 (a fictional treatment of her own life and faith journey over the previous decade); *The Disciple of a Saint,* 1907 (based on the life of St. Catherine of Siena, whom she regarded as the "prototype of all women idealists"); and *Brother John,* 1927, (a fictional re-telling of early Franciscan monks). She wrote biographies of St. Catherine, and of her contemporary Father James O.S. Huntington who founded the (men's) Order of the Holy Cross the same year SCHC began. She also wrote two autobiographies: *On Journey* (1937), and *My Quest for Reality (1952),* two years before her death.[12]

Within the early decades of the 1900s, Scudder helped organize the Church League for Industrial Democracy in the Episcopal Church, an action group hoping to keep alive the "tiny spark of radicalism" that had inspired resistance to WWI and her own pacifism. In CLID, she hoped to unite radical <u>and</u> conservative Christians around social justice issues. Previously, VDS had lectured at the Episcopal Theological School in Cambridge, MA, undoubtedly a

---

12 Corcoran 4, 34, 87.

first Episcopal woman thus featured. These talks were subsequently published as *The Social Teachings of the Christian Year* (1919). One of her arresting metaphors pointed out that Labor had first appeared at the Manger, in the form of poor working shepherds from the fields. They were shortly followed there by Wisdom, the three kings. "Socialism in those days hovered on the horizons of Utopia," she would write retrospectively.[13]

In early life, both Morgan and Scudder considered themselves Christian Socialists. But in the 1920s, EMM acknowledged that her financial inheritance was essential to supplement Adelynrood and Society expenses. This, in all honesty, disqualified her from full claim to that principled label. VDS remained more overtly socialist than EMM even as aging lessened her involvement in public protests. Her maturing sacramental theology led her instead toward quiescence and retreat.[14] Plus she was realistic about the modern woman and her times: "Surely there is room for a corporate life [like Companionship] that is more spontaneous, flexible in form, motivated by special religious aspiration, and with no claims on control of outward life, [nevertheless] organic, united, consecrated...Our closest model [might well] be the Third Orders of the Middle Ages."[15]

Another Episcopal critic in the same era provides instructive contrast with Scudder. Once launched into radicalism, Bishop W. M. Brown (Arkansas) got carried away, pursuing it all the way out of the church. Along with Scudder and others, Bp. Brown cited the intellectual and religious influence of Church of England priest Frederick Dennison Maurice, and the American Protestant cultural critic Reinhold Niebuhr. Brown knew VDS as a fellow churchman concerned with "class consciousness;" but his discovery of Darwinism and science in the early 1900s migrated to a Marxist position, along with outspoken racism. His fellow bishops' disapproval spurred rather

---

13 Corcoran, *Scudder 10*-12, 65, 97. *On Journey,* 163. Scudder wrote *Socialism and Character,* 1912, (dedicated to favorite student Florence Converse), which argued that a classless society combining Marxian hope and Catholic doctrine would be ideal (191).

14 Lears, No *Place of Grace*, 202-213.

15 (12-13), Vida Scudder, *House of Holiness* (pamphlet), reprinted 1964 from *On Journey*.

than quelled his extremism. Finally, Brown's rebelling against "authorities" burgeoned into rejection of core Christian doctrines: incarnation, the trinity, even the divinity of Jesus. After his "conversion to science" in 1913, he broke with Scudder and others on the critical edge of Episcopal thought. "He never understood the real difference between a genuinely concerned liberal approach to social justice issues, and extremist radicalism...a tragic, poignant story."[16]

The **Companion Conference** of **1909** had posed three revolutionary questions, still pertinent a century later: "<u>What can the church do to aid social justice? – What can the SCHC do? – What is the duty of the individual Companion in this regard?</u>" Then (and today) Companions' answers emphasized the "duty of *studying* to learn real conditions." VDS' comments reiterated EMM's ideal: "our Society" of women are "living in the world, in touch with the intellectual movements of the day, and loyal to the Church [yet] *studying* as well as accepting its teaching."[17] As early as the annual **Companion Conference** in **1911**, Companion Ellen Gates Starr presented a "thrilling" report of brave Chicago women shirtwaist workers on strike. Another Companion addressed "Our Church and the Negro."[18] In 1918, Companion Genevieve E. Cowles offered the design for the fresco she would paint in the Connecticut State Prison. These were unusual involvements for genteel Episcopal daughters and proper churchwomen of that day. EMM's euphemism, *knowledge of conditions*, was a typical upper-class understatement of the mandate requiring Companions to grapple with economic and industrial realities. They must see humanity in all its guises and not avert their faces from its ugly truths.

Of course both VDS and EMM urged Companions to keep abreast of their times by reading journals and news magazines such as "the *Nation*, the *Survey*, and pamphlets by the National Civil Lib-

---

16 Ron Carden, "The Bolshevik Bishop, William Montgomery Brown's Path to Heresy, 1906-20" *Anglican & Episcopal History 2003, Vol LXXII #2*, 197-228, quotations on 202, 211, 227.

17 Morgan, *Memories*, excerpt 1887, 4-5, italics added. *Annual Report* 1909 Companion Conference, 93,114.

18 1911 Companion Conference *Annual Report.*

erties Bureau." They each expressed "pity" for unawakened clergy and self-centered congregations who disdained humanitarian involvement in programs for the poor. If Episcopal preachers thundered against racially segregated labor unions, Scudder believed that Companions should pray against money interests and Christian apathy.[19] By the 1930s, Scudder's pacifism led her into the non-denominational peace organization Fellowship of Reconciliation.

The Gilded Age of Scudder and Morgan's youth, characterized by huge "robber-baron" fortunes and decorative excess, saw market values and business-culture assumptions infiltrate all American institutions. Worship in mainline churches took on a tone of cool, elegant rationality that feared emotional extravagance. In that Episcopal culture, Companions could represent an embarrassing exception though there was nothing inherently suspect in women praying together. Strangely, however, Companions were known to study economic and material inequities—a clear social aberration. Scudder and Morgan aimed at a Christianity enlarged beyond the evangelical emphasis on "a private pact between man and God." They dreamed of transforming the church into an "active humanitarian instrument" through prayer and influence—in and of themselves unchallengeable activities for women.[20] The **1941 *Annual Report*** carried one of many Society appreciations for VDS' stature in the larger society, e.g. saluting her reflection on the Malvern (Scotland) Declaration of the World Council of Churches, as "the salt of Adelynrood that <u>never</u> loses its savor."[21]

Retiring from college teaching in 1927 gave VDS the freedom to study St. Francis and his followers, and to meditate on Francis' Counsels of Perfection. "Religion is the leaven, not the loaf; the church as a whole is loaf, not leaven...[and] minority groups

19 Scudder ed., *Letters*, 52-53.

20 Lears, *No Place of Grace*, 1991, 24; Jean Strouse, *Morgan, American Financier.* (New York: Random House, 1999) 218-219; Vida Scudder, *The Church and The Hour: Reflections of a Socialist Churchwoman* (1917), quoted in Markwell, *The Anglican Left.* 119-131.

21 *Annual Report 1941*, 60..."a bloodless revolution due to the long slow permeation of Christian principles...[is] the best thinking in the church for many generations." Corcoran, 60-61.

within it have always had a prophetic role. The Way of the Cross [is another way of referring to] Christian revolution." An Institute of Franciscan Studies, held at Adelynrood, 1933, importantly invited participants to discern Francis's influence in the present world. Along with friendships of church figures such as British mystic and retreat leader Evelyn Underhill, VDS reported involvement in as many as fifty-four reform societies, primarily by subscription. The Church League of Industrial Democracy was her truly vital concern, she reported.[22]

When she wrote the autobiographical *On Journey*, she called it "a relief to speak in my own voice," not needing the voices of saints like "John or Hilda." She often announced her independence from restrictive dogma: "A Christian life can only be believed in from within...a creed is no wall, but a gate leading into a new country. And that country is as elusive as any earthly landscape...including holy language...to each his own Christ, as to each his own landscape."[23] Her pamphlet about Adelynrood, *A House of Holiness*, celebrated the joy to be found "in one's own mind!" She welcomed the medieval wisdom of withdrawing to a cloister when active life was finished, the "cell of my heart" as St. Catherine of Siena called it. Scudder even pondered her life as a "defeat"—unsuccessful (in worldly terms) in teaching, in reform issues, or in books. But her ultimate comfort was the sacrament: "one does not draw near the altar alone: the moment of the most intense self-realization, God-Realization, is communion," being in community, the essence of Companionship.[24]

Vida Scudder's Contribution To Retreats

The form of spiritual renewal known as retreats, previously an experience unavailable to Episcopal laity or Christians who weren't

22 *On Journey*, 348, 354
23 Ibid. 361.
24 Ibid. 405-07.

Roman Catholics, was the Society's gift to Episcopal thought and practice. In the schedule of the very first **Companion Conference, summer 1886**, EMM designated a Day of Retreat. By 1900, the Conference incorporated two retreat days, led by supportive clergy, e.g., the Right Reverend Charles Brent. Between 1901-15, SCHC quietly institutionalized two-day retreats and after 1915, three-day retreats—a new element in Protestant laywomen's spiritual lexicon.

SCHC Retreats became a regular part of the Adelynrood summer schedule, along with "constant intercessions, novenas...and a few other [Roman Catholic rituals] not available in the ordinary [non-Roman Catholic] 'vacation houses'." Adelynrood emphasized "the *spiritual* side of rest," a place of refreshment for those "not likely to come in contact with, or who from prejudice or constraint might not accept invitations to retreats in religious houses or...religious orders."[25] All Adelynrood conferences (except the Companion Conference each August which was totally filled with Companions) welcomed ecumenical seekers—Roman Catholics, Quakers, Greek Orthodox, representatives from the Federal Council of Churches (predecessor of the World Council of Churches), guests from foreign countries, nationally known activists like Jane Addams of Hull House, suffragists, active Socialist women, doctors, nurses and other professionals, college students, church school teachers, and members of Episcopal organizations like Girls' Friendly Society and the Altar Guild.

A January **1949** *IP* carried a thanksgiving that the Episcopal Church at large was finally "learning its need of retreats." That year VDS published *Retreats at Adelynrood*, a journal essay later reprinted as a pamphlet and widely circulated. Three-day retreats are crucial for busy, active women, she observed. A retreat experience allows one's mystic sensibility to open, revealing the "commonplace [as] sacramental." Retreats are an instrument uniting liturgical worship and personal devotion, nourished by daily readings from religious

25 Scudder, ed. *Letters*, e.g. 143

classics such as St. John of the Cross, St. Augustine, Eckhart, *The Cloud of Unknowing*, Plotinus, Woolman and Fox. Modern voices— Berdiaev to John Bennett's *Communism and Christianity*, Toynbee, scientist duNuoy, Alan Watts, and Edith Hamilton—were considered appropriate for retreat reading, but not newspapers or radios. Silence was to reign from 10 a.m. to 4 p.m. each day, and always overnight after Compline until breakfast. "The title of our Society [and] our constant prayers for justice and unity ensure our devout attention to the social revolution now in process," Scudder recorded. "But it is from the Interior Life [generated in retreats] that all social change must proceed."[26]

Vida Scudder's Companion Formation

Vida Scudder developed the role of Companion formation and became its longest-serving leader, Companion-in-Charge of Probationers, actually outlasting Emily Morgan's (1884-1937) tenure as Companion-in- Charge by nearly fifteen years. Her influence remained central even as physical debility circumscribed her movements greatly.

In her writings, VDS defined the Companions as "a group living [their individual lives] under definite vows, strengthened by a corporate prayer life, and aiming to specialize in spiritual goals." Traditional monastic life would have required women to be "outwardly separated from the world, wearing a garb, and entirely occupied with religious activities under obedience to a central authority." In

---

26 Vida D. Scudder, in <u>Inward Light</u>, #34 (Spring 1949), 10-13; Ibid. The archival harvest of statistics about SCHC retreats is surprisingly sparse, attributable in part to Companions' focus on quality rather than quantity. A sketchy survey found that fifty-one were registered for the annual open June retreat in 1949; in 1952, fifty-two attended, and in 1953, seventy-eight. In 1968, thirty-six June retreatants were registered, and at a 1969 retreat there were thirty-nine Companions and nineteen visitors. In 1973, sixty-two retreatants, thirty-seven of them Companions, attended an August retreat. Some twenty-four different clergy and bishops were invited retreat leaders before 1959, including Fr. Huntington of the Order of the Holy Cross, and the Reverends Moran Weston of St. Philip's in Harlem, New York City, S. Whitney Hale of Boston, and Theodore O. Wedel, Warden of the College of Preachers at Washington [D.C.] Cathedral. Presiding Bishop Frank T. Griswold conducted a retreat in the summer of 2000 for more than eighty registrants, about two-thirds of whom were Companions; other recent leaders were the Right Reverends Thomas Shaw, SSJE of Massachusetts, and Carol J. W. H. Gallagher of Southwest Virginia. In recent times laity, both men and women, have also led retreats.

Scudder's reformulation, Companions were to wear their vows *invisibly* while cultivating them deeply through prayer, study, intercession, and a daily discipline.[27] She believed that "the trouble with religious orders for many spiritually minded American women is [its] limits on their corporate freedom...and its medieval models."[28]

In 1917, Scudder melded praying with action and intervention, Companionship's dual thrust: "Intercessory prayer...is not easy to believe in or to practice. But intercession unites most perfectly our love for God and for our neighbor; it is here that the last danger of spiritual self-culture is overcome, and that the Self is merged in oneness with redeeming love...Social intercession is in a peculiar sense the prerogative, duty, and self-expression of a catholic democracy." Her wording captured the obligation of women to enlist in the reform of "what exists" in favor of Christ-centered "spiritual defiance" of the world's inequities [as in Walter Wink's thematic epigraph, Chapter 1]. EMM had stated that each woman joining the Society "makes a *profession* of intercessory prayer [emphasis added]."[29] Scudder amplified *profession* to incorporate "the secret, creative forces of thought and desire. To put the matter simply, God not only demands but also I dare say needs our cooperation, on the spiritual as well as the material plane. The Cross bearer of the universe, as He passes in our midst, does not act *for* us, but *in* us."[30]

During its first half century, SCHC was often the target of silent opposition from its own denomination's churches. Public rhetoric could denigrate or be "willfully blind" to any activity of Christian women beyond conventional fund raising and church suppers. But VDS believed that many "intellectually restive" churchwomen were not afraid of being criticized for supporting progressive social movements. And she appreciated the Society's customary commit-

---

27 *Papers of the 29th Annual Companion Conference*, August 18-25, 1925, "The Life of the S.C.H.C.," 8-9. Archive, Byfield, MA.

28 Vida D. Scudder, in Inward Light, #34, Spring 1949, 10-13; Ibid.

29 Vida Scudder, *The Church and The Hour*, New York: E. P. Dutton and Co., 1917, 119-21; *EMM Annual Letter 1938*, quoted in *SCHC Annual Report 1938*, 14.

30 Scudder, *On Journey*, 384-386 (italics added)

ment to hospitality, established by EMM. In editing the *Letters,* she recognized that EMM's "instinctive thinking" was outdated, having been shaped by the "limits of her inheritance and social class tradition." But VDS also knew that EMM had possessed "a heart [that] overleapt all barriers."[31]   In other words, EMM's founding ethos, supplemented and contextualized by VDS's historical scholarship and updated models of saintliness, created the twentieth century Companionship. Both VDS and EMM would have seen their vigorous idealism tempered as the Society became more conventionally middle-class Episcopalian in the 1950s. But back in 1889 when VDS had entered the SCHC, as many as fifty women "would scarcely have believed that eventually all my tenderest relationships would be found or formed within it."[32] Companionship provided her the sisters she had never had.

Vida Scudder's Later Years

In 1944 Vida Scudder selected from and published EMM's *Annual Letters to her Companions.* Her editorial contribution was the introduction of each time-period. EMM's cousin Emily Sophie Brown, also a Companion, furnished the biographical preface. Today we see this product as an effort to create a theology of Companionship, to establish the *Letters* as sacred text for future generations of Companions. VDS wanted the book to "rank with the *Spiritual Letters of St. Francis de Sales,*" influencing her choice of excerpts.[33]   She favored EMM's more didactic and theological prose over personal details and illustrative anecdotes. Her emphasis portrayed EMM as a gifted child of her era, born to privilege and status, but dissatisfied with any life purpose or vocation that did not combine sacramentalism with real-world engagement.

After Scudder's mother died in 1920, VDS' own home became

---

31 Ibid.

32 Ibid. *119.* See Author's notes 267-269 for probation process.

33 Vida Scudder's editorial introductions to each chronological section.

a "Companion house" that included her Companion (and former student) Florence Converse with <u>her</u> mother, who had moved there in 1919, plus Companions Lucy Smith and Helena Dudley. After Scudder retired from Wellesley (in the 1930s) and devoted her time to writing and the Society, she organized a Summer School of Christian Society Ethics at Wellesley under the auspices of Church League of Industrial Democracy [her pro-labor organization within the church]. Though age and physical debilities began to restrict her movements in the late 1940s, she remained personally and vitally involved with SCHC Probationers.[34] On New Year's Day of 1953, the year before she died at age ninety-three, in one of her many letters to Probationers, VDS made this observation: "Since dear Miss Morgan left us, her Society, which sometimes seemed almost too dependent on her personality", has experienced "a new phase of power:" the kinds of women drawn to SCHC are those who "never quite found their religious needs met elsewhere."[35]

Scudder's summary statement as Companion-in-Charge of Probationers registered organizational concerns that still resonate today: the "grave responsibility" of sponsoring new Companions, "the variety of impulses and interests that draw [women] to us, and the slow integration of these in that Way we tread, by light shining from the Cross." Her concluding lament, forever relevant in a non-residential religious association, sounded like a shepherd mourning for lost sheep—"names still on the list of Probationers, apparently lost, [with] nothing in the records from or about them."[36] She urged a policy "limiting the [allowable] period of preparation" [probation]. "Busy, seriously-minded women" need an end-point for establishing "those habits of inward discipline and faithful intercession" that constitute our Society's aims—"however humbly we Companions confess our failures in regard to them." More than a year of probation was necessary, but anything indefinite was not

---

34 Corcoran, 10-11, 65, 108.

35 Vida Scudder Papers, Adelynrood Archive, Box 53, to Martha J Gibson, January 1, 1938

36 *Annual Report* 1942, 54-54,

helpful. Also, Companions should "crystallize" Society policies for invitation and admission, leading to "greater care in extending invitations [to potential Companions]." Once explorers or visitors have actually entered the probationary process, it is "presumptuous" to label "one person's vocation less valid than others." Twenty-one Companions had been admitted in 1951: five clergy wives, five others also married, four teachers, and "only eight under age forty." VDS realized also that she represented the end of Companionship's early organizational informality. Her parting shot addressed that awareness: the probation process "is not the only point where our old and informal experimental ways are yielding, perforce, to more definite methods."[37]

In mid-**1943,** after retiring as Companion-in-Charge of Probationers and while editing EMM's *Letters,* VDS presented the paper "Per Crucem Gaudium: Companions in the Way, Retrospect and Forecast," at the **Companion Conference** whose theme was "The Crosses in our Lord's Life." She opened with recollections of the Society's founding, choice of emblem [the small plain copper cross stamped with the initials SCHC] and official Companion prayer, "an ancient prayer" of which Miss Morgan never named the source.[38] "What that prayer and its portrayal of the cross has meant to us down the long years!" She recalled the **Companion Conference** of **1913** whose theme was also "The Cross." The present Conference was taking place in an era when "ordinary religious thinking and theological study are held in poor repute, the Mystery of Atonement ignored." Yet "our little Society remains, held by its title, to find its conscious center in the study of that Holy Mystery [the cross]."[39]

"Let us not miss the significance of [our era's] increasing stress on the corporate, the social," VDS urged. We must all be "public

---

37 Ibid., 53-55

38 "Give us grace, O Eternal Father, that we strive to keep the way of the Cross and carry in our hearts the image of Jesus crucified. Make us glad to conform ourselves to thy divine will, that, being fashioned after his life-giving death, we may die according to the flesh and live according to the Spirit of Righteousness; through the same Jesus Christ our Lord and only Savior. Amen."

39 *Annual Report 1943, 3*

minded" rather than "private minded," and look at "the huge needs of the world until our own shrink to nothing." She further recalled that fifteen years earlier, in the first Conference after Miss Morgan's death (1937), the Society was also studying *The Cross in Modern Thought*. At that time the cross had been juxtaposed *against* corporate life, church, business, the state, the nation's society, and international relations. As she began to face old age and death, VDS intended a more optimistic and harmonious picture.

Unlike EMM, VDS never hesitated to claim the Society's part in the "vital" movement (led by British Archbishop William Temple) that "awaken[ed] the Anglican Communion to labor's call for justice." That movement had actually altered the image of a proud, stuffy English Country Parson to the image of an alert, contemporary missioner active on harsh city streets. She praised EMM's 50th (1934) anniversary Letter written from the Oxford, England Conference on Christian Sociology. She warned that the Social Gospel in America could "weaken" emphasis on the Kingdom of God, by allowing church folk to downplay "the creedal truths" of cross, death, and resurrection [here citing the renowned theologian Walter Rauschenbush, who had addressed the **1916 Companion Conference**]. Thankfully, this Companion conference continued to stress the Kingdom of God as *the indispensable basis of Christian thinking.* "There is nothing more striking in the religion of today than the revived emphasis on sin." Though many Americans shrink from the phrase *Original Sin*, "the [ongoing] pageant of history" undermines "facile Victorian trust in Progress," and the "conflict with Sin ever continues" [here she credited theologian Reinhold Niebuhr]. Her orthodox stance challenged a war-disrupted world.

Companions are quintessential "Children of Process," she maintained, using 'process' in its contemporary meaning of "continuous unfolding or enlightenment." Companions are crucified with Christ on his Liberty Tree and thus situated in the Way of the Cross - *Gaudium Crucis*. Once again she cited the dual emphases of

Companionly vocation, uniting "those interior disciplines we have [honored] from the beginning, with wide social vision," in "fellowship with the great movements sweeping [the world] toward a new social order." To 21st century eyes, VDS was over-optimistic about the world's "soon accepting the possibility of controlling all forms of corporate life through the power of God's grace and the laws of the Kingdom of Heaven." However, the ultimate goal toward which Companions were vowed to strive had to be Christianity's triumph. In 1943, "issues racial, international, economic, and political call for <u>our</u> witness, the kind that those who carry in our hearts 'the Image of Jesus Crucified' [from the official Companion Prayer] can best offer," she concluded. "We must dedicate ourselves anew."[40]

Scudder's international connections continued expanding through the 1940s though she was less administratively involved in the Society. Words and ideas were always her contribution: she continued sending SCHC letters and reports right up to the year before she died. She remained the Society's prophet and goad. Her "pathway of the Cross" lecture was one of her valedictory performances in the public forum of Companionship conferences, another (of which we have no copy, presently) her 1944 paper on the race issue. That presentation, reportedly well over an hour in length, was inspired by the publication that year of the first broad study of American racism, *American Dilemma*, by Swedish social scientist Gunnar Myrdal.

In her 1992 oral history, Companion Isabel Pifer reminisced about her Sponsor, "Mother Vida Scudder." Pifer had worked with Bedouins in Egypt, returning to the US in 1963 to a paid job administering settlement houses in Cambridge, MA, where she joined the nearest Episcopal Church, St. Bartholomew's, then an all-black congregation. Later in her retirement, she helped establish the SCHC Cape Cod Chapter. VDS was a "remarkable outgoing and affectionate spirit, a bubbly kind," Pifer recalled; (yet) she was also "a typical

---

40 *Annual Report* 1943, 3 ,7,11,13, 16 phrases excerpted and rearranged.

New Englander who was never demonstrative. But you knew that she cared deeply for you. She'd kept in touch with me overseas, of course, and I heard from her regularly until she died. She was the one who said to me, 'I use the daily newspaper as my intercession paper!' and taught me to do that...O how I loved her."[41]

In June of 1954, as Miss Scudder prepared to take an afternoon nap, she remarked weakly to Companion Winifred Hulbert: "My mind is so tired. After ninety-two years of work it has a right to have a rest. And at the end comes the hardest discipline of all... [One has to accept] that discipline with great courage and fortitude." She also murmured with bemusement "that I who have been for so long a radical socialist should end my days in this beautiful house...as a spoiled old lady... so many kind people caring for me." Hulbert's note ends with the following benediction: "Her hearing was entirely gone, her marvelous eye-sight almost entirely so. She was indeed ready to go."[42]

The *"Memorial for Vida Scudder"* appearing in the 1954 **Annual Report** was written by Companion Florence Converse, her partner of sixty years. Converse enumerated the range of interests and connections with which VDS had enriched the Society: "We have prayed, because of Miss Scudder, for her friend Evelyn Underhill, for Toynbee Hall in London, for college settlements, for Women's International League for Peace and Freedom (WILPF), for the American Federation of Labor, and for the Fellowship of Reconciliation. Adelynrood housed an Institute of Franciscan Studies in 1933, thanks to her." And Converse quoted a Harvard professor, husband of Companion Evelyn Cameron, to illustrate the empowering impact of Scudder's life and prayers. "If the principles of [St.] Francis touch the social order today in...few places...they touch it to the quick. We can escape the radical thoroughness of his principles only at the peril of our souls. Francis deemed that when he had something a poor man

---

41 Oral History 1992, Mary Steigner interviewer, 11. Adelynrood archives.

42 Vida Scudder, Box 2 File 9, Adelynrood archives. These final quotes were typed up after she died.

lacked, he had robbed that poor man. Those sentences should burn themselves into our souls in honor of Miss Scudder—who, upon the death of EMM, had opined that when our Society was founded, "only the Holy Ghost knew what it would grow into."[43]

The physical departure of VDS wrote *finis* to the Society's founding era. As a collective, Companions awaited a new infusion of vision and spiritual vitality.

―――――――――

Here we leave chronology for two earlier Companion views on these founding pillars. One is the mid-twentieth-century (1955) word-portrait of both founders by Companions who knew and remembered them personally. The second, written in the 1990s, offers an up-to-date lens on the founders' differing perceptions of Companion finances and public visibility in relation to social issues.

The 1955 reflection, drawn from personal experience with EMM and VDS, is typical of the 1950s "consensus history."[44] The 1994 paper titled "Spiritual Tensions in the Early Days of the SCHC" analyzed the two founders through a late-20th century historical lens that enjoyed the freedom of naming conflict and disagreement. It identifies contrasts in their personalities that would have been unthinkable, "too critical," even perhaps invisible, in the 1950s. They are summarized here, in reverse chronology.

Companion-in-Charge Clarkson's Opening Paper for the **1994 Companion Conference** began with the shared perspectives of EMM and VDS, then moved to their differences on the issue of the Society's public activism—in SCHC terminology, *taking corporate stands*. Their similarities included passionate honesty about their own self-knowledge, and a "prime, practical preoccupation with working people." Their most profound shared conviction was that Intercessory Prayer be justly seen as "an instrument of the Holy Spirit."[45]

―――――――――――

43 *Annual Report* 1954, 41-43, emphasis added.

44 A perspective described in Jacquelyn Dowd Hall, "Women Writers, the 'Southern front,' and the Dialectical Imagination." *Journal of Southern History* LXIX#1. Feb.2003, 4-38.

45 SCHC *Annual Report* 1986, Elisabeth H. Clarkson's Opening Paper of Companion Conference, "Christian Responses in a World in Crisis," 8-9.

Clarkson traced the Society's attitude on public stands back to 1917, when the Companions successfully petitioned our church's General Convention to act against abuses of labor—"to force the church to recognize its social responsibility." The Church had claimed that position rhetorically but not legislatively.[46] Jane Addams (a guest at Adelynrood) and other Companions from Hull House in Chicago were part of the Companion discussion over this petition, a dynamic element encouraging public action. Copies of the resultant petition were signed by EMM, VDS, Helena Dudley, Ellen Starr, and Florence Converse, and circulated to all Companions as well as to Convention delegates. Bishop Lawrence (MA) later reported that this petition had been crucially influential at the General Convention.

Self-questioning ensued within the Society, however: was it true Companionship to use the name of SCHC to imply the whole Society's commitment to a public stance that all may or may not have supported? Each woman [conservative, liberal, radical] having been vowed to *spiritual* Companionship but not necessarily to *public or political* unity? Was a public (group) stance essential in the SCHC commitment to Social Justice? Or was it more political than theological? Over the next sixty-three years, fears of potential divisiveness over any such corporate public actions were reflected in the Society's opinions. A statement issued by the Executive Board in the 1970s, reaffirmed in 1984 and again in 1990, has prevailed: "the SCHC is not by nature a body for the taking of public stands." *Individual, conscientious stands* on social justice topics remain the high goal and ideal of Companionship, thanks to EMM's own large-souled "genuine equanimity [toward] diversity of conviction," and VDS's lifelong advocacy.[47] Clarkson's graceful summary called VDS "our incendiary Companion," one who had welcomed "tests of heroism" and "readiness of sacrifice;" she was a Companion who knew she was "controversial...who loved the masses but was bored and

---

46 Chrisman, Miriam U. *To Bind Together: A Short History of the SCHC*, published for the SCHC Centennial, 1984, 71-72.

47 Ibid. 10, 11.

irritated by ignorant and stupid people." For VDS, "the power to love was not [her] natural impulse but a gift of grace."[48]

The year after VDS died, at the **1955 Companion Conference** in the Society's seventy-first year, two long-anticipated essays titled *The Prophetic Visions of our Founders* paid tribute to the two founders. Companions Emily Sophie Brown (Miss Morgan's cousin) and Winifred Hulbert chose key words or concepts for each founder: <u>hospitality</u> and <u>intercession</u> for EMM, concern for <u>our manner of living</u> [today it might be called life-style or mindset] and <u>life as a trail</u> or pathway, for VDS. Hulbert's adjective for VDS was "ethical;" Brown's for EMM was "hospitable," making her an earthy, practical model for Companions' use of time and money. Morgan's ideal was "personal holiness," while Scudder's was a "transformed social order." Together, the two women embodied the Society's two-pronged calling: the sacramental *philosopher* forming a goal orientation that challenged Companions' inner consciousness and outer actions, and the *philanthropist* who modelled inclusive, generous, self-giving leadership in the community's life of prayer.[49]

Both founders were fiercely honest with themselves, each despising what they deemed "fake" and "imitation." To be less than *real* was to be inauthentic, ungenuine, insincere—today, phony. Naturally, such determination opened their eyes to much of the falseness in the elitist ethos of much of the Episcopal Church as they experienced it. Both had a time of rebelling against formal religion. Even as teen-agers, each was repulsed by the church's rivalry over theological and churchmanship issues—rabid low-church militants *vs.* overly-precious high-church ritualists. Even worse was the church's disconnection from the "real life" that EMM and VDS intended to live. That "real life" required unblinking acquaintance with and friendship for those on the edges of their worlds. Their

---

48 1986 Opening Paper, Clarkson, quoting Emily Sophie Brown, pamphlet 8.

49 Companion Conference papers, 1955, *The Prophetic Visions of our Founders*, 1. EMM by Emily Sophie Brown: Pt 2, VDS by Winifred Hulbert – pp 11 on. All quotes hereafter from this booklet except where noted.

disdain for what was "fake" armed them against the Boston- and Hartford-society prescriptions of proper dress, calling-card rituals, and elegant afternoon tea. The intense, doubting young Vida had prayed: "O God, if there is one, make me a REAL person." Young Emily, horrified "by the inequity between privilege and poverty" as factory women trudged up the road to the textile mills, feared that her only spiritual alternatives were "atheist or hypocrite." Her instinctive embrace of tired laborers finally "brought her [in touch with] the Christ she sought."

If ardent self-honesty was their initial bond, a second was the new idealism of educated 20th century American females: the desire to use an aroused consciousness for improving the lot of the poor in their own city neighborhoods. Like many religiously committed young women seeking a channel for their moral energies and intellects, EMM and VDS needed a prayer-*and*-service connection with *reality*. For them, that was accessible only through personal involvement with those in need. And the ground of both action and service was intercessory prayer. When the Society had expanded to 120 Companions, EMM cautioned that belonging was not important in itself, only for the "strength it gave them to work for others." VDS wrote that for her, connection with "social reality" carried an additional benefit: mental stimulus. She famously observed that "the monopoly of consorting wholly with like-minded folk" would be total anathema. Her vocation saw Christianity as societal, not just personal, salvation; Christ's message was the only one that could bring justice to a harsh, unjust world. Well into old age, Scudder cherished the idea of eternal battle between light and darkness, the vigorous combat between the forces of Good and Evil.[50]

The contrast between them came in the way the two defined vocation—differently, supplementally. Miss Morgan saw *"vocation"* interpreted through and nurtured by the SCHC. Unlike traditional

---

50 *Annual Report* 1989, 8; "Social Christianity" was another term for "Social Gospel"—see Gary Scott Smith: *The Search for Social Salvation; Social Christianity and America 1880-1925*, Lexington: Lanham Pub. 2000.

religious orders (Roman Catholic sisters or Protestant deaconesses) set apart from the world, EMM wanted Companions to live "in the world" but use their "individual influences, social or otherwise, [on] the serious religious, educational, and social problems of our age, first by prayer and then by battle." Adelynrood the House was to be "like Adelyn's heart, a community life lived simply but broadly." Her cousin Sophie Brown could discern in the adult EMM a residue of Victorian manners that Morgan thought she had shed: Adelynrood community life should be full of "princesses of courtesy, gracious-ness, and helpfulness," in almost "old-fashioned" ways. In EMM's role as "ultimate arbiter" in the Society, "playing referee" may have become tedious enough that her mother's ideals could seem useful. They could compliment EMM's great-souled hospitality and open-armed theology.

Miss Scudder, a scholar of many phases of Christian history, was the mental giant who located the Society in the long procession of "minority groups that exist from time to time." To her, SCHC's dis-tinctive *vocation* offered "modern spiritual-minded women [whose occupations keep them in the daily world] a center for corporate life lived spontaneously, under no [human or churchly] authority" yet remaining "organic, united, consecrated." In her eyes, SCHC was a "modern pioneer among those historic [prophetic] groups [that] from time to time have enriched the church and released its powers."

Hulbert's 1955 perspective emphasized Miss Scudder's convic-tion that religion was the sole "clue" capable of transforming hu-manity, of being an "action-philosophy" or mission statement. In the words of Bishop Parsons (Diocese of California), VDS was one "to whom church meant a *challenge to sacrificial adventure* rather than a *bulwark of the accepted order* [italics added]." Scudder's em-phasis on cleansing an evil world may also be seen as a religious mantle intended to protect herself from the Communist hunting of Senator Joseph McCarthy. For all her radical sympathies, Miss Scudder's vehicle of reform was not the political party identity the

Senator enjoyed exposing. Through her life, Scudder's overarching commitment was to let her ideal of Christian Social Justice go wherever it led. She was fearless about "offending any who did not meet her standards of Christian life."[51] According to Hulbert, Scudder had often described herself as "overawed" by the revolutionary and paradoxical character of Jesus' teachings, a discovery succeeding generations of Companions would repeat. VDS had dared hope that her last years on earth would turn out to have witnessed "a veritable Christian revolution." Hulbert's conclusion credited VDS with the "prophetic meaning and [envisioning of a] practical goal toward which human hope was [surely] moving."

After 1941, Companions and the succeeding Companions-in-Charge (Emilie Hurd, Elizabeth Cook, Grace Lindley, and Jeannette Booth) would honor EMM for the breadth ("catholicity") of SCHC membership and the Society's avoidance of ecclesiastical politics. ["I never heard the phrase 'high church' applied to us," a Companion now in her 80s recently observed.] They would revere VDS for her civic idealism and theology, and her deep grounding in historical and spiritual Anglo-Catholicism [without thus labeling it]. Rare in that competitive religious climate, both appreciated "*every* religious expression of the human race." "Truth is a sphere," Scudder had written; "no one can see the whole of it." C-in-C Huntington, who would be elected in the late 1950s, saluted the two-pillar heritage of Companions as the "fusion of the prophetic and the mystical in EMM and VDS."[52]

---

51 *Op cit*, 21, 22
52 Virginia Huntington's *Memorial*, by Lee Beaty, 1983. Archive, Adelynrood.

This 1959 group photo, showing Companions in prayer caps, was taken to commemorate the Society's 75th Anniversary.

Commentary about the church and racial issues is captured in this 1954 drawing by Allan Rohan Crite, son of Companion Annamae Crite.

1952 Christian Education Conference attendees pose at Adelynrood.

Chapter 4

SCHC
1941–1954

"Our holy flame in a time of global agony"

Vida Scudder, Per Crucem Gaudium, (paper) 1943

This chapter's introductory quotation is a typically ardent phrase from Scudder's **1943 Companion Conference** paper *"The Way of the Cross."* This chapter's bookend is her death in 1954 which signaled the end of what both VDS and EMM called the Society's "informal experimental period." The narrative focus of this timeframe is the Society's literal struggle to define the vocation of Companionship without the active presence of the founders. Organizational rigidity lurked, a result of the anxiety about preserving EMM's noble vision. Polarization threatened between Companions for whom social justice issues were paramount and those whose primary focus was their own spiritual development. While the founders lived, open bifurcation could be avoided. But as VDS summarized in her 1943 paper, the 1940s were a time not only of global agony but also of anxiety over direction and identity among Companions.

Outside the Society, war generated huge changes that we today call modernization. Retrospectively the most troubling new aspect was the nation's, and the Episcopal Church's, still-reluctant admission of racial inequality. A few Companions had sent petitions about race to the *IP* beginning in the early 1900s. And a lonely beacon pointing toward a Christian awakening was an experimental interracial community, Koinonia Farm, founded in 1942 by two Baptist ministers.[1] If Companions talked among themselves about race, they probably assumed SCHC was already enlightened on that issue: there were indeed a few African-American Companions. However, in the Society's typically discrete, typically Episcopal records, a Companion's race is never listed and thus visible only contextually. Further abroad, occupied Japan would absorb some "Americanization;" the Marshall Plan's enlightened assistance would promote European recovery from war damage, and the imposed partition of Palestine would establish Israel and decades of Middle-East confrontations. At the same time, African colonies began throwing off Anglo-European domination.

Fortunately, Companions' spiritual horizons about the concept of racism were broadening in the US, thanks to reading about abruptly-evacuated West Coast Japanese-Americans during the War. After that came refugees and displaced persons fleeing the war in Europe. China wars and the Communist revolution would force Christian missionaries, including a number of Companions, to leave. Domestically, the anti-Communist scare was underway within the US, led by Senator Joseph McCarthy. On the home front also, these years saw housework revolutionized by a flood of consumer goods as postwar factories turned from armaments to refrigerators, washers, and dryers. [The emergence of mid-20th century American middle-class culture is vividly captured in Doris Kearns Goodwin's *No Ordinary Times*, 1994, dramatizing the expanding of minds and lives during the Roosevelt years, 1940s-early 1950s].

On the church scene, the first Bible translations challenging the King James' language of scripture appeared, presaging other upsetting changes. The post-war Episcopal Church also woke to the need

---

1 *Interracialism and Christian Community in the Postwar South: The Story of Koininia Farm*, by Tracy Elain K'Meyer, Charlottesville, University of Virginia Press, 1997.

for more relevant religious education, thus initiating a new curriculum to be called *The Seabury Series*. A first religious-institution role for women, many of them Companions, also began: professional careers as DREs (Directors of Religious Education) in large, multi-staff parishes. These currents shaping the Episcopal Church's self-understanding naturally began to influence the SCHC

The first four Cs-in-C following EMM's death shouldered the Society's leadership during this transition. Companions' concerns and challenges have been traced, here, from the published record of **Annual Reports** and *IP* intercessions, year by year. Social Justice petitions in particular offer an accessible index of the times, and demonstrate concretely the impact of the external world on Companions' religious self-understanding.

The Society–1941–54

1937-41— Emilie Hurd's caretaker regime, after which three elected Cs-in-C assumed Society leadership.

1942-45— Elizabeth Cook was the first elected Companion-in-Charge (Jessie Degen, Assistant C-in-C). Cook led 439 Companions and 43 Probationers. Adelaide T. Case was Companion-in-Charge of Probationers from 1942-45, succeeding Vida Scudder.

1945-51— Grace Lindley (Emily M. Crosby, Assistant C-in-C) shepherded 445 Companions and 30 Probationers. Deaconess Jane B. Gillespy was C-in-C of P, 1945-51.

1951-55— Jeannette Booth (Emily Sophie Brown, Assistant C-in-C) led 470+ Companions and 35 Probationers. Dorothy B. Weske was C-in-C of P.[2]

A 1959 *Cumulative Index* noted that Companion dues were

---

2 *Select Index* 1959. These years display fairly static numbers, a quantitative note neither EMM nor VDS would have dignified with attention since their concern was spiritual and personal, rather than numerical. Today, calculating the Society's brightest glow in terms of numbers alone, the period after WW I (1925-40) was the early-twentieth century apex of the Society. In that segment, with EMM and VDS both alive during part or all of it, the number of Probationers sometimes rose

$4 in 1948, $5 in 1950, and $7.50 in 1955. Participant-historians, the SCHC Recording Secretaries (following Carolyn W. Brown who served from 1906-36, the first thirty years) each served four-year terms. After 1915, Corresponding Secretaries also served two-year terms from 1915-1942 (except Irma Titus, who served from 1942-1948). The Society's financial stewards, the Treasurers (first appointed in 1906), were Nina E. Browne, 1906-1915; Harriet B. Harmon, 1922-30; and Alice M. Bartlett, 1930-58.

EMM herself had produced the *IP*s for eighteen years, from 1884-1912. Clara G. Tracy then became editor 1912-21, and Grace E. White, 1922-37. From 1938 on, *IP* editors served four-year terms: Dorothy B. Weske, Elsie Wickenden, Alpha W. Barlow, J. Gwendolen Morse, and Mary Grey Barron, up to 1953. During the period covered by the *Cumulative Index (1884-1959)*, some 66 (out of 479) Companions were listed in enough Committee activities to require more than one line in the *Index*,[3] a proportion of organizationally engaged Companions that persists into the present time.

During these transition years, much of the prophetic dynamism that had emanated from Miss Morgan & Miss Scudder (as they were always formally addressed within the Society) now came toward the center from the geographic edges rather than radiating outward from the center. Companions who were missionaries and teachers in distant, non-Anglo or non-middle-class settings imported their wider-world perspective into the SCHC via the *IP* and summer conferences. This direction of current nourished one strand of the Companionship's collective mindset—focus on breadth of outlook, plus spirited religious advocacy for social issues on which local parish churches rarely took a public stance. The other "mind" in the Society focused on spiritual growth, a definite rule-of-life and prescribed religious tasks. Balancing these "two minds" required juggling the organizational, administrative, and program needs of Adelynrood and

---

to 50 per year.

3 Aug. 19-24, 1941 *Annual Report*, 55, 18.

the Society amid the spiritual commitment to praying. A quiet joust-
ing for dominance began to emerge between them. Meanwhile, gas
rationing and four-million war-production jobs were luring many
women into factories (though not many Companions), along with
many poor black Southern Americans who brought their Jim Crow-
restricted lives into proximity with Northern white Christians. In
April 1942, some 120,000 Japanese Americans from the West Coast,
over 80% of them US citizens, were forced out of their homes, jobs,
and farms—evoking sadly little protest from the churches. Actually,
one Companion in California sent an anguished *IP* petition for her
Japanese friends, but neither she nor others criticized the government program of incarceration itself.

CHRONOLOGY:
Intercessions, Annual Reports, and Newsletters

Vida Scudder's 1943 phrase, "global agony," was a coded reference to World War II, the painful backdrop of Companionship during this time. President Roosevelt declared war on Japan Dec. 7,
1941, and shortly thereafter on Germany and Italy. Jews in Europe
started to feel the heavy hand of Nazism that forced them to wear
the demeaning yellow-star armband. With war anxieties deepening,
the theme for the **1942 Companion Conference** was *Thanksgiving*. Conference papers presented newly urgent calls for ecumenical and interfaith social action among Jews/Catholics/Protestants,
through existing vehicles, e.g. the World YWCA, the International
Red Cross. The **Business Meeting** opened with thanksgivings for
the first elected C-in-C, Elizabeth M. Cook (who would serve only
during the war years, 1942-45).

That announcement in the *Annual Report*[4] was nearly over-
shadowed by a second internal Society issue: Vida Scudder's failing
health required her to relinquish the role of C-in-C of Probationers.

---

4 A summary of Companion Conference and Society information, titled the *Secretary's Report* of
   (Year) was first published in print form in 1906. Its name and function became the *Annual Report*
   in 1947. Scudder, ed. *Letters*, 85.

Her successor, Adelaide T. Case, PhD, was "a greatly respected and admired professor of Christian education at the Columbia University School of Education." [She would later become the first female to teach at an Episcopal Seminary, ETS in Cambridge, Massachusetts. As a single woman, however, she was not allowed to stay overnight at the seminary, recalled Frances M. Young (admitted to SCHC in 1938). [Case had to commute from New York City weekly, by train.] Scudder's resignation elicited two profound responses: regret at the undeniable end of the "founders' era," and gratitude for the years of loving care "expended on our Beloved Society [that has established] an intimate companionship of spirit around the world." Retiring C-in-C Hurd observed: "[Scudder's] retirement marks a transition in our corporate life, the seriousness of which we all realize. We know that she cannot be replaced. But we should be untrue to her and to the memory of Emily Morgan did we fear for our future. The Spirit who has hitherto guided us to leaders of outstanding quality will guide us still."[5]

An example of the Society's post-Morgan administrative steps, its maturing method,[6] was the newly established *Committee on Artistic Planning* for Adelynrood. Its mandate was to create specifications [today called Guidelines] for Adelynrood décor that must combine principle, esthetics, and theological stewardship. Its platform statement in the **1942 *Annual Report*** aligned SCHC esthetically with the Church Army [a Church of England version of the Salvation Army], the Salvation Army, Quakers, and historic Puritans, all dedicated to the Life of the Spirit: "External goods are not the most important thing for us," the report began. "Still, the educational and social backgrounds of many Companions taught them that visual beauty was an essential element in spiritual ex-

---

5 *Annual Report* 1941, emphasis added.

6 EMM's own administrative style was idiosyncratic, not compatible with any Robert's Rules of Order model, and less democratic than she "truly" intended. As VDS editorialized, EMM couldn't resist paying any bills that came directly to her, thus undercutting the Society's sense of financial responsibility. And though she was a genius at social and personality management, one "had to have a sense of humor to enjoy her conducting Executive Council and the Finance Committees." Scudder, ed. *Letters*, 182, 234.

pression." The Incarnation is a doctrine and belief that accepts the outward and the physical, even glorifying it. "Our Companion House must be made rightly beautiful—to express [visually] the life and order of our House and the Society's principles." There was to be "no 'period' furniture; no inlay; no mahogany; no gimcracks; no so-called Victorian furniture, but rather something that might suggest the frontier, or the peasant, made by the same kind of hands that made our beams and rafters."[7]

The report then listed more principles: comfort, never primary but always basic, must not be ignored; door curtains or "portieres" hanging in the bedroom doors on both sides of the long upstairs hall should be harmonious in tone and color. No pictures should be hung where too-dark walls inhibit their appreciation. "A dead oil finish or stain on furniture, an old English oak or natural wood finish" was preferred over paint. Avoid "small bric-a-brac [such as] small holy water stoups where no blessed water can be put in them."[8] The report wove together the Society's organizational evolution, its spiritual vision, and external standards of beauty: "SCHC came into being long years before [the present] Adelynrood, [from] a company of those who saw a vision of the ineffable beauty of the Spirit [that] accepted suffering [turned into] healing." Invoking the spirit of Adelyn Howard, and of founders EMM and VDS, "outward expression of this beauty [at the House] is inadequate [and] must always be so. Meanwhile we trust in the Spirit to lead us, in its own good time, to ways of permanent outward beauty, as to the restoration of all our souls."[9]

All the *IP* petitions cited from here on bear the *date of their appearance in the IP,* rather than journalistic or factual time. In each case, they are samples or examples of the more than fifty petitions in an average issue of the *IP.*

---

7 This standard illustrates the burgeoning interest in folk-art and peasant-culture viewed as more "genuine" than Victoriana, as well as rejecting commercial modernization. Lears, *No Place of Grace, 1994.*

8 *Annual Report* 1942, 46-47.

9 Ibid.

1942— *Note: phrases in quotations are from the IPs.*

The **January** *IP* rejoiced that Episcopal missionaries in Hawaii and other places abroad were safe after the attack on Pearl Harbor, and prayed "quiet justice preserve us from hate." A Companion asked that "one of our [domestic] Bishops" rise above his bigotry and give "the bread of life to his colored folk, now denied it because of race."[10] Companions generally worried about the "lawlessness of youth in crowded cities, no jobs and poor housing as the factors actually responsible for their state," a somewhat rare prayer in white 1940s Episcopal churches. There were prayers that leaders of the Negro race and their white friends "solve" [resolve] efforts "for the spiritual welfare of our soldiers and in the training camps" [segregated and unequally provisioned] newly established by the draft, and that "the Negroes, excluded from Holy Communion in some of our churches, keep their faith in face of this unchristian treatment."

The **March** *IP* carried prayers that "our nation become more truly Christian in recognizing Negroes, Jews and other races as God's children & our brothers," and achieve "an end to discrimination against Negroes in employment, in teaching, and in the Army & Navy," as well as relief for peoples starving under Nazi occupation. Thanksgivings were offered for the life of our beloved Founder EMM; prayers asked that Christians become "aware of racial discrimination within [our] church" and "that the church become what our Lord wants it to be." There was a thanksgiving for Vida Scudder's many years of shepherding Probationers and for Adelaide T. Case, soon to assume that responsibility. The prayer "that the Body and Blood of our Lord be given to Negro boys & girls in Talladega, a segregated college in Alabama," accompanied a plea for raising the status of the Negroes employed in defense and war-product factories, segregated and unequally paid. Some individual Companions sent in petitions for the safety of family members in the military.

---

10 It is probable that many petitions about race discrimination came from Martha Jane Gibson, a Companion teaching in historically segregated Talladega College, Alabama.

ed: Mrs. Jamura, a Japanese visitor, seemed to "embody the spirit of cooperation with self-respect and resourcefulness."[15] A highpoint of the Social Justice Conference was Vida Scudder's major paper analyzing Swedish social scientist Dr. Gunnar Myrdal's study of race relations [titled *An American Dilemma*], exclaiming: "what implications this book has for us as Christians!" The Rev. S. Whitney Hale from Boston led the retreat on the topic of *Incarnation*.[16]

In **December 1944**, a thanksgiving on the *IP* title page announced that Emily Malbone Morgan's *Annual Letters to Companions*, edited by Vida Scudder, were now in book form, "a permanent treasure for fresh inspiration new from them as from her [in the original version]; for the record of her life set forth by the only one who could so richly portray it [the biographical introduction by Morgan's cousin, Emily Sophie Brown], for the loving care of the editor [VDS] and publisher [E.P.Dutton and Co., copyrighted to the Society itself], and for every detail—for all who brought this perfect gift to us."

1945—

[Intercessions in this period usually avoided the use of personal names except, occasionally, that of the Companion requesting the petition. Gradually, more names and illnesses, e.g. alcoholism, began to be specified in the late 1940s-50s.]

Missionaries in foreign locations were listed, including the new "colored bishop David W. Bravid Harris of Liberia," along with the new international ecumenical organization called the World Council of Churches. Christians must feel "deep unity in prayer with our Jewish brethren over the agony of [the war-marred establishment of] Israel," plus "responsibility for a just, lasting peace." A Compan-

---

15 *Annual Report* 1944, 36-37.

16 *IP* thanksgivings celebrated all missionaries, the special presence of all races and nationalities at Adelynrood during summer 1944, Archbishop William Temple's influence, the Federal Council of Churches [predecessor to the National Council of Churches], the General Council of the Anglican Communion, and the quest for unity among India, Burma and Ceylon churches. At present no copy of Scudder's 1944 paper has been found.

ion requested prayerful support of the Dumbarton Oaks proposal to establish the United Nations, which Companions were urged to read about in the *Readers Digest,* and to support by writing their congressmen. One prayer hoped that Japanese-Americans being relocated from the internment camps to the Connecticut Valley would experience "Christian consideration, and opportunities for good social adjustment." They also prayed for the "spiritual power" of chaplains in the Armed Forces. A Companion prayed "for all religious, particularly the Episcopal Sisters of St. Margaret and of St. Mary," and for breaking down "white soldiers' prejudice...toward their fellow fighters of the Negro race, that those from whom equal sacrifice had been demanded" not experience discrimination in civilian life.

In **May**, a thanksgiving in heavy dark type rejoiced in "**our country's order and stability in the crisis,**" and "**for the noble leadership and peaceful death of our President Franklin Delano Roosevelt.**" Separate thanksgivings noted his "noble personal qualities," his work for Social Justice, his sponsoring of the Tennessee Valley Authority that brought electricity to millions in mid-America; his being a "champion of the Common Man, his Christian stand upon racial questions, and his allowing Japanese-American citizens to serve voluntarily in a segregated army unit" [becoming the most highly decorated military unit of the war]. The paragraph ended with thanks for his work toward peace, the Atlantic Charter, the Four Freedoms, and for quotations from his speeches, including the phrase "an end to the *beginnings* of all wars."[17]

In **June**, thanksgivings named the "solemn gladness of VE Day, the dignity and reserve of our generals at the German surrender," and prayed for an end to fighting in Japan. Prayers asked for strength to face the "past tragedy and future tasks," including the world's determination to "organize permanent freedom from war, based on justice and economic peace." Special prayers blessed the San Francisco conference founding the United Nations, in order that

---

17 *IP* May 1945, 19.

"victory might prevail over hatred and the desire for revenge." There were hopes that "the fine work our church" did among "interned Nisei [American-born Japanese citizens] may continue to help these loyal Americans in their restored freedom, and help others to accept them ungrudgingly for what they are proving themselves to be [loyal Americans]." Such enlightened petitions were rarely visible in newspapers, or discussed in the average Episcopal parish. A petition asked for "clear thinking in the subject of relations between differing races in USA," for justice to "those of the Negro race who are members of our own communion," and that employers and workers cooperate in post-war industry. A special blessing was invoked for the new Secretary of Labor, Episcopalian Frances Perkins, the only woman in the President's Cabinet, and the major intellect and spirit behind the legislation that created Social Security.[18]

July-August 1945. Blessings were asked for the two daughters of Evelyn, Companion, in American Friends Service Committee work this summer. There were thanksgivings for the end of the war, plus "liberation of the atomic bomb from war service." [There was no mention of the atomic destruction of Hiroshima.] A darker petition expressed "a rising [sense of] horror of the immorality prevalent in many walks of life," and also asked that the surrendering Japanese "be given grace and wisdom" including the emperor, leaders, counselors, and people, "helping them to accept their hard situation with right understanding, and to cooperate with the UN in building a better Japan." There was a special thanksgiving for General Douglas MacArthur and the Japanese occupation; he seemed to combine "a soldier's with a statesman's insight in adjustment between Japanese psychology and the UN."[19]

Following the death of C-in-C Elizabeth Cook, Companions invoked the Holy Spirit's leading, and offered thanksgivings "for those willing to take committee leadership, particularly in the difficult details and responsibility of matters relating to the House." There was

18 *IP* June 1945, 7.
19 *IP* Aug. 1945, 12.

also praise for Miss Scudder's guidance of many, many Probationers into the Society and thanksgivings for her continued Companionship. An oblique petition for "better community life" at Adelynrood asked, "that a Companion may overcome the habit of making critical remarks and may grow in love." Personal petitions with that focus were very rare indeed, as if Companions felt constrained to share requests for prayer only on loftier problems and issues. Personal thanksgivings, however, continued to be plentiful.

1946—

A Companion lamented, in **January**, "the baleful restrictions on Jewish immigration to this country," but thanked God for President Truman's dealings with a contentious Congress, and invoked a "just settlement in the difficult problem of Palestine." Christians must pray and work, they urged, for improvement of mental hospitals and orphanages for "those in custody of the state," for improvement of "dangerous working conditions in our mines," and for "repentance" among "negligent stockholders." Copies of the Scudder edition of EMM's *Letters* were announced as available at $3.50.

In **March**, petitions appeared for a "cessation of bitterness toward Japan," and for a conference on disarmament: "If you want this effort made, pray and write your legislator NOW," one Companion urged. Petitions prayed that "civil war between Manufacturers and Laborers [would be] averted." Deaconess Gillespy, the new Companion-in-Charge of Probationers, was blessed, as was a new Hospitality Fund to help Companions with travel expenses to Adelynrood. There were thanksgivings for a new Probationer, Annamae (Mrs. Oscar) Crite,[20] mother of the Bostonian African-American painter Allan Rohan Crite. He would later donate his series of paintings *Stations of the Cross* to the Adelynrood chapel.

---

20 At this time she led her church's altar guild and was a long-term student at the Harvard Extension night school, finally earning an award for excellence but never putting her credits together for a degree.

The **May** *IP* recorded "great thanksgiving" for "an interracial charter signed at the YWCA's recent national convention"—the first majority-white public institution to expressly disavow membership race discrimination. Another petition invoked a rare plea for orthodoxy: "return us from [the prevailing] shallow Christian humanism to the profound wisdom of catholic theology and the great Christian doctrine, and to the blessings of Holy Unction, and also for a Companion's ecstatic joy in the life of a tiny black kitten witnessing to the tender love of our Creator." Combining lofty theological goals with love for a pet was unusual in an *IP* petition. Finally, another asked "thanksgiving for the lovely, joyous life of our founder Emily Morgan, for all those who helped her here, and all who have carried on since her going," perhaps evoked by the now-available book version of her *Letters*.[21]

Here follows a summarized paper from the **1946 Companion Conference**, presented in a different font to set it apart from *Intercession Paper* citations.

In her **1946 Companion Conference** Opening Paper, C-in-C Grace Lindley reported discussing with her bishop whether she "needed" to become a Companion: surely the church itself should provide her with all the "companionship" she could want. He advised that joining the SCHC would actually lead her "more and more into depth of the church's meaning." This day she thankfully named the "Christian intimacy, the Christian sympathy" she had found in Companionship. When we kneel in chapel for our fifteen minutes of intercessing, it's not just us as individuals praying, but the Society praying through us. Each of us is enlarged by the corporate power of SCHC, "but each individual also pours her strength into and through SCHC." Titled a searching "*Wherefore?*" her paper articulated the Society's mood of uncertainty.

Lindley named the concept "Paradise Chapter" [perhaps the first time it appeared in print] as the gift that allows Companions to live NOW in two worlds at once, to "think Christianly of death." Our former C-in-C Elizabeth Cook is no further away now than last summer, Lindley

---

21 Prayers included the UN, the relief of suffering in Europe and Asia, the US President and his cabinet, and the work of the Society of Friends in Finland, Germany, Austria, Yugoslavia, France, Italy, and Holland. A special prayer honored German Christians who kept love in their hearts through war and surrender, the Dutch Christians who sheltered Jews, and Christians in Japan who had kept the faith.

observed; through prayer companionship we are in eternity with her, here and now. She reminded Companions that the "precious element of Anglicanism honored by our Companionship" is its dual Protestant-Catholic heritage, reference to cooperation amid conflicts over high- and low-churchmanship (never named). And over whether or not we take *corporate stands*: "Miss Morgan would not want us NOT to change, if the times demand change: our choices are NOT doing or not doing, but method [or organizing principle]: should this Society, acting as a society, undertake a definite [unified] thing to pour its united energies into, at this time?" Or should our Society continue, "to inspire us who work as individuals" through local religious and secular organizations? This is one of the few times the Society's record included open grappling over emphases about corporate public action in "the Way of the Cross." The C-in-C's suggestion [reiterated in 2000] was that each Companion attack <u>one</u> task at home and report back on it the following summer. The worst "worst thing" would be to <u>NOT face up</u> to an issue or conflict.[22]

The **1946** *Annual Report* also contained the most direct statement of then-prevailing SCHC "secrecy policy" found thus far. This is an interesting historical note for today's Companions who puzzle over the secretiveness of 1950s-60s Companionship, troubling in its similarity to college sororities. The C-in-C, discussing a proposed conference to acquaint young people with praying and intercession as a way of life, suggested that such a gathering have an alternate name, perhaps something like "St. Martin's Comrades," to prevent *any publicity "or any sort of promotion"* about the Society (italics added). Realistically, SCHC was a vocation rather than a "club" one could join out of interest or curiosity, and this attitude may well have protected the Society from having to disappoint inquirers, as well as helping avoid anything that smacked of self-promotion. Quoting the C-in-C: *"Hidden* [sic]—that has been and must still be the quality of our [Companion] life, and of our gifts. Reticence has been our great safeguard. [Inference suggests that it also covered any attempt at interference from church officials.]"[23] The 1946 retreat topic was the *Foundations of the Christian Unity* and *Social Justice* theme committees. Daily petitions in the *IP* were grouped under those themes plus

---

22 Companion Conference *Annual Report* 1946, 11, 12.

23 *Annual Report,* 1946, 67; IP, Jan 7, 9; Feb 7; March 7.

Christian Mission, Social Justice, The Nation, and on Saturdays, *Needs Personal and General.*[24]

Later (**October 1946**) there was a thanksgiving for C-in-C Lindley's leadership, and "the manifest desire of the C-in-C that each step forward be a truly *corporate* expression" of the will of the Society, the result of "weighed opinions of us all." Yet corporate public stands on social-justice issues that could be seen as political continued to be feared. There were continued pleas for "protection of the ideals of the Society and its forward look" [from or for what only implied]. Any topic that elicited conflicting stances was smoothed over in published material, alluded to rather than named—an apparent modification of EMM's forthright style.

Thanksgivings came with the observation that the current Layman's Movement [promoting the leadership of lay churchmen instead of clergy autocracy] was significant enough to be news in *The New York Times,* along with noting that many returned military were entering the ordained ministry. Episcopal seminaries reflected this new student population. A special intercession asked, "that America-the-privileged...live above pettiness, partisanship in elections, and [be able to] face issues in the light of justice and for the common weal." Finally, thanksgivings at a corporate communion saluted the Dec. 10 birthday of founder EMM, as well as the United Council of Church Women and its president, Companion Georgiana [Mrs. Harper] Sibley, along with World Community Day. A petition invoked "a more vivid and intelligent realization of the danger of racial prejudice in the country, and the conviction to overcome it in the way of Christian brotherhood." Prayers "for the new social and economic order struggling to birth all over the world" referred to African and Asian nations emerging from colonialism. "Replacing the cynical faith in the profit motive" must be united with the joyous dynamic of Love and Goodwill.[25] The euphemism in such stately prayer phrases left events or problems unspecified.

---

24 *IP* daily themes had begun to be more specialized in 1917: the general theme of *Missions* separated out prayers for *Reconciliation of Classes.* In 1930, that theme was renamed *Social Justice.*

25 *IP* 1946, Oct 6, 9.

1947—

The **January** *IP* prayed for many Church institutions: for missions, for the new Presiding Bishop Henry Knox Sherrill, for seminaries, hospitals, prisons, and overseas missions. A special petition focused on the federal investigation of the Monroe, Georgia lynchings that could help establish right principles for ending racial conflicts. The term "lynching" appeared in the *IP* far more frequently than in most other Episcopal Church or other Christian publications.[26]

In **February** many petitions addressed the issue of race, requesting forgiveness for the "still unintegrated race relations" that "set our government back" in the esteem of other nations; for better housing and education for our Negro citizens, for eliminating "slum conditions for home-loving and children-loving Negroes," and for our white "indifference or blindness to such conditions." One Companion prayed that Americans wake up to the "inconsistent, temporizing nature of dealings between white/Negro citizens," and that God could move "many Christian Negroes to work among their own race."[27] March petitions for the first time prayed for "displaced persons in Europe," as well as for Gen. Marshall's plan to help rebuild war-torn Europe.

The **May 1947** *IP* cover featured, in bold type, a "**Thanksgiving For The Life Of Our Founder [EMM]; And For The Ideals Of Her Foundation, More And More Revealed With The Passing Of The Years**." Another Companion gave thanks for the daily inspiration of the *IP* and *Manual*, our heritage, and "for a peach tree in full bloom in a city yard." Thanksgivings greeted the "rarity" of a healing service at St. John's Church, Washington DC, the constancy and for-

26 Concerns were expressed also about inflation, financial depression, the rights of Conscientious Objectors, the American Friends Service Committee, UNRRA, and our soldiers in Europe acting "like gentlemen in their dealings with those they control," blocking a drift to dictatorship in emerging nations, and for strengthening devotion to Francis [of Assisi] and the Stigmata of the Cross.

27 A decade after EMM's death, the GI bill was passed—a great landmark in American higher education that made college education available for the first time to an entire generation of men, many the first in their family. This legislation however established anti-gay thought and customs, creating a "straight state." Legally excluded were many blacks that had served in the military, and anyone accused of homosexual tendencies. *Journal of American History* Dec. 2003, 90 #3, 935-957, "Building a Straight State: Sexuality and Social Citizenship under the GI BILL" by Margot Canaday.

bearance of a Companion's Japanese Christian friend, and Attorney General [Thomas C.] Clark as "a man completely sold on Civil Liberties." Also, a petition gave thanks "for the Presidential Committee on Civil Rights" helping to "make that REAL to all citizens, and to remove the blindness that still makes lynching possible [emphasis in original]."[28]

VOLUME 1 NUMBER 1 NEWSLETTER, dated **MAY 1947**, announced its aim as trying to "fill the long-felt need" of many Companions for "<u>news of each other</u>, plus essential information about direct and indirect matters of the welfare, spiritual and practical, of SCHC [emphasis added], paid for by the Hartford Chapter and others, "to avoid depleting our beleaguered national treasury." A note of Societal anxiety followed: the times call heavily on the spiritual resources of each of us. "The Society needs to review where we are going, corporately and individually." If this *Newsletter* contributes to "a clearer understanding of the Way, it will have accomplished its purpose."

A list of tasks for which Adelynrood volunteers were needed is familiar (if dated), e.g., to set up for afternoon tea; to pass out fresh linen at stated times; to help clearing tables, washing silver etc, when needed; occasionally to dust the House and clean other than one's own room. Agenda items for the August **Business Meeting** would include a memorial for former C-in-C Elizabeth Cook, and a decision on Summer Conference topics, either "Religious Education and the Crisis of Today," or "Companions' Relation to the Industrial Situation." Also: a place and date for the 1948 Winter Conference, and the thorny problem of publicity: how should SCHC promote non-Episcopal groups using Adelynrood facilities—for hospitality, but also to bring in income? Should the *Newsletter* be continued? If so, donations outside the dues structure would be required.

The 1947 Winter Conference hosted by the New Haven, New York, and Philadelphia chapters was held at St. John Baptist Convent in Mendham, NJ, and chaired by Rebecca H. Morton, attracting forty-two Companions from ten chapters. Henderika Rynbergen discussed *Today's Needs in Industry and Minorities*, one of their studies of racial inequality. Deaconess Gillespy pleaded that Companions not refer to the Society by its initials: "our name is great; why do we rarely use it?"

<u>Notes</u> from the Executive Board (in the end pages of the *IP*) included: a report that an appeal to cover the past year's deficit brought in $3,100 from 130 Companions; an announcement of the Winter Conference

---

28 May 1947 *IP*, 3, 7.

1948 to be hosted by Baltimore/Washington chapters; Hospitality Fund limits; the possibility of an Industrial Workers Conference with Hilda Smith and the Hudson Shore Labor School; Religious Educators presenting a conference for children; a Visiting Day for Children in next summer's calendar being considered. The *Christian Unity Committee* urged prayer fellowship with women of other communions. There should be some neighborhood hospitality for Byfield friends/neighbors next summer on the agenda. Funds were donated to buy the new *1940 Hymnals* for the chapel. Brief biographies introduced newly admitted Companions.

The **September** *IP* brought thanksgivings for the Society of St. Margaret and its British founder, Dr. John Mason Neale, a century earlier, along with a plea for "true Catholic faith in our church." In **October**, there were thanksgivings for Olive Sproul [non-member] who faithfully laundered the Adelynrood Chapel linen for thirty years. One Companion wrote that two thousand places awaited workers in the church's various mission fields. The Faith & Order Movement (sponsored by the World Council of Churches) was studying the points of unity among the various creeds and liturgies. The *Social Justice* page carried a special petition for Edward Way, a young Negro Veteran in South Carolina deserving an honorable release, presently serving a life sentence for murder allegedly committed in self-defense against two armed whites. On the theme page titled *The Nations,* there were prayers for an Atomic Control Commission, and thanksgivings for the American Bible Society. Companions were urged to read "The House that Hate Built" in the October *New Republic* magazine; they were urged to pray that Congress ameliorate the plight of migrant workers, as fictionalized in John Steinbeck's *Grapes of Wrath.*

A second **NEWSLETTER, ADVENT 1947,** was a single mimeographed page. A published **Annual Report** with which it was mailed would now contain most Society information, a next step in organizational evolution. From then on the **Annual Report,** "fully printed and inclusive of all administrative information," should serve three groups of Companions: "those who were at Adelynrood last summer, who can nod and say yes, that is how it was; those who have been there sometime in the past, saying yes, that's how it must have been; and those who've never been," imagining it and wishing to be there sometime. It was hoped that both the *Annual Report* and the *Newsletter*, "perhaps insignificant in the sense of our spiritual growth," will yet "answer our prayer that we may be drawn to one another" in the bonds of Companionship.

The Third Winter Conference March 5-7, 1948, was announced for Seabury House, in Greenwich CT, to be led by four chapters: Hartford, New Haven, New York, and Philadelphia.

1948—

This was the year in which Pres. Harry Truman desegregated the US Military by executive order. The **February** *IP* led off with "Great & loving thanksgivings for our Founder EMM on the 11th anniversary of her death on Feb. 17; may she grow from Strength to Strength in the Vision of Being and Beauty." Petitions requested support for young women in Episcopal professional training schools [such as Windham House in New York City] who were preparing for a full-time career in church work. Also named were people starving all over the world, plus Gandhi, Nehru, and Palestine.[29]

Deaconess Potter, Companion in California, gave thanks for the newly-available drug penicillin; a Companion prayed that our senators and representatives would waste *less time talking* "while the world waits in need," and that the Marshall Plan in Europe be seen "primarily as an aid to recovery, not as a weapon against Russia." A note regarding liturgy change in parishes urged every church to celebrate Holy Eucharist on holy days even if they fell on a weekday.[30]

May, the *IP* month of thanksgivings only, included many thanks for the life of EMM, for her "high spirit of gayety [*sic*]" for the "fathomless depths of her human sympathy," for the length and breadth of her vision and wisdom, for all the treasures of her heritage in the Society of her Foundation for which we daily give thanks to God. For Companionship and all that it means." Several Companions

---

29 A <u>Notice</u>, page 11, cited the 1947 vote to cease printing the summer *Corporate Devotions Leaflet* (saving expenses)...but in 1948, the decision was made to issue it as in the past. Would Companions send word of approval or disapproval to the C-in-C? The number of *IP* pages was being reduced because of cost.

30 January 1948 *IP*, 1; 11.

contributed to this summary, since individual thanksgivings tried to stay within the stated word limit.

June thanksgivings rejoiced in Bishop Norman Nash's "bold stand"(Diocese of Massachusetts) approving Planned Parenthood, formerly a health and sexual issue ignored or considered too controversial to endorse publicly; and for Bishop Sherrill's teaching presence at the NY Jewish synagogue and seminary, plus for cooperation with the Methodist denomination; and for race relations in general. A thoughtful petition attempted to summarize the Companion mood: *"Pray that the changing trends now becoming evident in our life at Adelynrood, and incident to living growth, new interests, and new personalities, may bring us forward to where we would be, avoiding the evil of rigidities but never altering the ideals of our Foundation or destroying in the smallest degree the blessed quality of Adelynrood as the spiritual home of us all"* [italics added].

July-August: Prayers included thanksgivings for the progress of education and school missionary work in China, and for the 75th anniversary observance of "our own" Holy Cross Day. Prayers were requested for a brilliant, unstable son-in-law, become alcoholic since the war, for the whole Benedictine Order (Roman Catholic as well as Episcopal), and for all young Americans working in Europe this summer. Special thanksgivings were offered for the life and peaceful death of Adelaide T. Case, renowned Christian Educator and the C-in-C of Probationers after Vida Scudder. The retreat theme at **Companion Conference** was *"Christian Education in the Present Crisis,"* Bishop Block of California the leader.

In the **September** *IP*, "our chapel bell rang every hour on August 22, along with church bells all over the world" for the World Council of Churches meeting in Amsterdam, a high point of ecumenical interest. Petitions requested "the increasing enlightenment of the Holy Spirit on our special corporate vocations in the SCHC, and our possible function among religious Groups in the contemporary Church." A petition asked that more women seek lay careers in the church as

Directors of Religious Education. Blessings were offered for Companions Eleanor Mason and Florence Risley teaching at the Christian College of Madras, India, and for the inspiration found in the book version of EMM's *Letters*. Special thanksgivings were offered for the leadership of C-in-C Grace Lindley, and "for the presence of Vida Scudder in our midst on Companion Day, the deep inspiration of her paper [on race prejudice], and the many signposts she has erected for us along the way through her years of journeying." One Companion wrote: "May we go forth from this summer with new plans into possible new trends about the problems and opportunities of the modern day, and hold firm to the ideals of our FOUNDATION, preserving for future generations of Companions the spirit which drew us and bound us and inspired us within our Prayer, our Rule, and Intercessions" [the word "foundation" in this usage seems to refer to EMM].

October *IP*: Thanksgivings were offered for Episcopal Church radio programs, for those who broadcast and those who listen; for the United Nations charter; and for peace. One Companion prayed that God "overrule" the increase in race prejudice in America, Palestine, and South Africa, and that all who've been "blessed by retreats at Adelynrood become living witnesses to the truths received there."

November *IP*: Ten Companions, most having belonged to the Society for at least ten years, gave thanks for Vida Scudder's "probation training;" another gave thanks for the success of shock treatment to a mentally ill friend; and another thanked God for all those Companions who, in these difficult times, manage the financial affairs of the Society: "our zealous Treasurer and Asst. Treasurer, our careful Finance Committee Chair and its members, and our wise Trustees," a rare prayer mentioning finances. A petition written jointly by two Companions, "after serious study and discussion," appeared on the *Spiritual Life* theme page:

1- that each chapter realizes its responsibility to prevent war, by prayer

2- that each determines to find a way of expressing devotion to the Companionship more vigorously

3- that each physically able Companion plans an annual visit to Adelynrood, to maintain and strengthen the foundation of the Society

4- that all "weak links" in SCHC be strengthened [in order that] the cause of Christ's Kingdom may spread, and

5- that unquestionable loyalty to the church control all SCHC policies and programs.

[This petition may reflect increasing factionalism in local parishes and congregations, among other concerns—a threat to the surface harmony important in the denomination's image.]

December *IP*: Perhaps in reference to journalistic preoccupation with the threat of Communism and other menaces, the opening thanksgiving celebrated "living in one of the most exciting crises in Christian history"! Also, there was a thanksgiving for "dialectical clash of opinion and theory ever present within the living spiritual experience of the Church," for persistent faith in the UN, and for a little "group in our town who, when the noon whistle blows, prays each day for the family of nations." Thanksgivings were offered for the wise leadership of [the Rev.] John Heuss [chair of Christian Education leadership at the National Council of the Episcopal Church in NYC] and his efforts to "arouse" the whole church to the importance of its instructional teachings [the new Sunday School curriculum, *The Seabury Series*], for more church libraries in local parishes, for two Companions and their deepening love as they complete six years together, for Displaced Persons from Communist Europe, and for our own "tormented consciences" until the "evils of racial segregation are clearly faced and as a Church and society we move to Christ's own pattern."

1949—

The **January** *IP* brought thanksgivings for the increasing number of small Christian communities or groups. One Companion rejoiced in "weekly meetings" of her local prayer group, and another rejoiced that *the rest of the Church was learning to acknowledge its need of retreats,* a sense of pride-of-ownership among Companions [italics added]. There were petitions that Jews and Arabs would let pilgrims visit Bethlehem at Christmas, for a free election in Berlin, and for SCHC Sponsors trying to help each new Probationer "realize the vocation of the Holy Cross," in its "solemnity of obligation and in the fullness of joy and thanksgiving." **February** prayers brought increasing attention to the weakness of church school and Christian education in the Episcopal Church. They offered thanksgivings and blessings for Mrs. Eleanor Roosevelt's "unflinching human leadership," for Pres. Truman's strong humanitarian programs, for better fellowship among the varied races and creeds, and for the relief agency CARE.[31]

The *NEWSLETTER,* **APRIL 1949,** formatted in narrow pamphlet size, printed a note from China. A Companion, secretary to Bishop Tsang, reported that hospitals and schools were still allowed to carry on after the Communist takeover, and expressed American optimism as well as Christian hope: "I rather look forward to experiencing history in the making."

Winifred Hulbert, one of five Companions working abroad, reported "indelible impressions" of Europeans' courtesy at all social levels: they "unconsciously show a greater cooperation and sense of unity than we, in our unbombed America." She concluded: "the Cold War will inevitably turn into a shooting war unless Christian Americans really see to it that America carries out its international relations in a spirit of commitment to the UN."

This issue also carried what may well have been the first widely circulated statement about Companions' dues paying. C-in-C Grace Lindley's introduction was a series of questions: do you realize that every Companion is the owner of an estate, Adelynrood? Have you been

---

31 Feb. 1949 *IP*, 6. In the nation, a book, Lillian Smith's *Killers of the Dream*, seemed to light a fuse toward a Civil Rights awakening. Meanwhile, during the late 1940s, the nation was having a kind of "national nervous breakdown" about spies and Communists. Ted Morgan, "REDS: MacCarthyism in 20th c America," *New York Review of Books*, Feb 12, 2004, 21-23.

there? How recently? Can you come this summer? Can you make it an "old home summer?" Adelynrood, open from June 13-Sept 15, charged Companions $4 per day, and the previous summer had created a deficit of $500. Companions should invite friends to pay and stay, not just for new Companions, but also for their souls' refreshment.

Also included was an unusual numerical report that acknowledged rising cash concerns:

> TOTAL: 349 Companions, 131 Pledges = $2,241 by March 15, 1949
> 125 paid dues only
> 100 paid dues + an additional yearly pledge
> 1 @ $50
> 3 @ $100   **29 haven't paid dues for 4-7 yrs
> 14 @ $25   **87 haven't paid 1949 dues
> 22 @ $10   **65 exempt from dues
> 39 @ $5   **43 are Probationers who don't pay dues
> 27 @ $3

April thanksgivings were offered for Companion Miriam Van Waters' work over the past eighteen years with prisoners at the Framingham (Massachusetts) Reformatory for Women, for the Child Labor Committee in Congress having erected one more barrier against "man's inhumanity to man," and for a welcoming of Displaced Persons into the U.S. On the *Spiritual Life* theme page, there was an urgent prayer for Companions' recommitment to Adelynrood and the Society: "Let us pray earnestly for life at Adelynrood, for faithfulness in our daily offices and more [Companion] hours of prayer in chapel, the center of all our life; for the joy of spiritual Companionship, also for its discipline within our House; for our C-in-C, for Conferences and groups; and that in every trend of our life we may be receptive to the revelation of our Lords' all-encompassing Love."[32]

May: During the month of thanksgivings only in the *IP*, there were "thanks *more profound with every year* for the life of our Founder EMM, for her consecrated wisdom and wit; and for all that she built into this Society of her foundation, now entrusted to our keeping." Also there was a first-appearance of thanksgiving for an

---

32 JBG's telephone interviews with Companion Lee Beaty in 2002, 2003. Companions entering at this point noted more open competition between the material/social or purely spiritual emphases.

African Anglican, the Bishop of Zanzibar, and for a domestic missionary in Utah...and special blessings invoked for British Jews, "rising above prejudice," who help care for "Arab refugees," also for those in US "standing against racial and religious prejudice."

June: A Companion gave thanks for work with blind children, which had taught her "the reality of the unseen." Companions rejoiced in lifting of the Berlin Blockade, and that the UN had found building space in New York City. The 53rd annual **Companion Conference**, with Grace Lindley as C-in-C, was a "paper-less" conference.[33] Its theme was *The Disciplines of Daily Life: What it means to us as Companions.*[34]

In **October**, an ambitious petition hoped that Protestant groups would welcome and resettle a quota of 50,000 Displaced Persons in the next months. Canon Theodore O. Wedel, [Warden of the College of Preachers at the Washington Cathedral, and husband of Companion Cynthia Wedel, a widely known national churchwoman and one-time president of the World Council of Churches] presided over the admission of Companions at Adelynrood Chapel "in the presence of a very elderly saint, Vida Scudder," and led the retreat on *The Disciplines of Daily Life and its Meaning for Companions.*

The *IP* end pages printed *Late News from China* about the war's effect on Companions. Also there was a didactic (if prayerful) paragraph about retreats: "Worry while on retreat is just plain sin! Grownups need to learn to retreat as simply as children take a new experience: just sink into silence, realize the love of God, and meditate on whatever they find most helpful. To be simple is the way to garner the riches of a retreat."

---

33 A separate Notice in the *IP*: The 1949 Companion Conference will test the idea that Companions have "more to give" [contribute] than emerges through the activities of presenting or listening to papers. "The best part of the Conference was being with Companions" has long been the majority sentiment, so this conference will find everyone spending a good part of each morning in "groups at work upon light tasks. While hands are busy, minds work more freely, as we know." No one would be *pressured* to take part in work, or to join the same group on successive days. This trial structure may have aimed at increasing Companion participation in conferences, as much as at serious cost-cutting. The general theme was to be "*Service of God through Daily Work*" (though the Committee was still looking for a better wording). This programmatic experiment may have signaled restlessness toward the existing conference pattern, and an attempt to combine work and prayer in a more explicitly Benedictine pattern.

34 June 1949 *IP*, 3, 14-15.

November 1949 carried prayers for a conference of the Episcopal League for Social Action [formerly Vida Scudder's Church League for Industrial Democracy], for Russia, for Nehru's visit to the U.S. and for a boy of seven in an iron lung [a first reference to the polio epidemic]. On the last page was the announcement that a Chapel Memorial Fund had been established, its first expenditure to be the purchase of a "new white superfrontal."

1950—

The Korean War began. Ralph Bunche, ambassador to the UN, received the Nobel Peace Prize, one of the first African-Americans thus honored. Alger Hiss was tried for treason, and the singer, athlete, actor Paul Robeson received public vilification for his pro-communist sympathies, resulting from a stereotyped interpretation of his visit to Russia. As Episcopalians across the nation found various ways to face up to or deny their discomfort with new awareness of racial discrimination and inequality, "from the mid-1950s to the 1980s, full racial integration was a concept from which our national church leaders still shrank." But the "social reform" thinking that actually occurred, among Companions and others, focused on school desegregation and educational integration as its linchpin. It was a major step for white Christians who had not personally confronted inequality and the humiliations of racism, or faced the privileged mindset that accompanied their status because of white skin.[35]

> The **NEWSLETTER, May 1950,** (Donna Brian Gropp, editor) expressed thanks for the many ways in which our SCHC bond is maintained, including this product, "written words." She penned another plea that Companions support Adelynrood as their corporate expression, and renewed concerns for supporting the role of the Retreat House in the Society's corporate life, especially the need for Companions to attend summer conference and retreat programs.

> The 54th Spring Conference on prayer, "*Living according to the Spirit*

---

35 Gardiner H. Shattuck, Jr.: *Episcopalians And Race; Civil War To Civil Rights*, University Press of Kentucky, 2000, 83.

of *Righteousness,"* [a phrase from the Companion prayer] was planned by Chicago Companions. The bulk of the *Newsletter* consisted of chapter and personal reports, e.g., one from returned China missionary Marian Craighill. Companion Judy Clark wrote about living there under a Communist government: "I believe the fine foundation of the past 100+ years will stand up to changes, [although] a definite Communist re-education program against US teachers and clergy is being carried out. We try hard to yield on inessentials, and to persist in what relates to our faith. It is a wonderful privilege to be here and to be a part of history-in-the-making in a very conscious way. Yes, there are growing pains, but we ARE growing." In conquered and occupied Japan, 26 churches remain: "we help do our part in the rebuilding of Japan." About a dozen brief first-person biographies introduced recently admitted Companions: six clergy wives, a musician and YWCA worker, a public health nurse, teachers, and welfare workers.[36]

In **February**, thanksgivings saluted the efforts of the Department of Christian Education of the National Council that produced the first volumes of the new *Seabury Series* curriculum [the national Episcopal Church's response to the shocking statistics gathered from WWII Episcopalians in the military—a survey of various Christian denominations in the military had revealed that those identifying themselves as Episcopalian were more thoroughly uninformed about their church, their faith, and their denomination than any other].[37] Special thanksgivings were offered for authors E. Stanley Jones writing about Gandhi, Elton Trueblood on Albert Schweitzer, Dorothy Sayers's popular book *The Man Born to be King,* and a book about William Temple, the Archbishop of Canterbury, a leader in social justice concerns and considered a special "saint" by Companions.

April: Special thanksgivings acknowledged the Rev. Sam Shoemaker's mission at Trinity Church, Boston and a traveling U.S. mission by a spellbinding Church of England evangelist, Bryan Green. [Companion Helen Shoemaker, co-founded the *Anglican Fellowship of Prayer* with Companion Polly Wiley; they also co-founded Schools of Prayer that were held in various parishes during the 1950s]. Com-

---

36 *Newsletter* May 1950, 4-12; 5. Adelynrood Archive.

37 Feb. *IP,* 1950, 5.

panions prayed for the constructive use of atomic energy, for the "Displaced Persons" beginning to flood into the U.S, and for more "God-centered leadership" in our country and in the UN Assembly. There were thanksgivings for Alan Paton's interracial work in South Africa and his influential book *Cry, the Beloved Country*. Under the *Spiritual Life* theme, a petition prayed for new and "more courageous" Christian education: it must reach, inform, and inspire the younger generation, and wipe out the older generations' complacency in the face of competition from "dim-sighted forms of Christianity." More women's prayer cells were "springing up everywhere: colleges, schools, business places," and were greeted with thanksgiving. Then a self-caution: One petition warned that when tempted to resent the religious attitudes of "those who think <u>they</u> are right, remember that we too think we are right." This may have been an early allusion to the Rev. Billy Graham and the rise of public evangelicalism journalistically.

May: The first page of this month's *IP* [always entirely devoted to thanksgivings] honored Founder EMM and her friend Adelyn H. Howard, the "first Companion whose courageous, consecrated life influenced EMM so greatly." Prayers for the Society itself were thanksgivings for those assuming responsibility as officers and on committees, and for the blessed influence of former Companion-in-Charge Emilie W. Hurd, now in the Paradise Chapter. A Companion rejoiced over her "deepening joy" in use of the *IP*, and praised a "cripple in Lexington" who had spearheaded the community participation that resettled twelve displaced persons. On *The Nations* page, prayers supported a Peace Vigil in NYC under the auspices of the World Council of Churches and its 156-member denominations from forty-four countries, "to witness against the H-bomb which is a sin against God."

A **June** petition made indirect reference to the McCarthy hearings, asking for a US government that would "not assume guilt on accusation only" and would protect freedom of speech and the press. A Companion prayed that the U.S. try to develop a "sense of shame over the proportion of our wealth expended upon weapons," instead of on peace and welfare. Also, a petition asked that the wages of Conscientious Objectors, having been withheld during the war, now be sent to CARE for relief work. The **July–August** *IP* carried prayers for the courage of delegates to the 1949 General Convention as they were asked to vote for a vastly increased national budget. And a new *SCHC Manual* was announced, the first to be published since the 1930 edition.

In **September** a petition asked blessings on the new housing developments springing up all over the nation, and that "families in them may seek Christ." These prayers reflected the opening of vast suburbs, a housing boom whose first public symbol was Levittown, Long Island, NY, and its mass-produced, "cookie-cutter houses." This signaled the beginnings of a white exodus from city centers, and located Episcopal Church growth away from poverty toward segregated housing.[38] There was also a thanksgiving for "an old age free from dissatisfaction in any material matter" and for the blessings of being in Companionship over the past fifteen years. There was a thanksgiving for the "liveliness" of the community life at Adelynrood, and for deepened understanding among Companions along with our differing attitudes toward race relations "as shown in our Conference Discussions." Intercessions named the preoccupations of government appointees on Indian reservations that keep them from "*serving* the Indians." The **Companion Conference** retreat theme, "*Lord Teach Us To Pray*," explored the official daily Companion prayer.

The **November** *IP* carried one of the few prayers in this extensive Archive about marriage: "that men and women realize their union may be the means whereby another *SOUL* is brought into the world, to carry out God's purpose." This prayer may have reflected

---

38 Eric Avila, *The Age of White Flight: Fear and Fantasy in Suburban Los Angeles*, University of California Press, Berkeley, 2004.

the rising discussion of divorce and remarriage within the Episcopal Church. The end of 1950 included a prayer of thanksgiving for Emily Morgan, our Founder, on her December 10th birthday: *"May that date become our own Holy Day."*

End-paper <u>Notice</u>: Announcement that an Emilie Hurd Hospitality Fund was now established to assist Probationers coming to Adelynrood for the first time.

1951—

The Peace Treaty with Japan was finally signed, and the first full-color commercial appeared on television. African-American Pauli Murray, PhD, educator, lawyer, and legal scholar who would be one of the earliest Episcopal women to be ordained in 1977, published a landmark study of segregation that contributed to the eventual civil-rights legislation.

January: A Companion offered thanksgivings for our historical church doctrines, also for Ralph Bunche, the American "Negro diplomat" at the UN, and for UNESCO, the relief agency focused on children. There was a prayer for Peter Marshall, the popular chaplain of the U.S. Senate, and author of *Mr. Jones, Meet the Master*, as well as petitions for the immensely poor nation Haiti. [The Society of St. Margaret in Boston operated programs there, involving several Companions.]

March prayers supported the "spread of the church in the Diocese of West Texas," and hoped that many young women would join Deaconess Training Programs. Companions prayed for complete disarmament, and for Congress to put its "duty to the electorate" above politics. There were thanksgivings for small groups of women "informed on all levels about government problems like the League of Women Voters." Prayers lamented the arrogance of race and class, and "our (SCHC) self-centered in-look"—an interesting self-commentary.

The **APRIL** *NEWSLETTER,* **1951**, Grace Lindley C-in-C, contained routine Committee reports: *Chapel, Artistic Planning, Library, Building and Repairs,* and *Finance.* Donna Gropp retired as *Newsletter* editor, to be succeeded by Irma Titus, who wrote that the more time she resides at Adelynrood, the more she appreciates its unique fitness for our ministry of intercession and the more she sees "appallingly strong reasons why we should make the widest and fullest use of it." The Winter Conference held at Seabury House in Greenwich, CT, reported sixty-two present: seven from China. Florence Risley, who had worked overseas in the YWCA for thirty years, reported her post-war visit to Belgium. Althea Bremer, from China, reported that Christians there now must meet in peoples' homes, since Americans are no longer allowed to own or maintain property.

April: There were thanksgivings for a mission at St. Martin-in-the-Fields (Philadelphia) conducted by the Very Rev. James Pike, for a Vigil of Prayer at the UN building, for the great composer Johann Sebastian Bach, and for a Companion's deepening joy in his music as she grows older. Under *Social Justice,* there was a poem-prayer in stanzas, with the refrain: "*We have professed to follow thee, but have not had thy spirit.*" Another prayer cautioned against work that satisfies one's own self but is no help to others; another petition acknowledged that Americans' financial and geographic "security" protects us from knowing or caring how many have to live in fear, also our "beautiful homes that keep us from worrying about who lives in squalor."

June: Thanksgivings were offered for the safe exit of twenty-eight Companion missionaries from China, and for the domestically-awakened interest in Episcopal Christian Education, especially the re-vitalization of Adult Education in parishes. One Companion wrote: "Forgive our wrongs to people of other races and nations." The July-August *IP* blessed the work of CARE, and pleaded that migrant farm workers be treated as any human should be. There were also prayers for better housing for all races and colors.

September: Thanksgivings were offered for C-in-C Lindley's selfless six years of leadership and for the newly elected C-in-C Jeannette Booth, and for a laymen's conference on Christian Education, led by Companions Dora Chaplin and Cynthia Wedel.

Thanksgivings also greeted a first Adelynrood retreat specifically for clergy wives, and the radiant life, inspiration, and friendship of Adelaide Case [former C-in-C of Probationers and a Professor of Christian Education]. There was a petition urging volunteers to work in the Good Shepherd Mission in Arizona [still a missionary district of the national church]. **October** brought a petition urging more caution in admitting new Companions to SCHC, moving only when there is "an increase in the understanding of the aims of the SCHC, and what the Way of the Cross is." This indication of Societal concern was rarely expressed. A list of Companions formerly in China was appended.

November petitions contained pleas for the "emancipation" of labor everywhere, and for freedom from the terrible bondage to narcotics, the first time that issue was named in the *IP*. A petition asked that Christians tune in to "the abuses [manipulations] of advertising." There were two prayers for alcoholics. **December** thanksgivings remembered our first C-in-C and Founder, EMM, for her successor Emilie Hurd, and her successor Elizabeth Cook.

1952—

The US tested the H-bomb in the Pacific, the Maumau revolt erupted in Kenya, and a steel strike lasted fifty-four days.

January thanksgivings included praise for two MIT students who raised $63,000 to bring students from Africa and Asia for technology training that equipped them to return to their own countries and teach others. There was a thanksgiving for Vida Scudder's wise and patient nurture of Probationers and the entire Companionship, and for many Companions' selfless work among refugees, our "new Americans." There was the suggestion that all Companions should read Baptist missionary Frank Laubach's *Wake up or Blow up*. An appended Notice expressed Miss Scudder's thanks to Companions for her 90th birthday remembrances and her regret at being unable to answer each one personally.

In **February**, a Companion gave thanks for her 3-year-old niece's recovery from polio, and another rejoiced over the new publication *Anglican Theological Review*. **March** petitions applauded the daily five-minute radio broadcasts titled "This I Believe" that emphasized spiritual values. There were thanksgivings for Vida Scudder's many Probationers, and for the missionary district of Utah. Petitions were offered for the Very Reverend James Pike, the new Dean of the Cathedral St. John the Divine in NYC, and for the Billy Graham evangelistic mission in Washington, DC.

May 1952 *NEWSLETTER*—Jeannette Booth, C-in-C. The Winter Conference reflected the anti-Communist preoccupation of the era: "Communism is one form of power, a religion, but one of fear, not of love. A stronger religion only can meet a religion like communism. We have to demonstrate Christianity rather than merely talk." Newly-elected Jeannette Booth was introduced as a "product of Connecticut, as much as any nutmeg!" She had attended Mt. Holyoke College, did graduate work at Yale, and taught in Salisbury, CT. She first came to Adelynrood with a Girls' Friendly Society conference (an urban Episcopal ministry to adolescent girls), where she met Emily Morgan, Elizabeth Cook, and Leslie Townsend who drew her into Companionship.

A new SCHC chapter was established in Texas; an Index had been created for the *Letters of EMM*. A plan for an International Weekend at Adelynrood July 4-7 was made, and a retreat for clergy wives July 14-17. Committee Notes included reports from *Chapel, Garden and Grounds, House,* and *Library Committees.* From occupied Japan, Companion-missionary Elizabeth Upton, living with a Christian family, described their hardships: the times were very tight and "my one indulgence is the occasional *Reader's Digest.*" GIs were very generous with Christmas gifts to the Japanese, giving them wood they could burn for warmth, and toys. Interestingly, on Christmas Day, the *Nippon Times* published an 8-page supplement of Dickens' *Christmas Carol* as a means of interpreting secular Christmas and Christianity to a Buddhist nation.

Companions who were admitted in 1951 shared brief personal histories, e.g. Janet Barton Morgan. She has three children (ages 21, 19, 13), lives in Amherst, loves music, drama, and intellectual activity, and participates in her church's Women's Auxiliary, Altar Guild, and choir. She enjoys walking and bird-watching, is married to a Fine Arts professor (also an archaeologist) and has traveled to Greece five times, coming to love the Greek Orthodox Church. Becoming a Companion has been the best thing in her life.

> Others included a teacher who'd thought herself a spoiled kid until the "face of Christ" changed her; also Elizabeth Bennett Gwin, daughter of the Episcopal Bishop in Niobrara (working with American Indians), and Gladys Hall, a physically disabled Deaconess who was very active. Also, a visiting nurse, an overseas Red Cross worker who had converted from Unitarianism, and Bertha Spafford Vester, whose lifelong career had taken place in Jerusalem where she had survived two World Wars and the Arab revolution. This is a fascinating issue, as informative as today's Memorials in the published *Annual Reports.*

May thanksgivings were offered for Presiding Bishop and Mrs. Sherrill who conducted the inspirational admission service at Adelynrood, for Congressional debates about migratory labor, and for programs providing help to addicts of narcotics and alcohol. There was thanksgiving that the US had admitted 100,000 refugees per year for the past three years, and "for evidence of righteous indignation and enlightened consciences regarding racial and class injustices. And Lo! The Dawn!" [39]

June thanksgivings named the gift of Elima Foster's index to *EMM Letters*, and the good work of Alcoholics Anonymous. Prayers urged support of the five professional-training institutions under the rubric of the American Church Institute for Negroes, of the School of Indian Girls in South Dakota, and of Cuttington College in Liberia. Petitions prayed for conversion of the one-hundred-thousand Chinese in the US, 97% of whom are without Christianity. Under the *Social Justice* theme, a prayer begged *"forgiveness for our neglect of sharecroppers, migrant workers, and racial blindness; and for exploitation of the helpless through drugs, liquor, and gambling"* [italics added]. Companion Mary Morrison, a published Episcopal journalist, was admitted. A <u>Notice</u> from the C-in-C of Probationers requested that Sponsors hold any new Probationer papers from June 1 until September 15, to allow the clearing up of a waiting list. Miss Scudder's last book, *My Quest for Reality*, dedicated to the SCHC, went on sale to benefit the Emilie Hurd Hospitality fund. The **Companion Conference** retreat, led by Bp. Voegli, Missionary

---

39 May 1952 *IP*, 6.

Bishop of Haiti, addressed *Women's Responsibility in the Missionary Life of the Church.*

In **November** Companions prayed that the restrictive and discriminatory McCarran Immigration Act be amended, and that the rising tide of anti-Semitism in Germany be stopped. There were prayers for Christians and Jews behind the Iron Curtain, and for uprooted Arabs living in terrible misery in refugee camps in Israel. In **December** thanksgivings were offered for a new president of Talladega College, AL, friend of Companion M. J. Gibson. A Companion and her Probationer gave thanks that their rector and his assistant in a southern-border parish "decided to include a Negro student in the choir. May all Companions pray for peace, quiet, and a good reception to him."

1953—

Young Queen Elizabeth II was crowned; Dag Hammarskjold became the UN Secretary General; former General Dwight Eisenhower was inaugurated as President; and the Rosenbergs, husband and wife, were executed in the U.S. as spies for the Communists.

February: The new public ministry of Agnes Sanford and her husband, the rector of St. Stephens in Westboro MA, healing through prayer and laying on of hands, was greeted with thanksgivings, as was the Companion working among the "benighted Arabs in Jerusalem." There was a prayer for President Eisenhower, and one for the parole board in Massachusetts. Another petition prayed for the press and radio to realize their responsibility to guide rather than mislead. The availability of copies of Winifred Hulbert's paper, *Christian Responsibility in Human Relations* from the **August '52 Companion Conference**, was announced.

May: Among the May thanksgivings, one rejoiced that the gifted young "colored singer for whom we prayed" had won a much-coveted scholarship for a year's study in Europe. A petition asked for more Companion interest in prisoners, another for an "awakening of conscience to the American disgrace of <u>preaching</u> democracy and <u>practicing</u> inequality [emphasis added]," and another for a "prodigal father who has returned to his trusting motherless children." There was a prayer for the 3rd annual Adelynrood Retreat for Wives of Clergy, and for women church workers who were professional Directors of Religious Education. Companions were reminded that reaching out to bring new visitors to Adelynrood was everyone's job: each Companion should speak to her rector's wife, encouraging attendance, in the hope that the beauty and peace of Adelynrood could "inspire these women who must themselves be channels of these qualities to others." This was a typical expectation for women married to clergy in the 1950s.

June: There were thanksgivings for the recent conference at Seabury House honoring returned China missionaries, and for the way they dealt with their forced relocation. The retreat theme at **Companion Conference** was announced as *Social Justice in the World Today,* led by the Rev. Moran Weston, the "handsome rector" of the largest "Negro" church in Harlem, St. Philip's in New York City. Needs: more Companion volunteer sacristans at Adelynrood.

October prayers were requested for the Chair of the Finance Committee [an indirect allusion to the Society's financial anxieties] and thanksgivings for the year-round service of the Adelynrood staff to the Society. Thanksgivings were offered for the retreat led by Father Moran Weston, for the courageous stand of the Bishop of Michigan against racial discrimination, and for Episcopal work on the Rosebud Indian Reservation in South Dakota.

November: There were prayers for Haiti, for a newly established Benedictine monastery in Three Rivers, Michigan, for Japanese students in US colleges and universities, and for the Rev. & Mrs. Edmund Sherrill, missionaries to Brazil. A petition urged all churchwomen to combat "juvenile delinquency" in every location, along with all totalitarianism. A Companion urged that the "circulation of foolish, sensational newspapers may cease." Special thanksgivings were offered for Chaplain Howard Thurman, the African-American writer and retreat leader from Howard University in Washington DC, who has been "a wonderful help to us [white Americans] in recognizing our common brotherhood with men (sic) of all races."

1954—

Background: This was the year of Tupperware parties, popular in the new suburbs as a middle-class business opportunity for married, white, stay-at-home women. It offered a safely domestic way of making money outside of regular businesses. It was also the year that Senator Joseph McCarthy was condemned by the US Senate, that protesting Puerto Rican nationalists staged a shooting in the well of Congress, and the Supreme Court outlawed racially segregated schools.

January was greeted with thanksgivings for an inspiring talk by Companion Helen Turnbull. [She was then the Director of Windham House in NYC, a church-sponsored residence for churchwomen who wanted training to become professional Directors of Christian Education, and the background of many who became Companions in this era. As women, they could only 'sit in' on classes at seminaries, not be admitted as students.] Also, there were thanksgivings "for the mobility" of the American Friends Service Committee that "steps in whenever a particular concern makes itself felt." Under the *Social Justice* theme were petitions that atomic power be given only peaceful uses, and for a 25-year-old Negro (first sentenced at age 12, after a five-minute trial, to a chain gang in Georgia) hoping for extradition to NJ in order to obtain a new trial and justice. There was a prayer that "our judges of the U.S. Supreme Court make the decision on segregation guided by Holy Spirit." A physical condition, multiple sclerosis, unnamed in the *IP* before, now appeared, along with frequent prayers naming the disease of alcoholism.[40]

40 January *IP* 1954, 4, 7.

An **April** thanksgiving saluted the Rev. Vine Deloria of the Home [Missions] Dept. and Episcopal missions to the American Indian. His son was one of the first published national voices expressing the formerly-ignored view and voice of Native Americans. Also there was a thanksgiving for the brilliant contemporary-language rewording in the new Phillips' *Translation of the Epistles*. The **Companion Conference** retreat theme, *Christ, the Hope and Unity of the Church,* celebrated the 70th anniversary of the Society's founding.

> The *NEWSLETTER,* MAY 1954, introduced Hilda Andrea Davis (among others) in a short biography of new Companions, especially significant at that time because she was a successful, professional African-American. Born in 1905 in the nation's capitol, she'd always felt "cheated of my birthright because people in Washington DC can't vote." Her father was a government clerk supporting a family of eight children in addition to cousins or boarders. She completed high school in three years, went on to Howard University, majoring in Latin; she taught at the training college for black women, Palmer Memorial Institute, in Sedalia, NC, and headed the English Dept. at Talladega College in Alabama after earning her PhD from Yale. She became a Probationer sponsored by colleague and Companion Martha Jane Gibson, and also by Charlotte Atwood, a teacher from her high-school years. A member of the YWCA since girlhood, she also belonged to the National Association of Deans of Women. [This was an example of Companion background information containing no mention of African-American heritage except by inference.]

The front page of the **May** *IP* praised Evelyn Underhill's anthology *Of the Love of God.* In **July-August**, prayers were asked for the three great church conventions to be held in August: the Anglo Catholic Congress in Chicago; the Anglican Congress in Minnesota; and the World Council of Churches, in Evanston, Illinois. In **September**, there were thanksgivings for the management of Adelynrood, for the way it was administered, for the food preparation, and for the efficacy of each Companion's duty to help keep it going.

Six intercessions regarding desegregation appeared in the **October** *IP*: for desegregated labor unions, for the church facing up to the MORAL issues of segregation (recognizing it as sin), for the Roman Catholic Bishop who abolished racial separation in his

North Carolina churches, for the quietly desegregated Washington DC public schools, for the fine leadership of President Eisenhower in this step, and for the support of the Federal Council of Churches doing all it can to assist.

In **November**, ten big petitions gave thanks for the life of Vida Scudder, for her 60+ years as a Companion, and for her gifts to the Society. Under the *Social Justice* theme, there was a prayer that school children of the South, pioneers in the desegregation plan, find sympathy [among blacks and whites] and cooperate "to lay the cornerstone of a nobler society through Christian helpfulness." Also, there were prayers that all groups in the North and the South, facing the imperative to integrate schools, be courageous and have the capacity to change.

Further, Companions prayed that the conscience of all Christians be quickened to eradicate the "glaring social evils" of our treatment of migrant workers, sharecroppers, and American Indians. One specific petition said: "May God have mercy on those who preach hatred and fear in resistance to the movement to restore rights to Negroes as God's children;" another also prayed that integration in the Washington DC and Delaware schools proceed smoothly. A new mindset appeared in a prayer for the theme page titled <u>Unity</u>: *"That all Episcopalians mistrust every divisive conviction, and remember that every true Episcopal church is catholic, whatever its churchmanship, and acknowledge that its head is neither missal nor Prayer Book but our Lord and only Savior"* [italics added]. On the theme page of *Special Needs,* the first three petitions addressed the organizational "crisis" of finding a next C-in-C, and that she be willing to take the job. There were also prayers that each chapter and individual Companion be guided in finding younger women "qualified" to join the SCHC.[41] This period (the 1950s-early 1960s) was the apex of secrecy and selectiveness in the SCHC, expressed in terms of concern for the "appropriateness" of Companions-to-be.

---

41 *IP* November 1954, 8, 9, 10.

The **December** *IP* featured a quotation from Vida Scudder's *Franciscan Litany* (page 147 of the 1984 *Manual*) about the "perfect joy of Francis and his Companions." There was also an expression of thanksgiving and joy for "an hour in which a Companion and Negro friend gave thanks for the "quiet" prevailing in their southern town as Negro children came to school with whites." On the *Unity* page, a profound petition asked that Christians and Companions be willing to study *difference*, racial and cultural, to "uncover fundamental identities of belief and faith." There was also a compassionate intercession for those parents "protesting that Negro children were going to school with theirs, that they [white parents] be freed from fear."[42]

Benediction for Vida Scudder, 1954

Back in 1938, VDS had written one of her thousands of letters as Companion-in-Charge of Probationers to her Probationer, Martha Jane Gibson, then teaching at segregated Talladega College in Alabama. Gibson had not originally imagined she would be "concentrat[ing] on the race problem," but as a white educator in the Jim Crow Deep South was confronted by its realities and giving "all she had." This involved dangerous speaking in public against the lynchings that spread seemingly unstoppable terror through the Black South. Scudder's applause for Gibson's "work with the Negro and witnessing against the wicked injustice of his lot" then summoned her retrospective thoughts about <u>her</u> own commitment to social justice. Scudder lamented that if <u>she</u> had lived out *literally* what she idealized, she would have become "a thorough [Christian] communist."

Scudder's core belief, one shared by other white radical Christian thinkers in the first half of the 20th century, was that <u>all</u> social inequality grew out of the American socio-economic "market" system, including racial injustice. Throughout her life, "the larger issue

---

42 The entire issue of *Journal of American History*, June 2004, Vol 91 #1, was devoted to historical analysis of the Brown decision's results and effects, negative and positive.

facing civilization and Christianity" arose out of the "whole question of our social and economic organization," capitalism—a world operating on the profit motive, pitting the rich against the poor, and rewarding personal and corporate greed. Scudder's letter combined regret for her own falling short of her own ideals, and gratitude that this Probationer was filling an anti-racial "niche" in our flawed social world.[43] In 1954, just before VDS' death, Companion Gibson's Talladega years would come full circle as she brought a fellow faculty member, Hilda Davis, into the Companionship. The warmth and personal involvement exhibited by VDS were integral to her influence in the Society.

In November 1954, the Society honored VDS for the vital "shaping [of] our policies and ideals." A tribute published in 1955 praised her "lively provocative ideas, her generous knowledge of men and letters, and awareness of social problems" that enlivened countless summer conferences. As noted earlier, Miss Scudder's "brilliant and searching address of one and one-fourth hours" (in length) on *"The Christian Doctrine and Race Relations"* had headlined a 1944 summer conference. The study book that year argued that "the so-called Negro Problem" in the US was really "the problem of the white race, not the Negro race, according to us."[44] Her personal knowledge of and connection with early saints like Catherine of Siena and Francis of Assisi had established them in twentieth-century Companion consciousness, so that they seemed almost like present-day patrons and friends. In short, during her sixty-five years as a Companion, she had "quickened the conscience" of the Society. And at age ninety-three, she greeted death "eager for the revelations of the next life."[45]

---

43 V Scudder to Martha Jane Gibson, Jan 1, 1938. Vida Scudder, Box 1 File 1, Adelynrood Archive.

44 1944 *Annual Report*, 36-37—also tribute 1954 (1955 *Newsletter*).

45 From tribute in 1955 *Newsletter*.

Cover of *The Church Militant: Diocese of Massachusetts* November 1962 issue shows African American couple Bishop John and Companion Esther Burgess; Bishop Stokes on left, Bishop Frederic C. Lawrence on right.

Six Companions in Companion Day Dress, 1968.

1966 Companions dine together.

Chapter 5

SCHC
1955–1964

"Joy: the fulfillment of the truest self, an identification with reality, human and divine"[1]

Virginia Huntington, C-in-C
1958 Companion Conference: Through the Cross – Joy

Social-Historical Background

In this decade, the SCHC Archive accumulated volumes of artistic words and spiritual insight, often expressed in poetry. Psychology had emerged as a popular tool helping analysts understand the way groups functioned, in business and in the church. In fact, popularized psychology fueled a self-help/self-improvement movement. Companions, especially those who identified themselves as social justice activists, were disappointed with the more internalized focus, and longed for battles as dramatic as those that had confronted the founders. Wider-world conditions, of course, offered plenty of topics for intercession, e.g. prayers about the "horrors" under which Palestinian refugees were living. In this same era, however, the *Missions* Theme Committee began registering an attitude-change toward work among native peoples within the American church, and in overseas work. The Presiding Bishop urged that foreign mission work be turned over to local or indigenous priests at the

---

1 *Annual Report 1958, 9.*

earliest possible time. "Exploring the scientific, technological, ideological, national, racial, religious, and population explosion" topics during this decade revealed a "changed [view of] mission in a changing world,"[2] at the very time the Society's fascination with interior self-exploration was deepening. The surrounding American ethos was also being transformed from a production economy to a consumerist mentality—insightfully analyzed by Christopher Lasch in *The Culture of Narcissism* (1979).

The dismaying confrontation with "the real" that was already lurking beneath the surface of white Protestant America's self-consciousness was increasing openness about racial inequity. It would produce a mind expansion impacting Companions' vocation and environment for the next three decades, and beyond. "No image in this era of American culture [is] more replete with contradiction than white mainline Protestantism," author Charles Marsh reflected. News of the brutal mistreatment of black citizens began to seep into mainstream journalism, e.g. Fannie Lou Hamer's terrible beating in a small-town Southern jail for daring to try to register to vote, and encouraging other blacks to do so.[3] Companions faced a major challenge in coming to personal terms with this "new" guilt-inducing realization. Daily life inequities long endured by black Americans were finally becoming visible on majority-white Americans' moral and spiritual horizon, even though some Companion intercessions had named it earlier in the century.

To many white Americans, the idea of racial desegregation, if they thought about it at all, was subconsciously frightening—unimaginable. Privilege is always least visible to those who have it, as the black truism notes. But young American blacks in segregated post-WWII colleges weren't as awed by Jim Crow laws and the Ku Klux Klan as their parents' generation had had to be.[4] A few of them

---

2 Summary tracing these changes (May 1994), by Mary Kelley chairing Christian Mission (theme) Committee.

3 Charles Marsh, *God's Long Summer: Stories of Faith and Civil Rights, 1964*, Princeton University Press, 1997, 6.

4 David Halberstam, *The Children*, NY: Random House, 1998.

began to educate themselves in and practice Mahatma Gandhi's non-violent protests against everyday discrimination, beginning with segregated water fountains and lunch counters.[5]

Books by a Southern white author, Lillian Smith, had made an inroad into white race-blindness: *Strange Fruit* (1944) and *Killers of the Dream* (1949). She was the first author to link the issue of Black civil rights with the psychological and cultural health of white America.[6] Mainline Protestant churches in both the north and the south still gave little attention to their participation in a segregated institution. Episcopal author and white desegregationist, Sarah Patton Boyle, characterized her beloved Charlottesville, Virginia church in this era as the "absolute quintessence of white, classist, sexist, social conformity."[7] Sadly, "white Christians' generalized revulsion against racial injustice would not really discard most [legal] racial barriers until the 1980s."[8]

Further, most Episcopal churches were still characterized by a deeply internal formality (stiffness?) that governed gesture, action, and perspective. Episcopalians were often caricatured, by others, and themselves, as "God's frozen chosen," "Whiskeypalians." Individual Episcopalians wanted to avoid "standing out" in the congregation; they idealized orderly, dignified liturgy that was free of unprogrammed interruptions like "Amen" or "preach it, brother." In spite of that overarching climate of parochial conformity, and in contrast with it, Companions at Adelynrood were encouraged to experiment with discussion topics and forms of worship, unbeholden to any rector or vestry ruling about what was "proper."

After the landmark 1954 Supreme Court decision outlawing school desegregation, the same year Vida Scudder entered the

---

5 Ibid, Chapter 1.

6 Fred Hobson, *But Now I See: White Southern Racial Conversion Narratives*, Louisiana St. University Press, Baton Rouge, LA 1999, 23.

7 Quoted from JBG, "Sarah Patton Boyle's Desegregated Heart," 174, in *Beyond Image and Convention* (ed. Coryell, Swain, Treadway, and Turner, University of Missouri Press, Columbia, MO, 1998, 158-183.

8 First quotation, Marsh, 6; second quote, Diane McWhorter: *Carry Me Home*, Simon & Schuster, NY, 2001, 3rd quote, Ibid, 590.

Paradise Chapter, Companions began in earnest to accept the new ruling through intercession, to educate themselves and "ameliorate racial inequality."[9] As early as the end of 1955, some Companions had grasped the far-reaching implications of the first Black bus boycott in Birmingham, Alabama; a few also may have shared the outrage of non-white citizens over the murder of Emmet Till that same year. [Till was a Chicago adolescent visiting in the South who was brutally lynched for being unaware of the local taboo against a black boy's whistling at a white girl]. That horrifying event, so devastating to African Americans, could not have been unnoticed by white Christians, north and south, though no mention of it appeared in the *IP*. [For that matter, how many Episcopal sermons in local parishes thundered against it?]

After WWII, Companions and white women of conscience had become active in secular crusades for "community good," as it was known. Women including Companions expanded their church-based lives into a variety of reform activities, including the League of Women Voters. Companions participated in the anti-nuclear movement, the peace movement, and the campaign to provide relief for the refugees of war. And they were committed, rhetorically, to the *ideal* of racial justice. Founders VDS and EMM had established the norm of spirited discussion about thorny issues under the rubric of Social Justice. Growing acknowledgment of racial inequity in *IP* intercessions can be traced. Also, white suburban housewives were beginning a new business and social venture: Tupperware parties, a domestically approved form of consumerism and economic enterprise. This served as unwitting precursor to white women's move out of the home into other kinds of jobs in the 1960s.

True to SCHC Founders' emphasis on self-education about "actual conditions," new vistas opened for many white Episcopal women—often a first public experience across racial lines. Even so, many more educated white women were "converted to activism

---

9 Susan Lynn, *Progressive Women in Conservative Times: Racial Justice, Peace and Feminism 1945-1960s.* New Brunswick NJ: Rutgers University Press 1992,5 (YWCA Interracial charter).

about social issues through their churches [and Companionship] than by their churches."[10] This was the same accusation of indifference that EMM had leveled at her parents' Victorian Sunday religion.

The topic of race discrimination was gradually climbing to the top of the founders' paradigm of social inequality, formerly focused on industrial conditions. During their probation and summer conferences, Companions continued to study social-class inequities but began more and more naming racial inequality. The fissure eventually undermining what was called *consensus history* [embodied in the 1955 profiles of the Founders, chapter 3] began to widen into the new *social history* that acknowledged conflict and began to account for factors of race, social class, and gender in its interpretations. The major spiritual challenge for American Episcopal parishes and communities in this period was to acknowledge racism within themselves and their own churches.

In the 1950s, Companions and many white churches focused "almost exclusively on educational tactics." Schools were seen as "the magic carpet to racial harmony." In the *IPs*, the injustice of interning Japanese Americans from 1942-1945 had opened the eyes of some Episcopalians to racial bias; that was followed by a belated recognition of the historically derogatory treatment of Native Americans. Companions active in the YWCA were often in the vanguard of racial-justice awareness; they were also among the first to realize that a strategy of "moral suasion" was too polite to really "make a dent in hardened segregationism."[11] Companion Jane Schutt (who entered SCHC only later, in 1977) was one who worked quietly to include local Black churchwomen in the interdenominational organization Church Women United, in her Mississippi hometown. For her activism, the local white Citizens' Council awarded her with a cross-burning on her front lawn.[12]

---

10 Lynn, *Progressive Women*, 81, 165; most recently reprinted in *Guideposts*, Nov. 27, 2004.

11 Lynn, *op cit*, Chapter 2.

12 Lynn, *op cit*, 81, 165; most recently reprinted in *Guideposts*, Nov. 27, 2004.

As Sarah Patton Boyle named it in her autobiographical *The Desegregated Heart* (1962), *unlearning* racist perspectives was both painful and liberating. Her life-changing lessons impelled her to criticize national Episcopal Church leaders for public pronouncements that did nothing to support local activists attempting to combat segregationist practices. During this era of deep national anxiety about race, the bright spot for Companions was an already-existing program format with which they were familiar and totally competent: conferences. This standard plan for women's' gatherings, in the YWCA, in women's clubs and church groups, and in the SCHC, became a major vehicle enabling women to confront and unlearn racist expectations and stereotypes. In that regard, this organizational medium helped SCHC make genuine intellectual and spiritual contributions through consciousness-raising conferences that educated Companions and others in "actual knowledge of [racial and social] conditions" (EMM's euphemism). Alongside the new attention to spiritual and psychological insights, the external world's racial awakening constituted the other "new current" in the Society's context during this decade.

Chronological Overview from IPs, Annual Reports, Newsletters

1954—

The **1954 Companion Conference** theme, *The Christian Hope and the Unity of the Church*, shaped C-in-C Jeannette Booth's opening address, summarized at length from the ***Annual Report***.

> She first noted the Society's internal needs: "The deepening of [our] spiritual life and the management of the business of the Society must become integrated. Our administrative structure was not *imposed* on the Society, but developed [by us] to give order and integrity to our business [financial] responsibility, as well as to bring harmony and dignity to our daily living." This organizational structure is crucial for the "material" side of the Society, our retreat house. It demands careful "thought and our personal service, if it is to function." Her concerns included attracting

younger women to the Society, encouraging new Companions to undertake more of the organizational responsibilities, and asking older Companions to be welcoming to the new, "with no spirit of criticism."

Any organization of almost one hundred women worries perennially over Companions too distant to enjoy summer residence together: Booth hoped the Society could "find some new means of being true Companions to them." Her concluding challenge addressed the emerging racial awareness indirectly, asking Companions to act on these "1950s issues" in ways that would make future Companions as proud of us "as we today are of our founding generations." In a dual-focus Society, Companions live and pray amid "differences of opinion." The key to SCHC survival is the ability to be Companions: "we, and the larger complex society of which we are a part, in this country, must grow in the art of *living and working* together." She quoted an earlier chaplain to the Society, Fr. Whitney Hale, who had described SCHC as "a fellowship of uncongenial minds," thanks to the imperative that Companions honor each other's individual conscience and path of action.

At the annual **Business Meeting**, the *House Committee* reported difficulty finding summer House-staff employees, and the need for more volunteers. The committee on *Artistic Planning* praised the "natural outdoor charm [of Adelynrood], and the not-accidental simplicity of our interior arrangements." *Buildings and Repairs* reported reshingling the House, electrifying some of the outbuildings, strengthening the wall of the chapel, and adding four new toilet units. This *Annual Report* contained ten brief written memorials of deceased Companions, a short summary of the **Companion Conference** Bible Study, and summaries of the three Companion Papers that were presented. The last three pages named 119 Companions carrying officer and committee responsibilities.[13]

1955—

In the early months of 1955, *IP* petitions named injustices to Negroes whose civil rights were discriminated against, supported the work of St. Margaret's sisters in Haiti, and gave thanks for

---

13 *Annual Report* 1954: 19, 21, 21, 54-56.

the admission, in Japan, of our first Japanese Companion. Prayers saluted Vine Deloria, Native American spokesman in the Episcopal Mission to the American Indian. Special blessings were invoked for the re-organization of the former Woman's Auxiliary at the national church headquarters potentially linking every parish. Henceforth its name was to be the ECW or Episcopal Church Women, assuming that every churchwoman was automatically eligible for membership. Also there was a prayer that Trinity parish in Los Alamos, NM, become an influence for Christ among the atomic scientists stationed there.

A petition asked guidance of the Holy Spirit for all who were trying out *The Seabury Series* curriculum, newly published by the national Episcopal Department of Christian Education.[14] Companions were among the lay Episcopalians appointed to help with revisions to the 1928 *Book of Common Prayer,* a new task requesting SCHC prayer support. A Companion specifically prayed that her interracial study group in a southern city could help bring integration to the fore in a Christian spirit, also that Hindu, Buddhist, and Muslim citizens in India would awaken to Jesus Christ. There was a petition for "wetbacks" (the first time for that word in the *IP*) entering the US illegally from Mexico and Central America. Specific prayers focused on Episcopalians Carl and Anne Braden of Louisville for their Christian act of desegregating a local community [buying a house in a white neighborhood for their black friends], and their subsequent court and prison ordeals. Companions also prayed for penitence on the part of all who wronged them.[15]

A Companion offered thanks, in the **March** *IP,* for her attendance at a Jewish worship service, and for friendship with a young Negro preacher, plus for a young Negro woman taking part in the World Day of Prayer, the first of her race in that town to participate. One Companion prayed for the work of Bishop Tucker in Japan, and

---

14 J B Gillespie, "What We Taught." *Anglican and Episcopal Historical Magazine,* Jan., Feb., March 1955.

15 Anne Braden, The *Wall Between,* Univ of Tenn. Press, 1958, reissued 1999.

that God, in His own good way, would "control the emotions and reactions of intelligent Christian folk who are disturbed at prospect of desegregation, and that Christian Negroes of the South may continue to have the strength to accept various embarrassing situations." Blessings were invoked for all who were working for justice, e.g. the fine educated Negro who elects to stay in the South to work with "his people." Special thanks were offered for the great new labor organization AFL-CIO, and for a Companion's work on juvenile delinquency with the League of Women Voters. The Winter Conference at Seabury House produced a prayer for faith, understanding and justice in the nation's carrying out the Supreme Court order ending segregated schools. A special petition asked for lessening tension between the races and blessed a young Negro pastor who urged peaceful response: "don't let anyone pull you so low as to make you hate them back."[16]

May thanksgivings named [organizations] the Church Army, the World Day of Prayer, United Church Women, and the United Church of Christ in the Philippines. One gave thanks for a plan to have mobile teachers follow the migrant workers' children to provide them instruction. Another petition honored the "timeless sanity and deep discernment of great spiritual directors such as Ruysbruck, von Hugel, Evelyn Underhill," also "progress in welcoming our Negro Brethren in our churches and schools." Thanksgivings were offered for a conference by the peace organization Fellowship of Reconciliation, for the *Big Brother* organizations in cities, for Dr. Jonas Salk's discovery of the polio vaccine, and for the Triennial United Thank Offering ingathering [a women's special collection at the General Convention that acknowledged special thanksgivings with a monetary symbol]. A Companion rejoiced in the film *A Man Called Peter*, and also in the 10th anniversary of the UN. One petition reproved Episcopalians for not supporting the Bradens' struggle against Jim Crow housing, another for not acknowledging the

---

16 April 1955 *IP*, 7.

danger to families of alcoholism. There was a special SCHC concern: *"for all Companions coming to Adelynrood; for the leaders preparing **Companion Conference**, for the conductor of the retreat, for officers, and those with special responsibilities; for ease in the practical running of Adelynrood this summer, for a spirit of Companionship throughout every department of our work & organization; and that the ten days of **Companion Conference** be in all things directed by God, inspired by the Holy Ghost, and carried forward in spirit of our Lord Jesus Christ* [italics added]."[17]

The **May (1955) Newsletter** reporting on the Winter Conference at Radnor, PA included a tribute to Vida Scudder. It was announced that Companion Dora Chaplin was serving in the national-church Division of Leadership. A new chapter in Sewanee was welcomed as were Companions at St. Margaret's House in Berkeley, CA. Companion Jean Davis reported touring through rural housing in Alabama and found the prisons "shocking", the worst, a South Carolina boys' reformatory near Columbia that had no refrigerator in the kitchen, no towels, and a rotting dormitory. Her article urged Companions to write protest letters, pray, and telephone their congressmen.

At the **1955 Companion Conference** in August, C-in-C Jeannette Booth, reflecting the "Organization Man" symbolism, addressed the theme *"Corporate Life in the Companionship."* The novel *The Man in the Grey Flannel Suit* [later, a film starring Gregory Peck] had dramatized a new awareness of businessman conformity that allowed anti-Semitism to flourish, unquestioned, in large American corporations. Booth reflected that Companions find something precious in the disciplines required by *"our* kind of corporate life," training in miniature for the larger societal harmony toward which we pray. Companions may be more influential as a group in promoting our Christian conception of a corporate goal, but count primarily as individuals: our version of "corporate life" may

---

17 May 1955 *IP*, 8; July-August 1955, 9.

mean helping even one other person with her particular burden. Booth praised Miss Morgan for the "catholicity" and breadth (rather than partisanship) of Companions in the Society, and Miss Scudder for SCHC absorption in and knowledge of our catholic heritage. Booth's closing cited one of the earliest EMM letters to Companions (1887) in which she stated what became an oft-repeated motto: "Perhaps never were societies like ours so much needed, *as now*, to cultivate that inner spirit of devotion to Jesus Christ."[18]

The **Annual Report** also featured the long-anticipated profiles on *The Founders*, summarized in Chapter 3. Three Companion papers examined aspects of "Corporate Life at Adelynrood": *Prayer*, by Leslie C. Townsend; *Work* by Mary O. Evans; and *Play* by Marie L'Hommedieu. In the afternoons, Companions in small groups discussed "the place of Adelynrood in the corporate life of the Society." Was Adelynrood indispensable for Companionship? One response emphasized its sacramental significance: it is where young and new Companions experience themselves as "guests of God." Companion Gibson's experience, based on her teaching at a segregated college in Alabama, reminded Companions that they have vowed to "live with people of other races according to God's laws. We must be ready to speak [out] so that others see the Christian attitude, [and] learn to live in love and understanding with people of other races." Companions were asked "to engage as Christians with the great secular organizations, such as the NAACP, that are trying to right past wrongs." And in the *IP*, Companions were asked indirectly to pray about the wave of bombing and burning poor black country churches throughout the South: the petition as stated urged Companions "not to tolerate any longer the continuance of this evil [unspecified]."[19] The third day of the conference, Companion Evelyn Cameron asked: "Have we now a prophetic vision of the corporate life in our Chapters? And in the world?" This mid-century grappling

---

18 *Annual Report* 1955, 23.

19 *59ᵗʰ Annual Report* 1955, 28, 54, 55, 56.

with the definition of "corporate action" expressed renewed focus on the founders' legacy of being "prophetic."

The **1955 Business Meeting** increased Annual Dues to $10 per member, plus an entrance fee of $2, and offered to send a Society representative to each Chapter to *explain* the Society's finances and the Adelynrood-proportion of the total financial picture. The *House* and *Gardens and Grounds* committees had invested extra work setting Adelynrood "to rights" after the late summer hurricane in 1954. *Artistic Planning* ordered rugs from India through Companion Eleanor Mason in Madras. The *Chapel* Committee reported that the white nylon Prayer Caps were "washed and ready for use once more." [EMM had solved the problem of essential Episcopal head coverings for women in church by providing Companions with small white-net prayer caps such as Mennonites still wear. The 1960s ethos encouraged worship without head coverings, so they were finally abandoned except as

Close up of 1959 75th Anniversary photo, showing Companions' range of garb, ornamentation, and use of various head coverings, which were on their way out a few years later.

an historical artifact.] A discussion urged consideration of omitting a very out-of-date liturgy from the *1928 Prayer Book*, "The Churching of Women" [a ritual cleansing after childbirth]. It was noted that only a small number of Companions attended the Conference sponsored by the *Social Justice* theme committee. There was an urgent call for conference topics that could attract larger numbers, perhaps a 10-day leadership-training workshop in religious education and theology [since Episcopal seminary education was still closed to women].

In the autumn *IPs*, there were thanksgivings for the election of Virginia Huntington as C-in-C and the service of retiring C-in-C Jeannette Booth, and for the love and trust evident in the SCHC election. There were pleas that any states in the U.S. refusing to honor the Supreme Court decision be "overruled by Spirit of God." There were prayers also for stability in South Vietnam. **December** brought special thanks for the life of our Founder on her Dec. 10 birthday, for her hospitality and dedication, and for her achieving "self-control of a youthful quick temper that became high spirits in her old age." Also, there were prayers of thanksgiving for "the consecrated intelligence" of Companion Mary Morrison, who had led the **Companion Conference** Bible study, for a bi-racial congregation at an ordination in Columbia SC, for peace between Israel and Egypt, and for the gathering strength of the bus boycott in Montgomery, Alabama initiated by Rosa Parks.

White Christians were still largely unaware of the daily humiliations of segregation, as white Southern author Diane McWhorter has described it: "segregated public transportation was still the most unavoidable daily insult of Negro life. Blacks had to step into the front of the bus to pay their fare, then get off and reboard, through the rear door, to take seats in the back. Some bus drivers glorified themselves as enforcers of the practice—cursed blacks, shortchanged them, passed their stops, even pulled guns on them." Rosa Parks, one evening in December, refused to move to the segregated section. Her resistance gave birth to the bus boycott, which widened into the civil rights movement. It also helped fuel the white resistance movement.[20]

1956—

In February, the black bus boycott was in full swing, and in November, Russians crushed the revolt in Hungary. The Interstate

---

20 October 1955 *IP*, 9; McWhorter, Carry *Me Home*, 90; December *IP* 6.

Highway system had begun to expand just as segregation was finally banned on interstate busses.

The **January** *IP* featured a thanksgiving for the President of Georgia Tech College who refused to cancel a football game with a Pittsburgh team, although it included a Negro player. There was another thanksgiving for all "wise efforts to remedy serious racial conflict," and for Fr. Trevor Huddleston's work against apartheid in South Africa. The **February** *IP* carried thanksgivings for the inspiring mission work of Companion Carman Hunter in Brazil, and asked support for Europeans, Africans and Indians working to remove prejudice from Capricorn Africa. One petition quoted British historian Arnold Toynbee: we have "suddenly become one another's neighbors physically, while our hearts are still far apart..."[21] Companions' conscience was pouring an important interior-life pain into the vehicle of intercession.

May *IP*: A petition thanked God "that in these times of racial tension, our hearts may be refreshed by the thought that skin is not character and the human spirit is without color." There were thanksgivings that the faith of Montgomery, AL Negroes had been strong enough thus far to conquer any potential violence in their uprising (the bus boycott), and for all those unnamed Southerners who had been working for years, on Christian principle, to further racial equality. There was a petition for Northerners to acknowledge their own hypocrisy in this matter. **June** brought thanksgivings for the visit to Japan of atomic scientist Dr. William Pollard, and prayers that Negro teachers not lose their jobs after integration. There was a prayer of sympathy for the many fine Negro schools in the South faced with accepting difficult changes, also prayers that God strengthen the minds of Negro leaders dedicated to non-violent resistance, and for the vast number of Negroes on whom fell the burden of carrying out desegregation. There was a special prayer for the Black South Carolina schoolteacher, Septima Clark, who

---

21 February *IP* 1956, 8.

was fired for daring to join the NAACP. She later became Director of Education for the Southern Christian Leadership Conference's voter registration drive.[22]

Simplicity was the **1956 Companion Conference** theme, Virginia Huntington's first as C-in-C. Her Opening Paper noted the expressed concern that Companions were not finding the same crucial social-justice issues, as had the founders. "A young Companion [had] expressed disappointment at the multiple possibilities for social action *outside* the Society," which makes our Society "less challenging" than she expected. In this more complex organizational time, individuals must work "less conspicuously" [than many of our predecessors] but with no less social concern. How do <u>we</u> lay hold on the mystical and prophetic note of Miss Morgan and Miss Scudder, Huntington asked? We have the same costly faith resources, and we hardly need to "persuade" God of our good intentions, "since He already knows our need."[23] Another Companion had wondered: "Are we not in danger of being spiritual snobs?" Huntington warned that Adelynrood must open its hospitality and prayers to "theist, Christian, unbeliever, and materialist, [and also must] cross barriers of race, theology, and skepticism" as never before.

In the **Business Meeting**, discussion noted the "very scanty attendance" at Social Justice conferences in the past half-dozen years. The exception to that picture was the Conference on Penology chaired by Companion Miriam Van Waters and colleagues from her workplace, the Massachusettes Reformatory for Women in Framingham, MA.[24] Surely the Society has <u>not</u> lost its birthright of strong convictions about achieving justice, Virginia Huntington said, "first by prayer and then by battle" (citing EMM's

---

22 May 1956 *IP*, 9.

23 1956, 60th *Annual Report*, 5-6, 8, 10.

24 See Estelle B Freedman's "Separatism Revisited: Women's Institutions, Social Reform, and the Career of Miriam Van Waters." Chapter 8, in *US History as Women's History: New Feminist Essays*, ed. Linda Kerber et al, 1995. 177-188. Van Waters was praised by Eleanor Roosevelt as an example of women's public authority.

favorite double image). In our era, justice must be sought less in industrial arenas than in the economic—the tenant farmer, the migrant worker." And race? It has to be faced "right where <u>we</u> live, not just in the Deep South."[25]

The printed **Annual Report** announced its new format. The changes were to allow inclusion of chapter reports and twenty Memorials for deceased Companions (many quite lengthy), as well as two written reports from the **Companion Conference**.

July-August: The interesting sociological note in the 1956 *IP*s was the many new parish "missions" springing up outside cities, evidence of the significant new demographic being developed—suburbs.[26] There were thanksgivings for the restoration to full service of St. Luke's Hospital in Tokyo, for the missionaries again in Japan, including Companion Elisabeth Lloyd. And there was thanksgiving for Companion Cynthia Wedel, elected president of the (interdenominational organization) Church Women United. In November, prayers requested support for the Russian delegates to the National Council of Churches, and Companion Peg Tyson rejoiced that the University of Virginia's School of Nursing, where she taught and later became an administrator, had made improvements in both its training program and professional status.

1957—

Startling events were the Russian satellite Sputnik circling the globe, alarming the US about our scientific capabilities. President Eisenhower sent federal troops to enforce desegregation in Little Rock, AR; the national Civil Rights bill passed on August 29, despite Senator Strom Thurmond's (South Carolina) filibuster. Studies linking cancer with cigarette smoke were released, and Althea Gibson emerged as the first Black female tennis star.

---

25 Ibid.

26 Avila, "The Rise and Fall of Vanilla Suburbs in Popular Culture," in *The Age of White Flight*, 2004.

January *IP*: A Companion offered thanksgivings for Fr. Huddleston's book *Naught for Your Comfort*, the voice of a white South African Anglican priest denouncing apartheid, and for Victor Riesel, a liberal journalist, union activist, and radical NY City Jew who was attacked with acid thrown into his face [his vision was eventually restored]. There were thanksgivings for the establishment of the Detroit Industrial Mission, an experiment in witnessing for Christ in the competitive jungle of modern assembly line workers. A prayer offered the hope that "the integration process in the South [would] occur in a natural, friendly, and Christian manner, without undue forcing and with more understanding on both sides." There were thanksgivings for articles in church journals (*The Living Church* and *Christianity and Crisis*) that saluted the implementation of the Supreme Court's desegregation ruling in various areas. A petition praised an "independent school" that admitted students regardless of race, color, or creed; another hoped "not one of us within the Anglican Communion...would do anything that tends to divide rather than unite us." A petition asked for the relief of racial dissension so that people could live in peace, showing kindness and friendship to each other. Also a Companion asked that God "show us means for restoring the Chapel at Tuskegee Institute [an all-black college] destroyed in January by fire."

May *IP*: The all-thanksgivings issue saluted SCHC initiators EMM, Adelyn Howard, Harriet Putnam and Harriet Hastings, and gave thanks for EMM's vision, hospitality, and warmth of understanding for all races, ages, and life stages. There were thanksgivings for Vida Scudder, Nina Brown, and the gift of the Great Cross behind the House at Adelynrood, for past Cs-in-C Emilie Hurd, Elizabeth Cook, and Grace Lindley, and for every Companion in the Paradise Chapter. There were special thanks for all whose quiet "backstage" work made Adelynrood, the Society, and the *IP* function. A special thanksgiving named a wonderful "season" [a gathering of prayer and praise] with an interracial group from the Christian Social Relations branch of the Boston Council of United Church Women, which had sent out the following petition: "We praise thee, oh God, for the day-by-day acceptance of Christ's principles being applied to the struggle against Jim Crow [segregation] in Montgomery, Alabama." In **June**, Companions prayed for the Congress as it argued the nation's immigration policy. There was also a specific prayer that two young Negro boys in the Wooster School for Boys be able to continue there till graduation, and fulfill the high ideals of that school in their future lives.[27]

The Opening Paper of **Companion Conference 1957**, the *Vocation of Companionship,* by C-in-C Virginia Huntington, was filled with retrospective yearning for the "spirit of the great founders of our society, their gifts of mind and soul [as if] our days of greatness were past." She stressed the urgency of the Society's growth and change. Our "traditions" must also be remade, constantly evolving. To believe less would minimize the power of God's "vivifying grace." Companions' loyalty to Adelynrood and the chapters is not enough, Huntington warned: "the globe is our bailiwick." Recalling Miss Morgan's "sharing" about her hospitalizations, Huntington commented, "I read of her thyroid operation, she and I thus share one thing: throat surgery. In no other thing can I find similarity, alas!"[28] She closed with a quatrain, "Stretch me on Thy Greatness, Lord, /Who am mean and small;/ Fashion me relentlessly/ that I may grow more tall." A Companion in the annual **Business Meeting** questioned whether Companions were not in danger of becoming "spiritually ambitious," a coded way of referring to "private feelings of superiority" when comparing Companionship with other groups and denominations. The editor of the *IP* reported however that out of the entire 500 Companions, only 80 had bothered to send in petitions that year.[29]

---

27 1957 *IPs* February March April May June.

28 *Annual Report*, 1957, 8.

29 *IP* 1957 July-August, 5.

In this **1957** *Annual Report* were fourteen Memorials, the three Companion papers briefly summarized, and in the last three pages, names of office-holders elected and appointed: ACs–in-C (elected chapter leaders), Council, Executive Board, and Committees on *Finances, House, Buildings and Repairs, Chapel, Library, Artistic Planning, Garden and Grounds, Retreats, Far and Near,* and *Nominating.* It also listed the appointed "theme" chairmen, the trustees of the Endowment Fund, and a special advisory committee for a new bequest named after its donor, Ruth Mary Wilson.

September *IP:* Virginia Huntington's prayer for the observance of Holy Cross Day read: "O living Lord, who set the perfect pattern of brotherly love, give to people of every nation a new vision of the meaning of Christian brotherhood, a kinship that springs from unity in the Fatherhood of God. May they forget nationality and color in that freedom where the Good of one is the Good of all; that the light of the Kingdom may irradiate both our minds and hearts; in the name of Jesus Christ our elder brother." The **October** *IP* gave thanks "for the courage of clergy North and South, Negro and White, who have dared to teach and act their faith, despite threats and violence to themselves and their families." A petition also prayed that many small towns throughout the country discover the joys of harmony and gentle understanding to be found in the midst of many races—including Negro—and many creeds. [As historian Gardiner Shattuck noted in his volume *Episcopalians and Race*, this period of desegregation was much the hardest in small communities and isolated towns.] Another petition urged that Companions examine the uses of the word "crisis"—by whom, and for whom, at this time.

November *IP:* Concerns for racial justice broadened to include all dark-skinned peoples. Episcopal American Indian spokesman Vine Deloria was quoted: "One of the missionary teachers used to try to enlighten me on the proper attitudes needed by the whole missionary program today [including the white church]; we now see that she was RIGHT." It implied an acceptance of racial equality rather than patronization. One of Vida Scudder's many Probationers gave thanks for Scudder's life and influence. God was asked to strengthen Bishop Brown of Arkansas during the public torment surrounding Little Rock's school desegregation. Another petition prayed for "all caught in the conflicts of racial injustice and those actively working toward the rapid end of segregation; and for those of goodwill but afraid to become involved." In **December**, there were "thanksgivings that racial integration is beginning in a small parish, that the rector is wise, and the congregation showing change in its thinking." There were prayers for relations between Christians and Jews in Israel, and for an end to atomic testing.

1958—

Nuclear weapons test-control talks were taking place among the nations, Pope John XXIII was elected, the United Arab Republic was established, and the first U.S. space satellite was launched.

The **January** *IP* included prayers for the ecumenical World Council of Churches, and for Companion Cynthia Wedel, national president of Church Women United. Prayers asked "for an informed and Christian approach to all problems of segregation." There were thanksgivings for Companion Miriam Van Waters' 25 years as Director of the State Reformatory for Women at Framingham, Massachusetts, and prayers for Communists, especially for "our one-time Companions A & G who have turned from Thee to become one with *them*." A Companion prayed that white Christians would lovingly assist American Indians trying to break into modern urban living from reservation life.

March: Prayers were offered for a Negro boy in need of special teaching and that the other children at that school accept him "rightly," for the peaceful national integration of a border state, and for a new "suburban" parish in Memphis, St. John's, for the grace to repent our prejudice/hypocrisy toward the lives and communities of our Indian brothers, and their leaders the Rev. Mr. Deloria and his daughter Miss Ella Deloria [graduate of Columbia University, one of the earliest Native American anthropologists]. Recognizing that factions in parishes were taking sides for and against *Book of Common Prayer* revision, an **April** petition pleaded "that the whole church may use the exhortations after the Order of Holy Communion in the *Prayer Book*, as directed; also that the proper placement of clergy be taken out of church politics."

May: the thanksgivings-only *IP* honored Companion, leader and friend EMM—her joy, sympathy, gracious hospitality, and guidance of our Society through many years. A Companion gave thanks for the heartening clarity of Paul's epistles as translated by J.B.Phillips in *Letters to Young Churches*, another for each small note of more rational thinking about integration, and acceptance of it. There was praise for the awakening of many to helping the American Indians "strive to regain what of their history has been taken" [in land and cultural identity].

June: A petition supported the organizational restructuring of Episcopal churchwomen at the national-church level, led by Companions employed at national church headquarters in NYC, especially Frances Young, Executive: "may the "Woman's Auxiliary" (soon to be renamed Episcopal Church Women or the ECW) be richly blessed in the process of being transposed to the General Division of Women's Work of the National Council." Another prayer invoked parental guilt: "that parents realize something is lacking in their home life when their children get into trouble, and have the courage to rectify it." This type of pop-psychology flourished in the 1950s–60s.

July-August: prayers for those quietly working to make integration in the South a reality, and that "in the North we do all we can to further [fair] housing, work and decent jobs for Negroes, and for other minority groups in our own section of the country," also that God's love in our hearts overcome any sense of racial superiority. ·

1958 *Annual Report.* The **Companion Conference** theme was *Through The Cross, Joy.* C-in-C Virginia Huntington cited the surprising phenomenon of Old Testament Job being a contemporary cultural figure: a new play, *J.B.,* by Archibald MacLeish; a book *The Bible and the Common Reader* by Mary Ellen Chase; and *Job, Poet of Existence,* by Samuel Terrien (professor at Union Seminary in NYC). The **Annual Report** included thirteen memorials, summary reports on the theme retreats, and brief summaries of three Companion papers: Hilda Davis, Asst. Dir. of the Gov. Bacon Health Center in Delaware, "What Is a _Right Spirit_ Within Us?" Helen Turnbull, Director of Windham House [a NYC residence for Episcopal churchwomen professionals], "*Joy in Darkness;*" and Julia Capen, "*Joy Through the Power of Redeeming Love.*"

September: There were thanksgivings for the Rev. Kilmer Myers, author of *Light the Dark Streets,* helping initiate a new religious outreach of "inner city" ministry for the Episcopal Church. Two Companions offered thanksgivings for their forty years of homemaking, praying and working together. Prayer were offered for all Christian Missionaries being driven out of China. In **November,** there were thanksgivings for "clergy and people in a parish trying to remain integrated:" there were special thanksgivings *especially for white parishioners* [who] remain strong in their witness to the Gospel [italics added]." Prayers asked that people in large cities be concerned for the safety and cleanliness of ghetto streets, not just their handsome public buildings. A petition asked that Christian goodwill increase in the minds and hearts of those in embattled schools, plus thankfulness for places where school integration was proceeding peacefully. A Companion asked that Bp. Brown of Arkansas and the dean of the Little Rock Cathedral be given great wisdom, deep patience, and understanding, and that the Power of Love enable them to bring together the [school desegregation] factions in that divided city.[30]

---

30 1958 *IP* Sept. 5.

1959—

Alaska became the 49th state, and Hawaii the 50th; the Cuban Revolution brought Castro to power, and the big television quiz-show scandal erupted; President Nixon visited Russia; and in a cooperative declaration by twelve nations, Antarctica was named a scientific preserve. In the South, sit-ins continued. The new phenomenon of "kneel-ins" [mixed race demonstrators kneeling on the steps of an all-white church] brought desegregation to actual church buildings on Sunday mornings.

The **January** *IP* offered thanksgivings for a Companion taking two little Negro girls into her home, in Little Rock, and sending them to school, plus for all teachers of Christian education in Released Time school programs. **February** brought thanksgivings for British author Margaret Cropper's new biography of the first Church of England woman mystic and retreat leader, Evelyn Underhill, well known to American Companions through EMM. Prayers were offered for the League of Women Voters' water conservation program, for the labor movement, and for a parish in NYC that mounted a large public protest against the neighborhood's terrible housing, the only affordable places for the poor. Petitions asked that Christian faith be central in an emerging African country's freedom, and strength for the newly elected Presiding Bishop, Arthur Lichtenberger, whose wife Florence was a Companion.

March: There was a thanksgiving that some families exemplify the "ideal American family" by taking in mixed-blood children. In **April**, thanks were offered for Navaho work in Fort Defiance, AZ; in **May**, thanksgivings greeted Jan Struther's new hymn in the 1940 hymnal: "We thank Thee, Lord of Heaven, for all the joys that greet us." Specific thanks surrounded "a courageous young rector handling the delicate situation when Negro servicemen were moved into an all-white town, also for women who spoke up for the right, affirming the [reconciling] mission of the Church, and for good will that bravely solves the complex problem of racial integration."[31]

---

31 *IP* May 1959, 6.

· **June:** Thanksgivings were offered for the life and witness of our Founder EMM and the power of the Cross in SCHC's seventy-five years of vitality. There were intercessions "for a downtown parish seething with strife, starting from a vestry-majority fighting against integration and unity, for the rector and his staff, and for dear friends who are ringleaders in opposition to the rector on these issues." Prayers were offered for educated Negroes in a small Virginia town who were not being given a chance to use their education, as they would like to. One Companion urged that Christians name *lynching* a crime against society as a whole.

The **1959 Companion Conference** theme was *Fruits of the Spirit.* The Opening Paper for this 75th anniversary of SCHC by C-in-C Huntington was subsequently reprinted and distributed separately under the title "The Meaning & Purpose of SCHC [Part I]." [Confusingly, it was later also referred to as the Theme Paper for the 1962 Conference.] Fr. Huntington of the (male) Order of the Holy Cross, no relation to the C-in-C but long-time friend and counselor to EMM and the Society, was a featured guest. At this gathering, Winifred Hulbert also presented a Companion paper that opened with these sentences: "There is no subject that has caused more violent disagreement in our Society than Social Justice. And yet there is none during our 75 years of existence that has united Companions more often."[32]

C-in-C Huntington's powerful re-statement of the shape, identity, and vocation of Companionship, intended as a summary reflection on Societal custom and meaning, ranks in organizational significance with words of EMM and VDS. Here it is summarized extensively.

> Huntington expressed regret that EMM's earliest annual letters had not been preserved in full text until <u>1942</u>, when C-in-C Elizabeth Cook first arranged it. (They had been published in the printed **Annual Reports** from 1935-1942.) Huntington quoted Morgan's first *Annual Letter* (1885) in full, the briefest ever, announcing the formation of the first

---

32 Joan Russell, "A Polished Arrow" Spring Conf. 1997, unpublished paper, Archive.

Companion committee, a Library Committee.[33] EMM had also announced the beginnings of the Society's "intercession paper" which was to constitute the Society's ever-renewing prayer agenda, a compilation of "Companions' subjects of Intercession or thanksgiving [sent in] during the first three weeks of every month." Both organizational moves firmly established the *word-based culture* that would nurture the Society's prayer bond into the present.

Huntington next traced EMM's maturing spiritual leadership in relation to the institutional church, her ability to combine "daring and independent" ideas with the traditional. Throughout the *Annual Letters,* her analytic insight combined a masculine directness with femininity. Miss Morgan, "not an intellectual in the strict sense, nor a scholar," possessed a wide-ranging mind and spirit that could slip easily from banter and wit into the profound rhythms of devotion.

Among the SCHC traditions Huntington described was the origin of the sung Adelynrood Grace, a result of Miss Scudder's expressed wish, one day, "that we could sing it." Companion Elizabeth Lobdell (1873-1959), an early collector of Negro songs from the South, simply sat at the organ and jotted down the melody, "the only music [she] ever composed." Huntington also cited EMM's 1915 wit on the topic of Noise vs. Quiet: Miss Morgan remarked that the "mere announcement" of having quiet prevail after 9 p.m. made "every American woman fear her citizenship was being infringed upon!" Also, Huntington paid tribute to Vida Scudder's nearly thirty-five years as C-in-C of Probationers, crediting her catholic churchmanship as the healthy counterbalance to Miss Morgan's broad churchmanship.

Back then, the Society had more single women than today, and present Society leaders, "mostly in their 60s," have great need for younger Companions. We live in a vastly different world and SCHC must change with it. "If we today seem not to have the dynamic commitment to social reform" [like the Founders], we are already more involved in all kinds of the world's problems than it was possible for them to be. The tree of Companionship grows in the shadow of the Cross, a paradox—endurance of it brings joy, the tree itself becomes the Holy Rood."[34]

Huntington reminded each Companion of the obligation to question, when the aims of the Society seemed unclear, in what ways SCHC differed from other religious groups—a prayer group, a committee on social service, or interchurch work toward Christian unity. Her answer? Companionship was a hard-to-describe quality of life, though its

---

33 This was an important organizational step, providing Companions with religious study materials (theological and church-history tomes) otherwise unavailable to lay women.

34 *Annual Report* 1959, 9, 10.

"purpose" was easier because of the Rule, aims, and ideals stated in the *Manual*. The small prayer group around invalid Adelyn Howard had been very youthful: as EMM observed, "Only youth could have chosen such a name for an organization of spiritual Companionship!" Characteristics of the Society, since then, have been <u>breadth of outlook</u>, <u>mental vigor</u>, and <u>spiritual depth</u>, reflecting the dramatically different personalities of founders Morgan and Scudder. In the *Letters* EMM's forthright spirit cuts through externals to the reality beneath. For her, the religious climate was broad and evangelical in its inclusiveness, while for Miss Scudder, it was Catholic and radical. Miss Morgan had an Elizabethan gusto and sense of humor; today one imagines her a female Falstaff! Miss Scudder was the scholar, the intellectual with a swift mind and incisive speech. Huntington pointed out that reading EMM's *Letters*, and VDS's *On Journey* were the only means of truly "knowing" them and understanding the impulse that generated SCHC.

Adelynrood itself is something else, a distinctive matter. It is not just a "holy clubhouse," but a holy routine, a way of living. What it has offered during the seventy-eight years of life as a Society, and in the fifty years since Adelynrood was built, has been peace, the Great Cross, the Chapel, and the Oratory. The disciplines of the Probationary period make entry into Companionship like the experience of entering a convent, in many ways: ordered, structured reading, and the study of the simple, profound questions preceding final admission. It also acknowledges the tensions that inevitably arise amid a group of strong-minded women.

Is SCHC a "Third Order" religious group? Scudder would say yes, Morgan, no. What we are <u>not</u> is the ECW, the Daughters of the King, the Girls' Friendly Society, and all organizations who have definite aims, objectives, and programs. Rather, SCHC is a *"dynamic group dedicated to creative prayer."* Companions work individually in all kinds of areas, *not as a Society*. Companions *as a Companionship* sponsor no causes and are involved in causes only via individual callings. "Companionship is a dynamo, a powerhouse, an inspirer; *each of us has a vocation to Companionship*" but a devout churchwoman *per se* is not necessarily called to SCHC, and may find the "regulations irksome." Make no mistake; our Societal aims make demands—prick us to definite prayer, to action in social justice, to seek unity in ourselves and in the world.

Companions are also joyful! Laughter, what EMM used to call by the Latin term *"hilaritas,"* is part of Companionly life together. "Membership" is each person's vocation to the Way of Cross. Is SCHC also called to be useful to the larger church, according to the leading of God, especially now that clergy are more familiar with Society programs and retreats? That is ponderable, unknowable. One of the questions in the Admission liturgy is: will you serve God in the ministries of intercession, thanksgiving and simplicity of life? Companions answer: we will, by the grace of God. This is the real purpose of our being, and the true meaning of SCHC.

We are not "members of an organization," but "a Way of Life to be lived." Companions are not pledged to action in Social Justice, Unity, and Mission, but these are the common [shared] objects of SCHC prayer. SCHC does not sponsor work in them but provides the corporate activity of conferences to educate Companions about them. Through the Society's long years, Companions have withstood the temptation to sign petitions lending the Society's name to eminently worthy projects. But our essence is a quality, not a program.[35] [This 1959 admonition was likely related to the "corporate stands" debate, and concern over McCarthyism.]

At the **Business Meeting**, the *Finance* Committee suggested raising Adelynrood charges to $5 per day for Companions and $6.50 for guests, as well as welcoming outside participants at $8 per day at special Conferences. A budget of $30,043 was approved for 1960. Each Committee reported, including a new one established to plan refurbishing the Oratory. The Summer Calendar Committee urged better attendance (therefore more income) at weekend conferences. A special Commission was at work revising the *Manual*. 116 Companions attended **Companion Conference**. Chapter reports were very brief and sixteen Memorials were published in a separate section.[36]

1960—

The pace of public Civil Rights events quickened. J.F.Kennedy was elected President, and M.L.King Jr. was briefly jailed in Georgia; television initiated groundbreaking political debates between national presidential candidates, and war erupted in the new

---

35 *Annual Report,* October 1959, 3, 5.

36 Ibid, 22, 39. From her Memorial [read at Companion Conference 1959, by Henderika Rynbergen], former C-in-C Grace Lindley was credited with: 1-establishing a Winter Conference, now called Spring Conference; 2 –offering hospitality on July 4th to United Nations support groups; 3- encouraging more retreats for Companions and their friends; 4—Penology Conferences; 5-being a leader in the church of women and girls over 20 years, including in the Diocese of Newark, and in NYC, Executive of the national Women's Auxiliary and recipient of an honorary doctorate from University of the South; 6-determined to test the anti-discrimination law at a NYC restaurant and 7-a story of St. Peter, remonstrating when Jesus let unsavory people into heaven. Jesus said, "But Peter! These are my friends."

Republic of Congo. The birth control pill was invented, and seventy South Africans were killed over race policies; mainstream news reported lunch counter "sit-ins" in North Carolina. At the end of 1959, ESCRU [Episcopal Society Committed to Racial Unity] had been established within the Episcopal Church.

An interracial incident in the Episcopal Diocese of Alabama created newspaper headlines: a young black priest, Robert DuBose, in Montgomery AL, [chaplain of segregated Alabama State College], marched in a desegregation protest. The dramatic photograph showed him in his vividly Episcopal cassock, surplice, stole and biretta. The outraged diocesan bishop forced DuBose to go north in order to find a parish. A sympathetic young white priest, the Rev. Francis Walter, preaching the moral rightness of desegregation and supporting DuBose, was also forced to leave his Birmingham parish.[37]

January: "Togetherness," a major commercial theme, was evoking the image of a comfortable, white, middle-class worldview that symbolized contentment and stability in family and church. It presumed universal, widely shared views of loyalty and responsibility. No Companions actually named that concept in the *IP*s. One enlightened intercession noted that the only ultimate solution to the scourge of juvenile delinquency was decent housing for minorities.

In **February**, there were thanksgivings for Vida Scudder's life and work, especially her "delightful autobiographical reflection titled *On Journey*," and for the renewed post-WW II work of Nippon Sei Ko Kai, the Japanese Episcopal church. The Bishop of the Diocese of California (James Pike) attracted prayers hoping "he would grow in faith in Apostolic Way," an oblique reference to his earlier Roman Catholicism, and perhaps also to his feisty challenge to Episcopal cultural conformity [Holy Communion once a month and other Protestant practices.] Thanksgivings greeted a new retreat center at Taize, France, that welcomed all young pilgrims from any nation, of

37 Shattuck, *Episcopalians and Race: 119, 120-121.*

any or no religious background, a pilgrimage for reconciliation after the World War.

There was an appended Notice of Reorganization for the *IP* itself. Henceforth it was to be organized in seven sections, to heighten the intention and focus of each day, reserving Sundays for Thanksgivings only.

That **Spring**, there were prayers "for a Civil Rights bill that CAN be enforced" so that the privileges of free men could be experienced by all minorities, also special prayers for the Episcopal Sisters of All Saints, in Catonsville MD, and a 50th anniversary note memorializing the great ecumenical Edinburgh conference on World Missions in 1910. One petitioner hoped that the world is "not too late to rectify all the abuses of civil liberty on the racial issue," and prayed about the resurgence of racial conflict in Asia and Africa.[38] In the summer, an *IP* petition asked for "a new generation of men [human beings], destroying our complacency and indifference to injustices for refugees, Jews, Negroes, Mexicans, and the foreign born." And on a socio-historical note, a first-of-its-kind petition focused on a "teenage girl, Episcopal communicant, [who is] hysterically rebellious against devoted parents"—a portent of the incipient generational revolution.

The **1960 Companion Conference** theme was *Approaches to God*. Virginia Huntington's Opening Paper again reflected the Society's uneasiness about "the seeming apathy toward Social Justice," low attendance at "problem" conferences, and lessened involvement in outreach work in Companions' own communities. Unlike the Founders' generation, the majority of Companions were now married, including wives of clergy who had little time for work beyond home and parish. VH cited a Companion's observation that was almost an indictment: "As a Society, we are all too safe, too comfortably off in [terms of] security and privilege. Our intercessions reveal little preoccupation with society's problems." Indeed, there

---

38 Jan 8; Feb. 15, March, April, May 1960.

seemed to be fewer intercessions addressing the huge and difficult world conditions. "To involve ourselves more closely with poverty and loneliness," VH suggested inviting women from slum-area Rest Homes for a night of peace and beauty at Adelynrood.

A rare, separate description of Companion Day and Evening portrayed the Companion Procession from Portal to Chapel, concluding at the Great Cross where Companions sang the "beautiful canticle *Benedicite Omnia Opera Domini,* especially meaningful on a lovely day." In the afternoon, Companions gathered in the chapel for remembrance of Companions who had entered the Paradise Chapter during the past year. Brief sketches of Companions' lives (Memorials) were read, followed by a picnic, and "the traditional auction that resulted in a goodly sum as well as laughter." The final event of the day presented letters from absent Companions, later called the Far and Near Chapter.[39]

The **September** and **October** *IPs* carried many prayers for the huge "new" social problems of delinquency and inner city gangs. There were prayers for middle-aged men unable to find employment, for migrant workers, and for acceptance and for better treatment of Indian-Americans. Dag Hammerskjold, General Secretary of the United Nations, was inspiring work for justice among church members, and some Companions were praying that kneel-in and sit-in demonstrations be instruments "breaking down the walls of prejudice." Petitions supported the integration of lunch counters in four leading chain stores in 112 Southern cities; there were also prayers for the beginnings of CORE, the Congress of Racial Equality. A petition blessed Roxanna, a nurse in a mission hospital in Sudan that was eight days distant from other settlements. There were thanksgivings and blessings for the ecumenical brothers of Taize. An explicitly political intercession revealed misgivings about the election of President John F. Kennedy: it was a prayer "that the people of our country may have chosen aright in the recent election

---

39 *Annual Report* 1960, 45.

and that the President-elect, over-young and inexperienced, may ask for guidance." In fact, it continued, may the "entire incoming Administration [turn] Godward." As usual in **December**, the birthday of founder Emily M. Morgan was honored, with thanksgivings for the richness and simplicity of her faith, her beautiful presence, and her never-failing friendliness.[40]

The response to Sputnik gave rise to more science content in newspapers and magazines, and Rachel Carson's book *Silent Spring* helped ignite the environmentalist movement. In reaction, "creationism" emerges in the fundamentalist Christian response.

1961—

The first major international war-crimes trial convicted Nazi henchman Adolf Eichmann. UN Secretary Dag Hammerskjold was killed in a plane crash, and the Berlin Wall was erected. The first astronaut rode into space, the Freedom Riders were attacked in the South, the Bay of Pigs invasion of Cuba failed, and kneel-ins in churches continued. Gardiner Shattuck, Episcopal historian of this era, observed that segregationists were beginning to be "unpopular" but few white Episcopalians were among those strong enough to be outspoken. Companion Jane Schutt was one: her courageous story [when a KKK cross was burned in front of her house, 1963] would be reprinted in many religious publications, one as recently as 2004.[41]

January began with thanksgivings for any and every sign of peaceful integration, the basic prayer of white moderates. One petition expressed faith in the ability of men of racial differences to live in community, with brotherly love and respect for human dignity; prayers were offered for the Anglican Sisters of the Holy Paraclete, and for the social-justice witness of a devout Episcopal layman-lawyer in NYC, William Stringfellow.

---

40 Dec. 1960 *IP*, 11.

41 "Incident at 955 Pecan Boulevard," *Guideposts* Nov. 27, 2004.

February: Prayers were asked for missionary Peyton Craighill, husband of Companion Marian, and for Haiti and South Africa. Another Companion prayed "that the bewildered US Southland may be left alone (all outside agitators stay away) to the work of its own salvation." Prayers were offered for the great silent moderates in the South to find their voice and sound out clearly through the strident tones of extremists on both sides, also that the bewildered well-meaning Southerner realize the evil fruit of forced integration has sprung ONLY from the evil seed of forced segregation (emphasis in the original). There was a prayer for a Texas parish experiencing "a blow at the body of Christ" when a minority pro-segregation group took over the annual meeting and elected a vestry of their persuasion. Intercessions requested support for the work of ESCRU, for the POWs still in Korea, and for the consciences of great corporations.[42]

In **April**, thanksgivings were offered for the forthright leadership of the President [Kennedy] and for NATO, for "opening the eyes" of a parish guild of women who had operated exclusively, like a club, for students at Japanese universities who have lost all faith; and for Companion Estelle Carver, accompanying the renowned Baptist missionary, the Rev. E. Stanley Jones, on a world tour of church repertory theater.

In **May**, some Companions saw "promise" in the idea of a National Peace Corps that could occupy post-high school youth constructively, and also gave thanks for any and all progress in school integration.

The **1961 Companion Conference** focused on *Simplicity.* Virginia Huntington, C-in-C,[43] suggesting in her Opening Paper that Simplicity was more about churchwomen's *"over-busyness"* than a matter of "mink stoles and Cadillacs." What had been thought of

---

42 March *IP* 1961, 7.

43 Prevailing through the 1980s, Companion Conference Sunday morning had a Meditation concluding the previous three-day silent retreat, with memorials (orally presented) in the evening; Monday, Companion Day and Evening; Tuesday through Thursday: papers by an invited leader and/or Companions, and Bible Study; and Friday, a corporate communion as conclusion.

as self-denial, asceticism, and "naughting, viewed in a new light," [an early English theological term she employed to mean self-effacement], can be key to a "freedom of the spirit"—holding the material world more lightly. Her conclusion included a popular quotation from poet T. S. Eliot: "For us there is only the trying. The rest is not our business. Fare forward, voyagers [not farewell], only undefeated because we have gone on trying."[44] The structure of the ten-day gathering now included a three-day silent retreat and a service where Memorials were read aloud, plus Companion Day—a rededication service and procession, followed by Companion Evening hilarity or a hymn sing. The annual **Business Meeting** announced improvements including new beds in the upstairs rooms, a new hotwater heater, and spruced up gardens. Some Companions were furnishing bedrooms as memorials to their Sponsors; today a few such placards are still visible on Adelynrood walls.

The **Summer** of **1961** brought many Social Justice prayers, one honoring a New England town where "justice, truly expressed, operated a school system respecting race and color." Prayers supported Companion Frances Young, the new executive of the Triennial Women's Meeting [held at the same time as the Episcopal church's General Convention]. An awkward petition illuminated the then-standard ideal of many concerned white Christians: "for American Negroes, that they may come to feel a sense of common heritage with those of the white race who founded our country, and to understand that it was not a matter of color in this giving of a constitution to the present generation" [a reading of early American history that ignored the 1787 inscription of slaves' limited "humanity" in the U.S. constitution]. Also, thanksgivings were offered for Companion Dora Chaplin's contributions in the field of Christian Education, and prayers for victims of national disasters, as well as for more sensitivity on the part of the U.S. diplomatic corps [perhaps a response to the "ugly American" image in British author Graham Greene's novel of that name].

---

44 *Annual Report* 1961, 7.

In **October**, there were thanksgivings for the "beautiful, deeply impressive *Stations of the Cross*" [paintings depicting scriptural characters with black skin], presented to the Adelynrood chapel by Boston artist Allan Rohan Crite (son of Companion Annamae Crite); in **November** a petition gave thanks for the "valiant" Civil Rights stand taken by the Episcopal Church, and for courageous men willing to sacrifice comfort and embarrassment by participating in Freedom Rides. A Companion thanked God that Americans were coming to the full realization of the historic harm done by vicious segregation laws. Also another Companion prayed for enough volunteers to fill the need for Church School teachers in her parish.

December: A Companion noted that seven years to the day after the *Brown v Board of Education* Supreme Court decision, "freedom rides" were now riding into the nation's consciousness, and that regular television coverage of these protest marches was opening the nation's and the Society's consciousness about the injustices of segregation.

1962—

The nation lived through the Cuban missile crisis, a time when ordinary middleclass families felt the fear of potential war in their own neighborhoods. There was the horror of birth defects traceable to the drug thalidomide taken by women in early pregnancy for morning sickness. The Supreme Court ruled that Christian school prayer was inappropriate for public schools because it excluded all other religions. White moderates in poor, rural Southern counties faced the impact of active voter registration and its threat to local power systems. Black citizens learned it was important for them to keep showing up and attempt to register to vote, even if they were not allowed to do so. TV coverage was helping arouse the consciences of white Christians.

January brought prayers for a ban on nuclear testing, and for disarmament. **February** brought a petition asking for "the Holy Spirit to guide the Southern Regional Conference (the civil rights organization chaired by the Rev. Martin Luther King Jr.) meeting at the [Episcopal] DuBose Center in May." As always, there was concern for Companions unable to experience Adelynrood, and thus unable to fully experience the aims and fellowship of the Society. There were prayers for NATO, for Congress, and for children in families without religious instruction. In the **Spring,** there were intercessions for Haiti, and for Alcoholics Anonymous. There were thanksgivings that fifteen priests [all members of ESCRU], jailed for participating in Freedom Rides, were "the symbol of our faith in the unity of the races." There were prayers for the Peace Corps, and the international student exchange program Crossroads Africa. A thanksgiving was offered for Kathy, age 17, who delivered the baby she put up for adoption [the first time that topic was mentioned], and a prayer that she "take up her life again without bitterness, [as well as] praise for her loving parents' strength."[45] A Companion asked that Companions continue to pray for one another's "need" in addition to praying for the issues of the day. A thanksgiving was offered for the decision by the University of the South (Sewanee, TN) to accept students in the future without regard to color or race, and a petition that the use of peaceful resistance and picketing might actually prove to be a more efficacious strategy. **June** brought prayers for the Sisters of St. Margaret and their work in Haiti. There was an oblique reference to lifting the "pall of fear" in a small Texas town where an election "triumphed," although in what way was not specified. Blessings were sought for the Episcopal Theological School in Cambridge MA, for Taize, for migrants, for more southern churches extending welcome to visitors regardless of race, and for new relations between the US and USSR. A petition was offered for "grieving parents of an only daughter from a truly Christian home who [seems to] seek divorce for purely selfish reasons. May she

45 *IPs* March, April, May 1962.

grow in maturity and love, recognizing the anguish she has brought into the lives of those around her."[46]

July-August 1962: There were prayers from Ernestine Henderson's *The Church Woman,* for missions in Alaska, China, the National Council of Churches, and for ALL children. The **1962 Companion Conference** theme, August 14-24, was *The Holy Spirit In The Life Of Today.* Virginia Huntington, C-in-C, presented the Opening Paper, [published in the **Annual Report,** labeled *Part II* of her 1959 paper *The Vocation of Companionship,* already excerpted here and distributed to all as a separate publication]—confusingly labeled *Part I* of *The Vocation of Companionship.* In Part II, she stressed the spiritual rather than organizational dimensions of Companion identity: the hope of "finding, in the expanding wonders of our universe, the summons of the Holy Spirit to a fuller and more luminous life in Him." A proposed moonwalk in the news was reflected in her choice of language. She ended with a prayer of her own composition: "Holy Spirit, inspirer of all human activity, enable with thy perpetual Grace all that we strive to be and do in thy name. Be to us the Spirit that maketh all things new. Compel us to discard pettiness and to venture forth, resting in thee, into the uncharted future in the ocean of charity."

In the **Annual Report,** a rare public glimpse of tension over Adelynrood appeared. Some Companions were lamenting a loss of SCHC intimacy when outside groups rented the buildings; they were asking the possessive question: "who's it for?" Huntington's metaphor recommended that *corporate life* at Adelynrood "be stretched on the sacred beams of the Cross horizontally as well as vertically!"[47] Over 500 people attended conferences in the summer of 1962, in addition to a few regional gatherings. In all there were seventeen chapters, the newest in Western Massachusetts called the Berkshire Chapter.

---

46 June *IP,* 11.

47 *Annual Report* 1962, 7.

A <u>Notice</u> in the *IP*: The new format for the *Intercession Paper* was explained. "Each editor naturally brings her own emphasis and format to the daily themes, and strives to narrow the time lapse between the intercession's arrival and its publication in the eleven annual issues." Companions were urged to state the intercessory need with *only as much detail as makes it intelligible* to the reader. Also: whenever possible and advisable, intercessing Companions were requested to use full Christian names in place of initials.

The *Newsletter* of **August 1962** reported the coldest July in 40 years, requiring Companions at Adelynrood to build fires and distribute extra blankets after Compline. The new program venture was a <u>School of Religion</u>, a Companion-sponsored conference on theological issues and church history. Since women were not admitted to Episcopal seminaries, 48 Companions attended; "it made Paul, Luke, Thomas, James and even Judas seem like real people." [In 2006, it would be somewhat comparable with a one-week session of EFM (Education for Ministry), the Sewanee lay-adult-education program initiated in the 1980s.]

Improvements at Adelynrood included carpeting on the main stairway, and two new wing chairs for a corner of the living room given in memory of Companion Elizabeth Lansing. Two Companions donated an electric dishwashing machine, and the kitchen now featured a walk-in refrigerator, a stainless steel sink, and ovens, plus new lighting in the public rooms: kitchen, dining room, Common Room. The grateful husband of a Companion from Boston gave new beds (box springs and mattresses) for every room. In the chapel, "flowers, the battle ground of all Altar Guilds, were carefully renewed each day"...Also it was noted that Companions were reading the Psalms in unison "better," thanks to "gentle prods from the C-in-C to pause at the semi-colons!" It was reported that at a national church committee studying race issues among Episcopalians, Sarah Patton Boyle, white Virginia activist and author, had presented "Witness of a Lone Layman," a paper confronting Episcopal leadership with its lack of support for brave individual desegregationists isolated in white parishes.

In the fall *IPs*, prayers celebrated the post-war restoration of a thousand-year-old abbey in England, also the "new" [rebuilt] cathedrals in England, Coventry and Guilford—and a joyful Corporate Communion of Women. A Companion gave thanks for EMM's "strong unwavering belief [that] one individual in the certainty of [heavenly] reunion may [exercise] immeasurable influence." Another prayed that children of Prince Edward County, VA might have the "opportunity for a rightful education." A petition asked enlightenment for those in power who exercised it unfairly, closing the public schools to defy desegregation.

November 1962 brought prayers for Bp. Duncan Gray and the clergy of Oxford, MS, [who had stood up to white rioters at the University of Mississippi, popularly called "Ole Miss"],[48] and intercessions for African-American James Meredith [as he desegregated the University of Mississippi]: "during the terrible days of strain, grant him courage and wisdom, and pray for his family." By **December 1962,** many thanksgivings were offered for the life and death of Eleanor Roosevelt, for her deep Christian love of all mankind, and for her promotion of the full achievement of human rights. Other petitions gave thanks for her peaceful death, and her "spirit that continues to shed light in the dark corners of the world." A petition named the truly Christian work of KEEP [a program in the Japanese Alps helping restart grass-roots agriculture under the leadership of lay-Episcopal-missioner Paul Rusch, from Cincinnati]. Prayers were offered for the Detroit Industrial Mission where Companion-to-be "Muffy Paradise worked with her husband Scott," and for the Baptist missionary Frank Laubach's "Army of Compassion" with his motto for world literacy, "Each One Teach One."

1963—

President John F. Kennedy was assassinated; the 16th Street Baptist Church of Birmingham, AL, was bombed, killing four black Sunday school girls. The March on Washington for Civil Rights attracted more than 200,000 black and white demonstrators. An anti-nuclear test treaty was signed, and Gov. George Wallace [Alabama] physically "blocked the school house door" to prevent a black child from entering and desegregating the public schools. Pope

---

48 November *IP* 1962, 8.

John XXIII died; Pope Paul VI was elected. Black Americans were painfully aware that in the hundred years from 1863 to 1963, from the Freedom Proclamation to this date, little had changed: they still had no real freedom, no real equality of education or occupational access. Fortunately, the white Christian world was slowly beginning to acknowledge this reality.[49]

Early in 1963, the *IP* rejoiced in the Rev. John M. Burgess's election as the first Negro Bishop elected in a US diocese (Massachusetts), a landmark event in the Episcopal Church, his wife Esther a Companion. Sadly, Companion Connie Sharkey's 9-year-old son died in a sledding accident. Intercessions supported a young Methodist minister driven from his church in Mississippi, asked that the Governor and State of Mississippi be given a new vision, and that Sarah Patton Boyle's autobiographical book *The Desegregated Heart* receive wide use. A Companion asked protection for Alaskan native hunting and fishing rights, and for the peaceful resolution of the undeclared wars in Vietnam, in the Congo, and in India.

Spring: thanksgivings were offered for the joy of recently read EMM *Letters*, and for an emerging awareness of the Anglican Communion as described in the national newspaper *The Episcopalian*, plus for the U.S. mission of British evangelist Bryan Green. There were prayers that Negroes, having impatiently left parishes because of integration "snail's pace," would return. A petition supported the interracial group meeting in Columbia, SC, and the interracial wisdom in Septima Clark's book *Echo in my Soul.* Another gave thanks for the work and life of poet Robert Frost. A petition for a new parish in San Diego was followed with a thanksgiving that the Columbia [SC] Council of Churchwomen had invited Negro women to worship and work *with* them. A thanksgiving was offered for the School of Prayer led by Mrs. Sam Shoemaker [Companion] in March, with a lengthy report of her vivid speech. A thanksgiving was offered for the sense of community enjoyed among students' wives

---

49 *McWhorter*, 306; January, February 1963 *IP*s, 10,11.

at General Seminary [NYC], and praise for the life and spiritual gifts of the great Quaker retreat leader, Rufus Jones. A petition opposed the evil uses of nuclear power.[50]

June: Thanksgivings were offered for the work in Haiti of the Sisters of St. Margaret, and for Negro leaders' steadfast faith in non-violence. While giving thanks for S.P.Boyle's book *The Desegregated Heart*, Companions were urged to pray that "reading it by many may...change the hearts of both Southerners and Northerners, and of Negro friends."[51]

July-August: Thanksgivings were offered for the life of Edith Hamilton, scholar and translator of Greek myths, and for Emily Gardiner Neal's work with the Order of St. Luke that promotes laying on of hands for healing, a new practice in many parishes. A petition asked that Congress pass legislation guaranteeing the civil rights of Negroes and all minorities, and that in time all may realize God's purgative action through Little Rock, Mississippi, Alabama, Roxbury [MA], Harlem, and Chicago [scenes of protest and unrest]. A special thanksgiving was offered for the comforting picture of a Negro family "now living happily, with respect, in an outstanding Massachusetts community."

Companion Conference 1963, August 13-23, on the theme of *Intercession*, emphasized that intercessing was NOT a private enterprise between one's soul and God, but "a communal practice of the family of God." C-in-C Virginia Huntington's Opening Paper saw it as opening a public niche for the witness of Christian women. Intercession required *imagination*, carrying another's burden as if it were one's own, and *compassion*, the sublime word capturing the very nature of God and the human web. But intercession in this world? Bishop Burgess had reminded Companions that this is a dirty world: Companions can't specialize in only "good" news, can't read only the *Christian Science Monitor*! Huntington confronted the

---

50 March April May *IPs* 1963.
51 June 1963 *IP*, 10.

perennial question of whether group prayer is more valued than individual prayer. Companions know they are never alone, even when far from other Companions. Are we able to pray for Khrushchev, Castro, Franco, and Red China? For ideological difference? And is Christianity a paradox? Antipathetic? Yes. Simone Weil wrote: "If I am only filled with sorrow, then I am empty."[52] Intercession, Huntington concluded, is the cross on which Companions must stretch themselves, with humility: first, perpendicularly, in adoration, then outreaching, along the horizontal arm.

Deaconess Jane Bliss Gillespy's Companion Paper also addressed intercession and what it is not. It is offering to use one's will and love for God as channels of His spirit. "Intercessory prayer is loving our neighbor on our knees." Unfortunately, she lamented, some knees find themselves too stiff to bend.

At the **1963** annual **Business Meeting**, Adelynrood was enriched by the presence of Companion missionary teachers Eleanor Mason and Doris Wilson, returned from India, and Dorothy Stout from Japan. The council voted that August 28, the date set for the March on Washington, be observed as a day of prayer at Adelynrood. The Endowment Fund received a total of $6,037; the *Finance Committee* presented a budget of $48,618 for 1963-64. The *IP* Editor reported receiving approximately 22 submissions each month, a fairly small representation from membership of some 545 Companions. Due to publishing costs, the *IP* is restricted to sixteen pages, requiring many petitions to be shortened. It was requested that petitions be framed in a "pray-able" form.

Marion Rollins was elected the new C-in-C, and three papers were presented by Companions (Rollins, *The Theology of Intercession*; Dorothy Worrell, *Interceding for Social Justice*; Deaconess Gillespy, The *Communion of Saints*.) On page 61-62 of the **Annual Report,** a printed tribute honored departing C-in-C Virginia Huntington's eight years of service.

---

52 *Annual Report* 1963, 12, 21, 61-62.

NEWSLETTER 1963. This time a hot summer was reported. Nine Companions were resident the whole summer; three parish groups were present for retreats. The Conference on *Mission* and one on *Christian Unity* were both excellent but poorly attended. The House was filled to the roof (as it had been for the AA retreat) for the School of Religion, testifying to Companions' thirst for serious religious study. The library reported its 100 new books as "striving to keep ears and hearts open to the clamor of the troubled world beyond our serene salt marshes." Many Companions were planning to attend The March on Washington on August 28; those at Adelynrood would observe a day of prayer-vigil in the chapel.

The September *IP* featured a quotation from the startling new book *Honest to God,* by Bishop J.A.T.Robinson. Thanksgivings were offered for the outstanding leadership of C-in-C Virginia Huntington, for the School of Religion at Adelynrood, for an encouraging financial report, and a spirit of agreement in the Council, the Executive Board, and the **Business Meeting**. There were petitions that public schooling be restored to Negro children in Prince Edward Co., Virginia, for the Negro undergraduate admitted to the University of the South, for **Companion Conference** and for the NAACP to use "Christian ends to accomplish its goals in all areas." Another prayer expressed the hope that Negroes and Puerto Ricans might come to love each other.

The October *IP* carried thanksgivings for the "dignified, orderly" Civil Rights March of 200,000 black and white citizens in August, in Washington DC, and for the spirit of the Bill of Rights that "sweetened" the whole nation. A petition prayed that Negro children in <u>all</u> schools might be increasingly accepted, and that the cooperation of school officials become standard. There were thanksgivings for the courage of Negro children bravely entering newly-desegregated schools, for the spirit from the Anglican Congress in Toronto filtering down into local parishes, for a new religious order of women in India, Pakistan, Burma, and Ceylon, and for unity, including the unity of Church Women United. An intercession prayed that the people of this nation "be forgiven for the tragedy of the Birmingham church bombing Sunday Sept. 15." A thanksgiving was offered for the poem, *"For the Marchers, August 28, 1963"* by Companion Louisa E. Bilon, for students from Africa who come to the US to study and grow, and for US Ambassador Lodge in Vietnam. Earnest prayers urged more study about other religions: Islam, Buddhism, Judaism, and Hinduism. A Companion prayed that the church proclaim in prophetic tones that racial segregation and injustice are the result of man's callous sin against his brother.

A <u>Notice</u> appended to the **December** *IP*: The C-in-C of Probationers lifted the moratorium on submitting the papers of new Probationers, but set a limit of 40 to be processed at any one time. Alice Bartlett's paper, "A Picture of Miss Morgan," really a memoir and tribute, was published and sent to Probationers, and to all Companions who wished it.

The **December 1963** *IP* carried thanksgivings for the life of John F. Kennedy, for our founder EMMorgan and all her gifts, for the Anglican Fellowship of Prayer, and for ecumenical dialogue. An intercession asked "that the depth of the grievances of Negroes be better interpreted to the nation as a whole, and that churches be fully confronted with the consequences of the sin of racial hatred." One petition asked that God heal the heart of a young Negro girl dismissed from a church choir in the North because of her race, another that people of the U.S. "accept Martin Luther King's *acceptance of persecution* as powerful." Companions prayed for support for Jacqueline Kennedy and her children in their grief, and for all the Kennedy family, plus special prayers for the little girls killed in the Birmingham church bombing.

<u>Notice</u>: An in-house organizational <u>reminder</u> asked all committee chairs and officers in the SCHC to prepare "a step-by-step outline of procedures [today, Guidelines] for their successors in office," and send them to Hilda Bishop for the Society files.

1964—

In August, three missing Civil Rights workers were found buried in an earthen dam. President Johnson signed the Civil Rights Act covering voting and employment. Martin Luther King Jr. was awarded the Nobel Peace Prize. In South Africa, Nelson Mandela was sentenced to life in prison. Pesticides were discovered as the cause of fish kills in the Mississippi River, and the Surgeon General named cigarettes a health hazard.

In his book *God's Long Summer*, author Charles Marsh [referring to the year 1964 in his title] wrote that by then, it was "clear that any white clergyman preaching brotherhood and urging justice toward the black race could be run out of town by sundown." The Civil Rights movement was beginning to split. White Episcopalians were the symbol of unacknowledged white privilege, exacerbated no doubt by efforts of the Bishop of Alabama who did his utmost to block the progress of desegregation in Birmingham. M.L.King Jr, arrested there for public protesting, wrote his famous *Letter From Birmingham Jail*. The televised image of dogs and water hoses directed at Negro children in Birmingham revealed "the divided soul of white America."[53] Then, the march to Selma.

SPRING CONFERENCE 1964 featured *A Look at Suburbia and Eternal Life* by Companion Alice Mizner Lewitin. It was a farsighted examination of this influential demographic element for Episcopalians, and what "the overnight creation of suburbs" portended in the larger American culture. She cited two writers: first, Dietrich Bonhoeffer who championed "non-religious Christianity" yet affirmed that churches and clergy are indeed still necessary. Today's young are not so much individualists as shaped by *mass values*, an expression of the herd instinct or "mass culture" originating back in the 1950s. Typical young people of the 1960s seem tormented by the perceived need to conform, they have little interest in eccentricity, and like "pyramid climbers," seek wealth and exclusivity.

In contrast, the Rev. Malcolm Boyd, chaplain at Wayne State University in Michigan, had asserted that ideals *indeed* matter, that the young see middle-class, middle-class middle-aged *hypocrisies* in "religion, in formerly-pat answers that no longer function as answers." The church,

---

53 Marsh, *God's Long Summer*, September, 1999.

Boyd said, wants to tell the young "this is a world of profound, deep, purposeful meaning, rooted in God and each other." But what the young see in the church is brokenness and fragmentation. Lewitin questioned whether this perception sprang from a failure in our educational system; Marshall McLuhan had popularized the idea that knowledge is absorbed by differing means, one being non-linear learning."

Many Companions were reading English Bishop Robinson's disturbing book *Honest to God*. Was it true, Lewitin queried, that half the Episcopal suburbanites attended church in order to seek the "right" playmates for themselves and their children? yet another dimension of the quest for conformity? Is Sunday school only a busywork hour each week, "a spiritual babysitter for the average spiritually-illiterate American?" She cited French author Jean-Paul Sartre's "Hell is Other People," and agreed that this was "the age of anxiety." She noted that the esteemed Roman Catholic theologian Guardini said Christianity was not metaphysics or a matter of "belief," but of witness—not to an idea but to *the reality* of man. People don't go looking for the "Great Perhaps," but for the "Great Reality." Citing a 1964 martyr in Rwanda, Pastor Kanamuzeyi, Lewitin called on Companions "in suburbia, exurbia, and urbia" to know Christ truly, right within the agony of the world and the meeting of person with person, not just secure in the coziness of one's own piety.[54]

The **January** *IP* carried thanksgivings for Bishop Stokes' breaking the segregation barriers within congregations, for ESCRU, for the kindness and sweetness of a colored no-longer-young nurse's aid, and for the living testimony of Jackie Kennedy's dignified sorrow. **February** brought thanksgivings for President Kennedy's three years in office, for the consecration of the Rev. Paul Moore as Bishop of Washington DC, and for the Episcopal Church now taking an active stand for Civil Rights, especially twelve Episcopal clergy protesting segregation in Williamstown, Mass. Also there were prayers for three young men who could be put to death while jailed in Georgia. **March** brought thanksgivings that *Time Magazine* had named Martin Luther King Jr. their [cover] *Man of the Year*. There were petitions that the Boston School Committee become aware of social change, human rights, and dignity, thus able to accept desegregation. A petition asked that Companions consider

---

54 *Annual Report* 1964; image from Ramsey, Archbp of Canterbury, *Image Old & New*, 1963.

themselves daily "on pilgrimage," never passing a hospital or a prison without saying a prayer for its inmates.

In the **Spring** *IPs*, thanksgivings were offered for the life of British writer C. S. Lewis, for a magazine article on Wellesley College and Christian Youth, for an interracial drama (sponsored by NAACP) being presented in a parish, and for the Rev. Sabine Baring-Gould's 16-volume *Lives of the Saints*. A special thanksgiving rejoiced in the adoption of a long-awaited baby girl, and commended the assistance sent to a black church, St. James in Marietta, GA, after a fire, by the Good Shepherd Navaho Mission in AZ. There were thanksgivings for Sarah Patton Boyle's dedication to the cause of racial justice, and for "the Christian witness of two wives of bishops, Mary Peabody and Companion Esther Burgess, who allowed themselves to be arrested in St. Augustine, FL, as part of a Civil Rights demonstration."

The **June** *IP* carried thanksgivings for Bp. Stokes' Advance Fund in the Diocese of Massachusetts, for companion Emily Allen who was working with American Indians, for the new social-gospel book about street gangs, *The Cross and the Switchblade* by the Rev. David Wilkerson, and for Companions in California, including Ruth Jenkins. A petition rejoiced that the U.S. Senate had passed the Civil Rights Bill, AT LONG LAST [emphasis in original]. Another gave thanks for the annual Adelynrood School of Religion, and expressed pride that SCHC provided serious study-time for committed, educated Christian women. Special prayers were asked to strengthen all those who oppose extreme violence and hatred in our country, and that children participating in anti-segregation demonstrations be protected from hatred.

At **Companion Conference 1964,** the theme was *The Kingdom Of God*. Marion Rollins, C-in-C, opened with a quotation from C.S. Lewis' *Till We Have Faces*: how can we speak of face-to-face relations with God till <u>we</u> have been remolded, have "faces"? Today Christians must come to terms with *"The Cross and the Switchblade"* with people in all the religious and social groups Episcopalians don't usually "know." Restating EMM's mandate to study social problems, Rollins urged curing our human tendency to run away from the poor, from our own poverty, from fighting, from mourning, from the spread of alcohol and drugs, and from persecution. "Humility cannot be humiliated," Professor V. G. Simkhovitch had written [husband of Companion Mary Simkhovitch, the director of a major NYC settlement house]. While Fr. Moran Weston from St. Philips Church in Harlem, NYC, was preaching at Adelynrood, urging Companions to think about prejudice, his Harlem streets were echoing with the cry "Kill or Be Killed." Rollins' concluding quote was: "The Kingdom of God is to receive! To demonstrate!" Each SCHC chapter may display differing strengths and vitality, outside of and away from Adelynrood, she noted. But without Adelynrood, the Society would have no base, would lack what is "basic" to being Companions. We would not have the "powerhouse that established the norm" for the experience of Companionship.[55]

Conference papers by Companions addressed the *Parables*, Elizabeth Falck; *Utopian Visions*, Lillian Weidenhammer; and *The Spread of the Kingdom*, Dorothy Gilson—excerpted below for its new attitude toward foreign missions and the influence of cultural anthropology on working in a foreign culture:

A **1964** Conference paper, *The Kingdom Of God, Mission, & The Mission Field*, illustrated the new cross-cultural perspective on foreign missions. Dorothy Jenks Gilson, returned missionary, introduced her theme with a quote from Nicholas Monsarrat's *The White Rajah* (p352): "The white man's task in these islands is not to plunder, or merely enjoy, but to teach, serve, and liberate. That's the true Kingdom of heaven." That novelistic statement expressed the *why* of becoming a missionary, while the *reality* takes a longer time to grasp. Settling into a mission field, e.g. China, involves no central heating, damp sheets, the icy toilet seat, and mildewed shoes. Actually, only very slowly connecting with the "nationals" makes one feel inadequate, weighs heavily on the heart. Life is a bottomless pit of loneliness, for a while. But this "ebb tide" is actually the beginning of becoming a missionary—adapting to climate, food, lack of old favorites, feeling like the fishermen called by Jesus to leave all

---

- that is familiar to them and become preachers! Taiwan missionaries from U.S. and Western culture have to be self-sufficient. Yet to anyone who lives with perception, every culture offers a great deal.

The missionary learns "a culture unimagined before," although it is not so much learned as absorbed into the bloodstream. Chinese parents with no material THINGS, no heat in winter, no running water, no car, no refrigerator or TV, are ambitious for their children. Recently two visiting American ladies were entertained in a Chinese home that boasted more than average comforts. But they quizzed the daughter of the house about "baking a cake," with no realization that the family had no oven. The Americans were making polite conversation from their own culture and expectations, utterly insensitive to their hosts.

Gilson concluded that Americans in China were a "problem" for the Chinese: "we have to be considered Christian, since we are from a Christian country. But we use the name of God in a flip manner, we drink too much, we are too free with women, and we ignore Christian causes. AND by the way, in a society where grooming is innate, the slovenly appearance of *beatniks* hurts the US." Chinese Christians will attend any church near them, even if they are members in the Episcopal Church, a key factor when thinking about the future of Christian missions.[56]

At the **1964 Business Meeting**, committee reports included the conference on the Greek Orthodox and ecumenism sponsored by *Christian Unity Committee*; the *IP Committee* reported that only 66 Companion contributions had been sent this entire year; the *Missions Committee* conference featuring Japanese-American priest, the Rev. Daisuke Kitagawa from the National Episcopal Church office in NYC, had lamentably poor attendance. There were fifteen chapter reports, and brief memorials.

Executive decisions included discussion of plans to attract more Companions to Adelynrood, inviting all Probationers to be guests of the Society for one retreat, and offering them $35 toward travel expense if needed. Also, two assistants were appointed to help the C-in-C of Probationers process new Probationers. The decision was made to build a permanent year-round residence for a Superintendent of Grounds and Maintenance at Adelynrood, to insure year-round on-site care.

---

56 *Annual Report*, 1964.

NEWSLETTER **August 20.** A happy summer was reported, with no mention of concern about finances. The study conference on "heretics" had presented a pageant of historical characters. "Community sings" after Compline were accompanied by Sophie's violin with Irma at the piano; summer employees were the finest-ever group of waitresses. Companions attending from long distances were Dorothy Gilson (Taiwan); Jane Torrey (Korea); and Mary Bull (Canada). Dr. Daisuke Kitagawa led the Missions Conference, "Missionary Frontiers in the Emergent World Society," from the National Council, a prescient critic of the "white Western captivity of the Christian churches." He noted our "minimal awareness of the contributions from other cultures," and how more understanding might enrich "the American Christian enterprise." Fr. Weston of St. Philips Church in Harlem presented *The Human Understanding of Human Rights.* On Companion Eve, letters from Companions admitted in 1914, 1924, 1934, 1944, and 1955, the last five decades, were presented. A skit featuring Companions about to depart for the moon, eager to establish an SCHC chapter there, topped the evening.

In the **September** *IP*, there were thanksgivings for Fr. Wylie's meditations at the **Companion Conference** retreat, for Companions Marie, Isabel and Henderika who were preparing a new edition of the SCHC *Manual*, for Companions' progress in work among Indians, Negroes, migrant workers, and prisoners; also "for understanding hearts and cool heads in all civil rights matters." **October** thanksgivings were offered for Mrs. Harper Sibley's Prayer (Buffalo Companion) from **Companion Conference 1964**, and for Adelaide Rogers' inspiring Bible-study lectures that illuminate and expand Companions' understanding. Thanksgivings were offered for the many groups studying S. P. Boyle's new book, *For Human Beings Only.* Special prayers were asked for the Mississippi Freedom Project's registering of black voters, and for a truce in Vietnam.

November 1964: a thanksgiving compared the experience at Adelynrood retreat house with the fellowship among the early Christians. There were petitions for a Christian interpretation of racial problems among Mississippi clergy and for the organization ESCRU. In **December,** thanksgivings were offered for the image that "the real work of Christmas" begins when shepherds are "back with their flocks" [from Howard Thurman, the chaplain at Howard

University in Washington DC]. The birthday of founder EMM received a special blessing. And a petition from a Companion in Vicksburg, MS, prayed that "one law function equitably in Mississippi for both whites and Negroes." Special prayers were offered for President Johnson and his various advisors meeting on complex issues [possibly Vietnam], and for Bishop Bayne [husband of Companion Lucie] in Washington state.

1964 presented the nation with dramatic and painful civil rights events in Birmingham, AL. The ensuing decade would see an expanded focus on the War on Poverty along with deteriorating relations between white and black civil rights activists. Soon to come would be the Episcopal Church's Special General Convention, producing a belated *mea culpa* gesture and a remarkable institutional action—i.e. the Episcopal Church's attempt to act on new awareness of racial inequities. It did not honor or utilize the loyal Black clergy who had long embodied Episcopal liturgical and justice work within the church. The totality of full racial integration would work its way through white Episcopalians' relatively slow acceptance of change from the 1960s into the 1980s.

How Companions internalized and acted on this gradual consciousness change about race—and other external-world events—provides the context of the next chapter. The published **Annual Reports** still revealed little visible anxiety about SCHC's financial weakness, or of the necessity for reforming the internal culture of Companionship.

✝

The Society of the Companions of the
Holy Cross

ANNUAL CONFERENCE 1970

BE BLACK............AND BE THANKFUL
By Viola E. Pinder

This Paper from the Conference was in manuscript form
and was selected for publication by a committee of the
S.C.H.C. Council.

Chapter 6

SCHC
1965–1974

"O God be with us in the flame;
consume the ill, purge out the shame"

1968 Companion Conference Opening Paper
C-in-C Jeannette Booth

Introduction

Many Companions in the early 1970s may well have prayed the above words that concluded the C-in-C's Opening Paper at the **1968 Companion Conference**. It was a powerful social-justice statement, summarized below.

Despite the tumult of world changes and events, the printed *Annual Reports* in this decade continued to sound an upbeat tone—optimistic, positive; little in the published record referred to the Society's precarious financial situation. Print reticence about the Society's financial vulnerability may simply have reflected Episcopal politeness, a reserve about public airing of troubles. The SCHC leadership style seemed to favor encouragement. One Companion recalled feeling, at that time, that she "<u>needed</u> the Society to be *perfect,* needing to see it that way, since so much in the rest of my life wasn't [perfect]."[1]

Meanwhile, outside the Society, longhaired youth including

---

1   Personal interview, 2003.

Companions' children were emblems of generational challenge—to high school and church authorities, and to prevailing standards for clean and "stinky."[2] *IP* intercessions mentioned little of this particular upheaval, but a lot about the unthinking racism <u>within</u> white Christianity, along with the changing assumptions about overseas mission work. Behind the scenes, a few Companions were beginning to hone in on a looming financial crisis.

Another 1960s impact on the Society led to questioning the role and import of Theme Committees. The *Missions Committee,* for example, found that its submitted prayers were so "interwoven" with Social Justice issues that it no longer made sense to continue separating them, or sponsoring separate summer conferences. *The Missions Committee,* as such, was becoming superfluous, reported a self-analysis; was it possible to change, to better serve the Society? In 1972, the conference "Mission of the Church: A Call to Christian Action" would be sponsored jointly by the three Theme Committees: *Missions, Christian Unity, and Social Justice.*[3] These realizations began to challenge the comfortable view of "doing things the way we always have." By the end of this decade, 1974, SCHC itself would divide itself into Task Forces and undertake a major re-visioning and re-structuring process. One Companion who participated in that Task Force work recalled: "What the 1974 Task Forces had to confront was that *in order to save Adelynrood,* we literally had *to give it away.*" That rethinking was exhilarating, "the most exciting meetings I've experienced in my life."[4]

Not until they confronted the 1974 crisis could Companions begin to see administrative patterns that had become stifling, nor could they redesign a version of EMM's theological "hospitality" that fit the late 20th century.[5] The Society had to be shaken out of routine; Companionship vows had to be re-plumbed by a strong act of leadership.

---

2 "Flaunting the Freak Flag: Karr v. Schmidt," by Gael Graham, *Journal of American History* 91#2 (Sept 2004) 543-544.

3 Summary of Missions Committee report by Mary Kelley, May 1994.

4 Ibid, personal interview, 2003.

5 Ibid. personal interview, 2003.

This chapter is structured by first naming the changes occurring in Companions' church lives. Second will be the external context itself, a remarkable time of change culturally and nationally. The third section summarizes the 1974 crisis and plans for Societal change. And as this narrative reveals, leading up to that focus, Companion intercessions continued expanding in scope and awareness. Clearly it was time for the material fabric of Adelynrood to open out. The new ground of SCHC's spiritual extension lay in the very issues confronting the culture, the church and the nation.

"The flame" surrounding Companions in this decade included the nation's turmoil over anti-Vietnam War and Civil Rights protests, and two major ecclesiastical reforms: the ordination of women as priests (the first "irregular" ordination would take place in 1974), and revision of the 1928 *Book of Common Prayer.* Internally, Companions in 1972 were addressing stark challenges: Who are we as Companions, as Episcopalians, as Christians? Are we what we say we are? This self-questioning opened a door into the Society's identity and practices that paralleled the Episcopal Church liturgical renewal then being undertaken by the Associated Parishes movement. That group, in this same period, began re-connecting contemporary worship with its historical and scriptural roots—shaking up patterns that had become automatic in Sunday morning Episcopal liturgy. Today, in the early 21st century, it is possible to compare the revitalization of SCHC after its 1974 upheaval—the Society's version of the renewal that reshaped the Church's Sunday worship and rituals—with that liturgical reform. The "crisis of 1974"—the only summer in SCHC history during which Adelynrood remained closed—turned out to have been as crucial for the Society as was the reinvigoration of Episcopal worship.

Changes in religious practice seem to emerge in a time of other major social change. A first step toward ordaining female priests was Episcopal action making a Chicago deaconess the equivalent of an ordained male deacon. This recognition initiated that world-shaking mental adjustment.[6] The second major upheaval would produce a new basic tool for regular Sunday mornings, the 1979 *Book of Common Prayer,* to be followed by the 1982 revised *Hymnal.* Along with the larger white Christian awakening to sins against black Americans, women's ordination and *Prayer Book* revision forced people in the pews to shift mental images and adjust foundational religious practices. Those interested in Episcopal women's actual words about that shaking-up may read poignant 1980s–early 1990s interviews with Episcopal women, especially those of the older generation, in the 1995 book *Women Speak.*[7] Perhaps the single liturgical change that elicited the most visceral negative was modern wording of the Lord's Prayer, its ingrained rhythms hardest of all to surrender. Hadn't God dictated the *Book of Common Prayer* in Elizabethan, King James English, and signed it with Jesus' own signature?[8]

The Companionship's struggle over women priests within its own ranks, beginning in the 1970s, would similarly bruise or even end some relationships: hadn't the Society been created by and for lay women, at a time when women were totally excluded from church leadership and administrative participation? The effect of ordained clergy, even if they had been Companions first, might undermine this founding ethos of SCHC. Even when laywomen had been institutionally voiceless, except in church kitchens, Adelynrood experience had asked Companions to lead their own chapel worship. Urban church programs were beginning to experiment with more relevant connections between Sunday religion and industrial workers' everyday lives, e.g., the Urban Industrial Mission begun in Detroit, then moved to Boston. In fact, two of the 1970s

---

6 Episcopal Deaconesses as a new church role for women emerged during the same era as Companions—1889-1920—according to historian Rima Schultz. See "To Realize the Joy of Dedication and Vocation in the Grace Conferred in our Order": Deaconesses in Twentieth-Century Chicago. *Anglican and Episcopal History,* September 2004, LXXIII#3, 335-362.

7 Joanna B. Gillespie, *Women Speak of God, Congregations and Change,* Trinity Press/Morehouse Pub. Co., 1995.

8 *Anglican & Episcopal History 2003, Vol LXXII #2,* "Hoosier Episcopalians, Women's Ordination and the 1979 Book of Common Prayer" by Jason Lantzer, 229-254, (242, 243). Bp. John Craine, in 1971, ordained Jackie Means and Tanya Vonnegut Beck, creating a "media circus" over the Diocese of Northern Indiana, 236. (11 women would be "illegally" ordained in Philadelphia, 1974).

Companions articulating the challenges that precipitated the 1974 SCHC crisis were from urban locations—Philadelphia and New York City—where some all-white Episcopal congregations were already confronting race and class issues.

As if ordaining women and revising the *Prayer Book* were not earthshaking enough, the ultimate challenge impacting everyone, whether or not they could recognize it, was race—in all its previously unquestioned white, middle-class perceptions and assumptions. During 1958-68, the Episcopal Society for Cultural and Racial Unity [known by its acronym ESCRU] had come into being as the church's organizational response to the Civil Rights awakening. ESCRU served "not so much to speak 'for' the church as 'to' the church," offering Episcopalians a previously non-existent means of active witness, according to the Rev. Gardiner Shattuck, author of *Episcopalians and Race* (2000).[9]

A third challenge implicitly confronting the Companionship as well as the larger society was same-sex relationships. These had been taken for granted from the 1884 founding but without open acknowledgment. Until well into the late 20th century, female partnerships were an unremarked reality in the Society. Occasionally a rare *IP* thanksgiving celebrated an unnamed female couple's enjoyment of many years of life together. Episcopal reticence here was both blessing and bane: positive, in that Companionship was the rare religious fellowship where such unions were natural and acceptable, negative in that public silence denied or ignored the full personhood of the Companion couples. The **1978 Companion Conference** presentation by the Rev. William Doubleday finally brought the topic of homosexuality into public language within the Society.

In this decade, women in general began claiming a more public voice and authority in public events, e.g. criticizing the Miss America contest. In WASP (white middle-class Anglo-Saxon Protestant)

---

9 Shattuck, *Episcopalians and Race: from Civil War to Civil Rights.* (U of Kentucky Press 2000), 200.

culture, women for the first time began challenging gender barriers within professions and in many jobs outside the home. (By contrast, African-American women had long shouldered that weight, in addition to the burden of skin-color bias.) Thus race challenge was the catalyst rearranging all varieties of local customs and expectations, e.g., interdenominational women's organizations and community gatherings across racial lines. A new public view of racial segregation began to place white Christians on the defensive.[10] Journalist Blanche McCrary Boyd captured the feeling of being "a white Southerner in those times: northern suspicion, aroused by a Southern accent, made one feel "like being Eichmann's daughter: they don't assume you were guilty [of the Holocaust, of killing Jews] but they wonder how you've been affected by it."[11]

In a brief overview, here are some of the mind- and culture-changes in a single 1970s year, a wide-lens snapshot of the many rearrangements that are background to this decade's IPs.

1973 witnessed:

–the end of American intervention in Vietnam;

–the *Roe v Wade* Supreme Court decision legalizing abortion;

–the discovery of the Watergate conspiracies;

–the first Arab Oil shock forcing car owners, rich and poor alike, into long lines at the gas stations;

–Billie Jean King winning the U.S. tennis "battle of the sexes;"

–the film [*The Godfather*] about immigrant crime families, "foreign" to WASP Americans, sweeping the Academy Awards;

10 In its supporters' view, the "theology of segregationism" was equally Biblical--reinforcing the white-Christian duty to protect against racial "mongrelization" via black-white sex. This helps explain the depth of its hold on southern culture. In fact, "MLKing's genius was to transform what had been a legal struggle into a spiritual one" (144). Jane Dailey, "Sex, Segregation and the Sacred after *Brown*" in *Journal of American History 91 #1*, June 2004, 119-144.

11 Quoted from *The Redneck Way of Knowledge*, NY: Penguin Bks 1982, 7 in Bruce J. Schulman, *The Seventies: Great Shift In American Culture /Society / Politics*, NY: Da Capo Press, 2001, xiii; "*Following our Bliss*" by Don Lattin (book review by the Rev. Bob Cromey, *The Living Church*, Feb. 8, 2003).

–evangelist Jim Bakker claiming to be "God's television;"

–"ethnic" Americans demonstrating that their own cultures and customs had not been totally buried by Anglo-Saxon culture, e.g. 200 armed Indians occupying the hamlet of Wounded Knee and shedding some blood; and

–the Japanese American Citizens League proclaiming their "true Americanism," despite property losses and internment in WW II "concentration camps."[12]

At the end of this decade and the same eventful year that SCHC was thrust into its own agonizing reappraisal, the Voting Rights Act empowered thousands of first-time Black voters. A Black admiral in the Navy became a "first" in the nation's history, as did the first elected Black diocesan Episcopal bishop [John Burgess, Massachusetts]. White flight from city apartments to the suburbs gave rise to the new inner-city problems though some Companions had been praying about them before this came to national attention. School desegregation, the solution to this racial crisis idealized until whites mounted a stance of massive resistance, had been the white mindset visible in the 1960s *IP* petitions. At the **1970 Companion Conference,** a stunning paper by African-American Companion Viola Pinder personalized the revolution in racial perception for Companions who had had little exposure to black-American history or "ethnic-American" cultures. A predominantly white sisterhood was opened to the striking, new "black is beautiful" stream of culture— living testimony to the wisdom of founders EMM and VDS whose passion for studying problems of the times had schooled Companions to face rather than ignore reality.[13]

Christianity itself began to splinter into liberal and evangelical approaches in the 1970s, within and outside the Companionship, despite or perhaps alongside a heightened interest in ecumenism. And the new approach to religion in general was "New Age" reli-

---

12 Ibid, Schulman, xii xii.

13 *Annual Report* 1972, 77-78, 68,77; Pinder's paper was titled "Be Black...And Be Thankful."

gion reflected in the "me decade." That attempt abandoned allegedly "bankrupt" western religious traditions, rejected dogma and doctrine, and enjoyed shopping around in the "spiritual supermarket."
Its ideal was self-discovery: promoting openness and self-transfor-
mation, and new equalitarian relationships (including resistance
to honorific titles like Sir, Professor, even Mother or Father). At the
other end of the scale, evangelical churches were finding their voice
on political and religious issues, e.g. the issues of prayer in public
schools, and the Pledge of Allegiance in the classroom.

This particular cultural current was yet another mixed blessing for Companions: on the one hand, Companions were sheltered
from the extremes of religious experimentation through their well-
established Holy Routine and sacramental worship services; wide-
spread "focus on the self" in the general culture encouraged "tuning
in" to one's own religiosity, which Companions already endorsed.
Negatively, on the other hand, individual responsibility toward external world problems could seem less compelling. [This would be
one of the allegations in Companion Hawkins' pointed 1972 challenge, summarized below.] The good news about "working on"
one's own self, for Companions, was its affirming the irrelevance of
heavy theological argument and disputes over doctrinal fine points.
The "me decade" embraced a pop-psychology framework that could
slide into "therapeutic religion." Robert Bellah's influential book on
America's "Civil Religion," [Habits Of The Heart –1973] called this attitude "Sheila-ism." "I have to check out my own self with God,"
said a girl named Sheila, "so church itself is irrelevant...can't remember the last time I was in [an organized, established, denomi-
national] Church!" That experimental, middle-class mindset was
largely white, an unwitting indication that nonwhite peoples were
not free to indulge in such self-preoccupation in the midst of a racial struggle for citizenship rights.[14]

All this societal questioning inspired a "back-to-the land" move-

---

14 *Annual Report*, p100; Robert Bellah *et al. Habits Of The Heart*, 1973.

ment. The hippie mentality that created the *Whole Earth Catalog* in 1968 had engendered a re-thinking of the nature/human, artificial vs "natural" categories. A new Christian environmental theology would emerge fully by the 1980s.[15] Both rebels and middle-class nonconformists saw that arena as permission for a fresh (oppositional) "alternate lifestyle." A new awareness of the importance of "whole foods" offered the possibility of direct action and attitude transformation *right at home*, in one's local community—legislatively expressed in the 1973 Endangered Species Act. The phrase "reconciliation with the whole of creation" in the 1996 SCHC Vocation Statement reflects this perspective. Intentional communities—communes—flourished; individuals seeking yet another arena of *self-realization* wanted to opt out of modern consumer society, as well as out of the traditional family, church, and white middleclass culture.[16] By 1972, corporation boardrooms, the New York Stock Exchange, hotels, inns, and transportation systems were all in various stages of desegregating. Companion chapters, e.g. Buffalo-Rochester, began to cultivate influential African-Americans for the Companionship.

By 1970, an energetic trio of Companions in the Society's leadership—C-in-C Alice Lewitin, Ethel Colt, and their youthful spokesperson Michelle Hawkins—felt called to question the prevailing SCHC mindset, in response to external changes and in light of the looming Society centennial in 1984. These Companions, motivated also by bottom-line financial alarm, initiated a radical step introduced by challenging the Society's social-justice sensitivity. As will be evident in the 1972 *IP* citations, the racial consciousness of Companions would more easily be aroused by that kind of challenge than by financial warnings *per se*. The leaders' forward-looking plan did not take into account that their successors would be the "Joshuas" marching a reawakened SCHC into its modern Promised Land. Perhaps their anticipation did not proceed beyond the

---

15 Schulman, 88- 89.
16 Ibid. 91.

"Moses" role empowering them to lead the Society into a necessary (brief) wilderness.

The first step in SCHC renewal, called Task Force I, laid out structural parameters for the re-evaluation to be launched in response to that 1972 challenge. During 1973, Task Force II would then develop plans for implementing that outline. This in turn would lead to the major break in the Society's routine ("the way we've always done things") during the summer of 1974. The C-in-C herself and the Executive Board made the decision to suspend the 1974 opening of Adelynrood. To replace only the **Companion Conference**, Companions would instead meet at a Roman Catholic retreat house in Natick, MA, to discuss and act on the Task Force II recommendations. This announcement created a Society earthquake—"shock" was the word among Companions.[17] In a community built on routine worship patterns that have been made precious by history, repetition, and tradition, nothing could be more radical—or ultimately healthful—than a major break in routine.

Companions tried to "hold it together." Internal confusion sometimes pitted Companion against Companion after that summer. Those for and against women's ordination wrestled with that additional issue. Companions called to ordination had to struggle with yet another aspect of commitment: as a Companion and as a deacon or priest. Naturally the "crisis of 1974" released new energy and vitality. At the same time, personality issues engendered competition over the management of the reshaped Society. The print records portray the SCHC "crisis mentality" as precipitated by the accusation of social justice hypocrisy, which had the effect of glossing over purely personal motives. And under the hypocrisy charge, there was indeed genuine financial danger. But for a time after 1974, Society leadership itself became the arena of contested authority.

After that summer, a new theological and spiritual self-understanding began to coalesce. It would finally produce a sea-change,

---

17 Hindsight and reflection make it easier to value strong leadership than is possible at the time.

by the end of the twentieth century: there would be a rewording of the Companion vocation, a modernizing business-management approach to Society finances, a rethinking of the Adelynrood surround as suburbia encroached, and a comprehensive Program Committee responsible for planning the summer calendar of retreats and conferences. All this would impact Companions' relationship to and with Adelynrood. By the end of the 20th century, a year-round office facility, St. Clare (first called for by EMM in the 1920s), was dedicated(2000). This narrative of SCHC evolution after the death of its Founder concludes with the Society's 1984 Centennial.

Chronological Intercessions and Reports

1965—

A massive electrical network blackout of northeastern US & Canada affected some 25 million citizens in early summer. On the other side of the country, race riots erupted in the Watts section of Los Angeles, California. Washington finally passed the Voting Rights act that banned discriminatory voting practices, and more draftees were sent to Vietnam. The national government created a major "safety net for the elderly and poor," Medicare. Malcolm X was murdered in New York City, Winston Churchill died, and Civil Rights protesters marched from Selma to Montgomery in a major demonstration, the most newsworthy Civil Rights event since the 1963 March on Washington.

January: The *IP* opened the year with thanksgivings for the inspiring witness of Southern writer Sarah Patton Boyle, for the Episcopal Peace Fellowship, and for President Johnson's "war on poverty." Companions who read the Rev. Daisuke Kitagawa's book *Race Relations and Christian Mission* gave thanks for his challenge to a dated view of "foreign" missionary work. Also there were thanksgivings for Companion Esther Burgess', paper on "MRI, Mutual Responsibility and Interdependence" [a newly created national church program promoting inner-city poverty programs encouraging recipients' participation and self-determination], which introduced new ways of thinking and praying about poverty. A new voice appearing in the *IP*s was that of Roman Catholic Brother Michael Quoist's *Prayers from the Ark*.

Companions' petitions focused on the work of voter registration among Negroes in the South. One prayer expressed the hope that juries and law enforcement officials would become more "representative:" a Companion prayed that "it will be finally possible for a white-man's [*sic*] crime against a Negro to be successfully prosecuted and convicted." Prayers also supported the lunch counter sit-ins in Alabama, and those clergy forced out of parishes because of their interracial attitudes. There were prayers for the Mississippi Council on Human Relations and its newly appointed Director, and "that God's Love may penetrate the heart of Gov. Wallace of Alabama to receive forgiveness for his part in Selma, and that this may arouse segregationists to Jesus Christ." Blessings were offered for the families of those who had died in Selma, and one Companion prayed "the problems of all the Selmas of the South be solved in future without bloodshed."[18]

A Notice appended to this *IP* announced that this summer's **Companion Conference** would celebrate the 50th year of Adelynrood, and the many "traditions" of House and Chapel.

In **May 1965,** there were thanksgivings for "Adelyn and the group of girls praying with her, from which our SCHC grew," for World Day of Prayer observances in the South, for the much-quoted spiritual encouragement of the Rev. Howard Thurman, chaplain at Howard University, for "seasons of hope that constantly invade seasons of despair," for young people willing to engage in bringing about racial justice and non-violence, for the National Audubon Society, and for "the enormous gentleness" among Negro people.

During the summer, thanksgivings greeted a new ecumenical service for the elderly called Meals-on-Wheels, as well as a Se-

---

18 Feb March Apr 1965 *IPs*.

wanee Companion's help in preparing Negro students for integrated schools. Thanksgivings also named the growing "Retreat movement" in this country, and that a woman at the Adult Correctional
Institute of Rhode Island had finished her High School Equivalency
degree! Companions praised Taize and other ecumenical religious
fellowships, and young folk able to see the injustices and discrimination that exist all over our land, thus entering nonviolently into
the coming summer's racial strife.[19] Petitions prayed that the US
cease economic exploitation of underdeveloped countries. One
poignant intercession invoked "tolerance for the groping and often
somewhat ill-advised actions of the very young," an empathetic
Companion perspective on the generation gap.

> A *NEWSLETTER* sent out just before Companion Conference **1965**
> reported on the theme-conferences earlier that summer: The <u>Missions</u>
> conference focused on the newly independent African countries and their
> cultures; the <u>Social Justice</u> conference on American Indians had special
> guests: the Rev. Noah Broken Leg; Anne Uken (outstanding Dakota
> churchwoman and daughter of one of our first India missionary-clergy),
> and missionaries Elizabeth Clark and her daughter Betty Rosenthal,
> from the Home Missions Department of the National Church. Florence
> Converse, writer-editor and longtime companion of Vida Scudder,
> wrote an "Adelyn/ Emily Jubilee Hymn" to be sung on Adelyn's Day.
> Incidentally, two new shower and lavatory areas had been created on
> the second floor of Adelynrood, and new lights had been installed in
> the hallways.

The **Companion Conference** theme (August 17-27, **1965**) was
The Way of the Cross in Today's World. C-in-C Mrs. Wallace E. Rollins' Opening Paper asked: "Were you there when they crucified our
Lord?" Yes, she answered for Companions, because for all humanity the way of the Cross has to precede resurrection. The vocation
of Companionship, <u>our</u> "way of the Cross," is a choice, and choice
drives out self-pity. Intercessing Companions know and undertake
vicarious cross-bearing jobs. Across the world, the Christian church
is seeking new ways of superceding old divisions—through experimentation in interdenominationalism—in the Taize movement, in

19 May June July August 1965 *IPs.*

the Church of South India (United), in the United Church of Canada, and in the new role of worker-priests. The "shell of corporate self-interest is cracking in many places." Companion papers addressed "The Cross and Health Services," (nurse-educator Margaret Tyson), "The Cross and Legal/Moral Justice," (Grace Hamilton), and "The Cross in Settlement House Work," (Isabel Pifer).[20] The denominations cooperating in the Church of South India in 1947, for instance, included Anglican, Methodist, Congregational, Presbyterian, and Reformed. The United Church of Canada combined Presbyterian, Methodist, and Congregational denominations.

> An unusual <u>Notice</u> appeared in the printed **1965** *Annual Report: too many Companions were not paying dues or were being exempted from paying dues.*[21] This alarm clearly acknowledged that the largest part of operating expenses, including the costs of Adelynrood, was being drawn from the Society's Endowment and the Ruth Mary Wilson bequest—eating up capital, in other words.[22]

The **Fall 1965** *IP*s frequently named the Rev. M. L. King Jr. asking for "his control over the aroused Negroes of the South, [that they be inspired] to the nonviolent way [of demonstrating for equal treatment]." Jonathan Daniels, a seminary student from the Episcopal Divinity School, in Cambridge, MA, was shot to death at a rural southern crossroads store while working on Black voter registration. Thanksgivings greeted news that the Lloyd missionary family was safely back from Japan, and that the Industrial Mission was launched in Boston. A petition verging on preachment prayed "that M. L. King may retain his humility and not be led by success to dissipate his energies in lines or places not his province," perhaps referring to his taking the Civil Rights Campaign north into Chicago,

---

20 *Annual Report* 1965, 11, 85 ff.

21 Explanatory note: from the beginning, SCHC had practiced exempting dues from those Companions for whom such expense would be financially prohibitive. No Companion should ever be excluded because of inability to pay.

22 Ibid. 1965, 21. This background is carefully reconstructed in the 1985 paper "An SCHC autobiography of Money—Imagined, from Archive and Records," by Elisabeth H. Clarkson, SCHC Archive.

or to his open criticism of US military involvement in Vietnam. Another prayed: "Since men can't stop the Vietnam War, let the Holy Spirit do it."

There were thanksgivings for the life of Founder EMM, for all "forward movements" in our churches like prayer groups and social action committees, for teachers of adult religion classes; for "listening groups" across racial lines in local communities, and for a specific mixed-race /religion panel of housewives and professional women in a "Know Your Neighbor" program. There were petitions for a co-op factory (for those who lost jobs because of civil rights activity), and for Companions' increasing awareness of and protest against the "brutally dehumanizing practices against Negro demonstrators," and in Mississippi penitentiaries.[23]

1966—

Among major topics in the national scene were the government's admission it had bombed North Vietnamese civilians, the first comprehensive Auto Safety law (introducing seat belts), and the Supreme Court's Miranda decision that established the right of people being arrested to avoid incriminating themselves. China's "Cultural Revolution" was under way, and Indira Gandhi became the world's first woman prime minister. New attention began to focus on urban unrest and the "Crisis in American Cities."

January opened with thanksgivings for the Anglican history embodied in Westminster Abbey's nine hundred years, for a Taize retreat in France attended by Anglicans and Roman Catholics, and for the "successful" integration of a parish church in Sewanee.

February celebrated the life of Howard Clinch who had designed the Adelynrood Oratory and Chapel, the new ecumenical "inner city" efforts in Baltimore, the Women's Christian College in

---

23 October 1965 *IP*, 8. In December 1965, thanksgivings appeared for a Companion "bold enough to give thanks in the *IP* for the Gift of Tongues," implicit recognition of Episcopal discomfort with the idea of spirit visitation.

Madras, India, where Companion Eleanor Mason was principal, the Selma, Alabama, InterReligious Project, and a prayer by renowned African-American opera singer Marian Anderson.

March included thanksgivings for the wisdom that had originally selected the Companionship's signature themes, *Christian Unity, Social Justice,* and *Mission,* "still the three greatest needs of this bewildered, groping world," and for a Parish Life Conference on race.

April brought petitions for the plight of sharecroppers, rebellious youth, and current attempts to "rethink and rephrase traditional religion" without "prejudice or frivolity: pray for the writers of the new [revised] *Prayer Book.*"

June petitions prayed that churches draw together interdenominationally, as well as liturgically, and that Companions not fail to pray for other racial groups in their focus on Negro-White relations.

The **Companion Conference 1966** theme, *The Cross in Contemporary Life,* continued focus on the centrality of the cross in Companionship, begun in 1965. SCHC emphasis on "the cross," symbol and spiritual fact, was (and remains) the major if not the one element binding Companions together—amid recurrent reasons for disagreement. Margaret Ann Young's paper, *The Cross and Professional Life,* presented a new perspective—her experience as a Director of Religious Education [the only lay-professional role available to women in the church at that time] in a large suburban parish. That new role was practical rather than theological, a linking of domestic *and* professional roles. She verbalized what many 1960s Episcopal women in the "transitional middle-class" were experiencing. Keeping "the Way of the Cross" in a life of expanded contacts, including business relationships new for women formerly confined to homemaking, meant "sanctifying the accidental in our lives," finding the holy in unexpected places and people. As new horizons opened careers to white middle-class women outside the home, they were enjoying a sense of discovery.

Other Companion papers presented were Florence Risley's *The Cross in Contemporary Life* (which introduced the phrase "computer civilization" to SCHC petitions); and *The Cross and Race Relations*, in which Martha Jane Gibson, called for the elimination of "the caste system" in the South, and cited our "ominous white Christian tendency to gloss over the morality issues in race and slavery." Male speakers instructed Companions in the "new curriculum" of the Episcopal church: the *Ministry of Listening*, by the Rev. Theodore Wedel, Canon at the Washington National Cathedral; the new ethics by the Rev. Gibson Winter; poet and priest, the Rev. Chad Walsh; and the Rev. Reuel Howe, a leader and trainer in the emerging field of Group Dynamics. Companions were urged to *really listen* to voices previously ignored by white Christians, those in the civil rights and poverty programs.

A **JUNE** *NEWSLETTER* (just before Adelyn's Day), named the Cloister Garden "a Lovesome spot," and praised the Garden Committee. The old woodshed next to Serene Meadows cabin had been outfitted as a hangout for Companion night owls; San Damiano rooms had been rewired. A conference on "Christian Conversation" sponsored by the *Committee on Church Unity* attracted 10 religious—six Roman Catholic and four Episcopal Sisters of St. Margaret. An interesting conference had discussed Harvey Cox's book "*The Secular City.*" A retreat for (black Episcopal) women from St. Cyprian's, Roxbury, MA and one for alcoholic recovery were well attended. Negative reactions were expressed to the new practice of nuns relinquishing religious habits for "street dress." And a letter left in an Adelynrood room wished its next occupant "all the same peace and joy [as I experienced]. Being here was the nearest thing to heaven."

The **September 1966** *IP* printed a prayer from the Rev. Michael Murray of All Saints Church, Worcester, MA, "that God will restrain the passions of both Negro and white rioters, and all who harm innocent people; that Negroes [will] use their civil *responsibilities* as well as civil *rights* so that whites may see that only as they work WITH rather than FOR their black brethren will they be showing true Christian love." This reflected the goal of national Urban Poverty Programs, to empower the participation of the poor in decisions about their own programs. **October** thanksgivings rejoiced in all those identifying with the social-justice struggle through teaching, and in the new Sunday morning church format that encouraged adult study during the time children attended Sunday School classes [thanks to the new *Seabury Series* Christian Education curriculum]. And petitions were offered for the interdenominational, interracial Friendship Groups organized by United Church Women in Ann Arbor, MI, and for Black educator Mary McCloud Bethune, a friend of Eleanor Roosevelt.

The **November** *IP* carried thanksgivings for a conference of 450 Negro and White teenagers under the leadership of the Rev. Jim Breeden, and for those who are breaking down "ghetto walls." Thanksgivings were offered for Founder EMMorgan's great breadth of vision and Christian insight into all religious thought, also for former Companions-in-Charge Hurd, Cook, and Lindley, for many groups meeting in Living Room dialogues to discuss both the war and civil rights, for the Iona Community in Scotland, and for the devoted work of Navy Chaplain Hebert Bolles in Vietnam. Petitions asked that "misunderstandings" of certain minority leaders not halt efforts toward their goals, and also that Negro citizens assume their true responsibilities.

1967—

Major news items were: the first heart transplant, massive Vietnam War protests, Detroit race riots in which forty people died, race riots in Newark, and the 6-day Middle East war in which Israel seized Sinai and Gaza. The first Black American, Thurgood Marshall, was appointed to the nation's Supreme Court; champion boxer Muhammad Ali was imprisoned for refusing to honor the draft. New voices appearing in Companion prayers and papers were poets T.S.Eliot, Robert Lowell, Edith Sitwell, Kenneth Patchen, and Leopold Lenghor, African poet and national leader.

January: Thanksgivings were offered for U Thant of the UN, and the 40th anniversary of the ordination of Presiding Bishop Lichtenberger (husband of Companion Florence), for Companion Elizabeth Goudge (British novelist) whose compiled volume *A Diary of Prayer* is still found in the Intercession desk in Adelynrood Chapel [2005, Intercession bookcase in the Library], for the Episcopal church in Japan [Nippon Sei ko Kai], for the International Christian University in Tokyo, and for the Presiding Bishop's Fund for World Relief. Petitions asked that the spirit of Sarah Patton Boyle and the late Lillian Smith—white Southerners honest about segregation—might come to prevail throughout the South, and for the Jackson, Mississippi Community Organization called C. O. G., as well as for the Episcopal Church in the Diocese of Mississippi.[24]

April: Thanksgivings were offered for the benefits of studying Dietrich Bonhoeffer's *Cost of Discipleship* "even so long after WW II," for cooperation between the Baptist and Episcopal Churches in Southern Pines, NC, and intercessions invoked for the terrible addiction of teenage drug abusers.

In **May**, [the month of Thanksgivings] the Buffalo-Rochester chapter gave thanks for Alice Brooks' 28 years in SCHC and her editing of the *IP*, for the spread of Sunday morning Adult Education classes in our parish churches, for the leadership of Companion Georgiana Sibley in the Rochester (NY) Council of Churches, and for the Peace Corps. **June** intercessions requested support for the work of native clergy in Alaska, the new Wall Street Ministry dialogue between business and religion, and the General Convention meeting in Seattle.

July 1967: Prayers were offered for Sister Daisy Kitchen's Church Army work, and her marriage to the Rev. George Pierce at Mission, SD, for the work with "colored youth at St. Paul's," New Haven, CT, for Sister Doris Mary of St. Margaret's mission in Haiti, and that Israel-Egypt military conflict be short-lived. Special prayers gave thanks for the Negro/White leadership that quickly reduced

---

24 Feb., March *IP*s.

the threat of violence during the recent Roxbury "confrontation," and for the years of cooperative effort. One petition asked: "Please hold before the Lord our white people who cannot see Him in the sufferings of our colored neighbors," as well as relief from hunger and lack of food among the Mississippi Delta Negroes.

> *NEWSLETTER* SUMMER 1967: a rainy cool summer. House improvements included bedrooms now equipped with silent switches (no more groping for the light bulb pull-cord); a fourth dining table in the "small refectory" as EMM called it (we call it the New York Room) and Jeannette Booth's gift of teacups and saucers; concerns that the Della Robbia porch is becoming shabby; Companions celebrating Adelyn's Day in Byfield learned about Adelyn's interest in the Winsted, CT, Memorial Hospital. One attending the Healing Conference wrote of this "first experience at any kind of religious house," thankful for its peace. Editor's comment: that kind of hospitality is "where Adelynrood accomplishes its purpose, and is Intercessory Prayer in action."

At the **Annual Business Meeting, 1967**, the Finance Committee reported a deficit budget, an actual overrun of $45,500, and that annual dues be increased to $10 in 1968.[25]

September: Thanksgivings were offered for the retreat led by Quaker leader Douglas Steere, titled *On Being Present Where You Are*. There were thanksgivings for the Anglican Fellowship of Prayer, and the work of its founders (Companions Helen Shoemaker and Polly Wiley), and for those who hate war but weren't Conscientious Objectors. Intercessions were offered for Companion Frances Young, appointed head of the Dept. of Women's Work at the national church headquarters in NYC, and for the rectors of parishes who used the reorganization of women's programs as an excuse to disband their parish ECWs, for seminaries, and for Bishop James Pike (California) plus those who "solve the problems created by him and by the church" [as he challenged many Episcopal-culture traditions]. Petitions invoked grace on intra-parish struggles with Liturgical Renewal, and patience toward those opposing it. Prayers were offered for minorities in race-torn cities, and for grace to admit its

---

25 *Annual Report*, 32; in her last years EMM had paid for secretarial help.

underlying causes. A Companion prayed that consciences of Christians be aroused to meet those causes.

October: Thanksgivings were offered for the summer at Adelynrood, and for the new clock tower at nearby Governor Dummer Academy that added its mystic sound to the air, along with petitions for workers to go to the "mission field of Four Corners Area" [where AZ, Utah, NM and Nevada meet].

November: Companions expressed thanksgivings for the many "streams of awakening in our time: racial conscience, ecumenism, liturgical renewal, and all the honest problems of the Body of Christ," for all "experiments undertaken to make traditional symbol, rituals, and words speak with a direct, contagious impact today," for the beginnings of Trinity Institute [a 3-day program of lectures at Trinity Church, Wall Street, NYC, presenting outstanding contemporary thinkers on current religious concerns], and for the UN Convention on Human Rights. A special petition pleaded for "no turning back" from our church's offering of financial help to black and poor organizations.

December prayers asked for a creative Triennial meeting next summer for the women of the church, with "farsighted leaders, excitement, and resolution," for an open-minded view of liturgy [in the face of all the liturgical experiments], and support for our Presiding Bishop's courage in wanting to give financial aid to the poor, a commitment to be adopted at the Special Convention. There were thanksgivings for the special UTO gift from the Episcopal Church Women for this program, for a Pilgrimage of Prayer under the sponsorship of Coventry Cathedral (England) and its iconic symbol, "the Cross of Nails," for the national church's acceptance of the ESCRU request that the church acknowledge its historic guilt in discriminating against black priests for white parishes, for the decision of the Cathedral of St. John the Divine, NYC, to postpone its completion in favor of sponsoring programs for the city's needy. Also, there were petitions for Mexicans crossing daily into El Paso, TX, for work, and for parents and those in "the older generation who were <u>trying</u> to understand today's young people (emphasis in original)."

1968—

This was the year that President Nixon was elected, astronauts traveled around the moon in space, and athletes at the Mexico summer Olympics staged a Black Power demonstration. The Democratic National Convention meeting in Chicago produced turmoil, protests, and arrests. The Soviets invaded Czechoslovakia, the Nuclear Nonproliferation Treaty was signed by 62 nations, M.L.King Jr. was slain in April, and Bobby Kennedy in June. President Lyndon Johnson refused to stand for re-election.

The **January** *IP* opened with thanksgivings "for Christmas, our Cosmic Independence day," [in the popular "mind-blowing" vocabulary of the '60s], for fine teenagers who seem to be revolting against "hypocrisy, sham, and musty conventions, " and for publication of a book of poems, *Inscape of Grace*, by Companion Virginia Huntington. Prayers asked support for the Presiding Bishop's call to direct real aid toward the inner-city underprivileged while not neglecting other forward-looking programs of our church. There were also prayers expressing its opposite: dismay over the poverty focus that had dominated the church's Special Convention in the past December.

February brought thanksgivings for Bishop Paul Moore's call to reinvigorate downtown Christian witness, rather than only planting new Episcopal churches in the suburbs (in *The Church Reclaims The City*), for the excitement of a new Episcopal Church magazine (*The Episcopalian*) that regularly included articles by several Companions (though not publicly identified as Companions), for congregations giving a "positive trial" to the new liturgical materials, and for a new ecumenical venture in which Presbyterian and Episcopal congregations shared the same building facility.

March: Petitions were asked for St. Margaret's Convent in Boston, for a Companion and husband's return to Voorhees College and their welcome by the Negro student body, and for Companion Isabel Pifer's "missionary" work in Boston, with Travelers Aid.

April: Petitions asked for the promise of effective Civil Rights Legislation, for WILPF (Women's International League for Peace and Freedom), and for the work of the National Church's Standing Commission on Liturgy. There was a special petition "for strength to see the shock of [and grace to understand the irreverence of] Hippie influence on ordination, i.e. psychedelic vestments and liturgy," for Episcopal churches that were developing Christian Education programs to fight prejudice, for Martin Luther King's April meeting in Washington, and for (South African) Alan Paton's prayer over "white Calvinists who see no wrong in the dehumanizing treatment they give native Africans."

May brought thanksgivings for the Rev. Sam Shoemaker's book *Extraordinary Living for Ordinary Men*, for the great unity evident among mourners at religious services for M.L. King, for his life, and for his tragic death. Thanksgivings were offered for the public dignity of the two young widows, Jackie Kennedy and Coretta Scott King, for the *Anglican Digest* and its Episcopal Book Club, for Urban Coalition groups in 35 cities, and for the softening of prejudices so that black and white citizens might begin to think of each other as individuals. A special prayer was offered: "Thanksgivings for the restraint of black communities where justifiable anger is not expressed in violence; and for the outpouring of sorrows and admission of shame by the whites of our nation."

June: Thanksgivings saluted a Companion's privilege in helping interpret this country to many who come to study or migrate to the US (volunteer work with Travelers' Aid), for increased financial giving within our church to make up for the million+ diverted from ongoing missions to the Special Program fund, and for the School for the Handicapped in Haiti. Petitions asked that the Kerner Report [on violence in cities, generated by racial discrimination and poverty] be implemented, that programs for the hungry and the homeless become the form of "riot control" to be used, and that white America work toward M.L.King's *Dream* "of a future where a child's skin color won't determine his life."

July–August: A Companion gave thanks for fifteen years in Alcoholics Anonymous, for the UN treaty on the positive uses of atomic energy, for American Indians involved in church-sponsored summer projects, for the *prayer of contemplation* that is itself activism in the Christian life, for those resisting the Trial Liturgy, for the more-than-fifty radio stations "broadcasting Jesus," and for Coretta Scott King and the Kennedy family. A petition asked "that Christian women...lead in dress reform for women and girls," (possibly a protest against bikini swimwear).[26]

> *NEWSLETTER*, end of **SUMMER 1968**: "For those who've never experienced Adelynrood, it's hard to define the quality: peace, order, gaiety, chatter, silence, prayer." Sophie Brown has retired, accompanied by Peter, her violin. The GARDENS have never looked lovelier: delphiniums, white dahlias, Shasta daisies, regal lilies (one stem sported 7 huge trumpet-shaped blossoms!); there were fierce green flies after the rains. Companions expressed thanksgivings for the new young waitresses in the dining room who were very enjoyable. Companion Lee Beaty with her new PhD from Yale was redoing the Library with great vigor and logic, making "the alphabet = the law!" The dream of having electric blankets at Adelynrood has come to fruition. "May our intercessions be much widened by the appalling needs of the world."

Companion Conference 1968: C-in-C Marion Rollins' stunning Opening Paper titled *"The Christian's Involvement in the Life of the World"* is summarized for its historical power and prophetic insight at this juncture.[27]

> Thanks to the Liturgical Movement returning us to early-church practices, a quality of corporate life experienced in a hostile time by the first Christians is now available to us. Involvement in the world is NOT optional. We ARE involved whether we admit it or not. Whites who try to move into the black world are told: "Whitey go home! Reform your own people!" Finally we've climbed aboard a moral bandwagon. However,

26 *IP* 13.
27 *Annual Report 1968*, 13-14.

the moral offense was there all the time: we whites needed blacks to "stab us broad awake."

Her <u>second</u> point: "the "<u>molten lava of change must pour through Episcopalians.</u>" Our church is wasting time debating Exchange of the Peace (in the new liturgy) and whether we stand or kneel. Some elders are so concerned about dress and hair as to be deaf to the youth-cry "phony." "It's dangerous to reserve a box seat among the saints and look down on the stage, where the real sinners are slashing around."

Her 3<u>rd</u> point: <u>up-to-date *tests for loyalty* exist not just in secular but also in religious society</u>...for us, who've enjoyed lifelong liberty, the *freedom we seek for others* remains the acid test: others cannot wait for <u>us</u> to inch along, finally granting theirs. As Jesus said to the women along the way to the crucifixion, don't weep for me but for yourselves and your children. Her interpretation? "Until the pain and anguish of the Cross become our own, *our* tears are irrelevant."

Her 4<u>th</u> point: We must <u>continually refresh our Christian behavior: watch for overused words</u>. What does "God's love" mean to a weary taxi driver, an underpaid garbage collector, and a hopeless migrant-worker father? We must give "new dimensions" (honoring the dignity of others) to the word "love." Tune in to what is humiliating to other cultures—as we have learned, today's racial militants refer back to some actual painful incident that turned them bitter. Our phrase "children of God" usually means only *theoretical* inclusiveness!

Her <u>5th</u> point: We must see the patterns in our prejudices, e.g.anti-Semitism is often the first step in accepting contempt toward another race. What if our pilots had refused to bomb Hiroshima? How many individual citizens are willing to stand up for conscience issues? She quoted the Rev. Moran Weston (a pastor to 4000 Episcopalians in New York City's Harlem) who led the Companion Conference retreat: During a civil war between black and white, more would be killed than in the Holocaust! She applied Jesus' words: "Are ye not as Puerto Ricans unto me, O white Anglo Saxon Protestants? Have not I brought up your WASP ancestors out of their old-world limitations?" Her concluding point: Christians must learn to combine <u>unilateral moral responsibility</u> with <u>multilateral, humanity-wide interdependence</u>..."O God, be with us in the flame; consume the ill, purge out the shame."

The **Business Meeting** acknowledged a budget imbalance: Anticipated income $55,622, anticipated expenditures $69,194 (not including capital on hand nor bequests, gifts), equals a $13,600 deficit.

A **1968 COMPANION CONFERENCE** paper by Mary Morrison, "The

Quiet Revolution" [first published in the *EPISCOPALIAN*, the national magazine for which she regularly wrote] identified one of the huge changes facing all white middle-class Christians: loss of that "cultural certainty" about the definition of "truth" that they had taken for granted, unquestioned. Twice in this century, two close-to-Christ leaders (Gandhi and M.L.King Jr.) expanded the nation's racial horizons and what was taken for granted as "reality." (Gandhi's autobiography was titled "*My Experiment with Truth.*") The truth about us has also been explored in the popular books *Games People Play*, and in C. S. Lewis' *The Screwtape Letters*. The WASP crisis is a concept crisis, awakened by civil rights: it makes us ask how could we have missed this truth thus far? On the day of Dr. King's funeral, a huge crowd walked the grieving street— but "the rich he hath sent empty away" (from the *Magnificat*).

September: Thanksgivings were presented for the Berrigan brothers' "waging of peace," and for the Episcopal hymnal presently under revision, edited to be more ecumenically inclusive. Intercessions were invoked against apartheid in South Africa, for a Negro priest's claim to equality and the opportunity to be hired in church work, and for an end to discrimination in order that *our* failure as Christians not make Negro clergy and parishes bitter, for the new Episcopal Society for the Ministry in Higher Education, and that Negro soldiers returning from Vietnam be enabled to find new equality of access to jobs and housing. **October** brought thanksgivings for the life of Presiding Bishop Lichtenberger, for the Shiprock Ministry to the Navaho, New Mexico [a location today known as the setting for Tony Hillerman mysteries]. Petitions asked that more young Japanese men be called to the ordained ministry in Japan, and that Adult Education classes in Episcopal parishes (initiated by the new *Seabury Series* curriculum) become a vital element in all parish programs.

November: Thanksgivings were offered for the Rev. Boone Porter's book about local parishes (husband of Companion Violet), for a prayer written by Companion Annamae Crite (mother of African-American artist Allan Rohan Crite), and for the Rev. Daisuke Kitagawa who had been interned during WW II and was now Episcopal representative to the World Council of Churches in Geneva.

There was a petition that the number of Eucharistic celebrations in parish churches be doubled, perhaps due to the influence of Liturgical Movement reforms and individual churchmen like Bishop James Pike. Intercessions were offered for the new organizational structure of the national Episcopal Church, an Executive Council, for the interdenominational agency *Church World Service* helping to resettle refugees in the US, for counseling centers established by local churches, and a request that prisons become opportunities for redirecting lives instead of mere punishment.

December: Prayers were asked for the San Pablo house in Phoenix, AZ, helping young men in trouble with the law, also for disturbed and almost despairing clergy.[28]

1969—

The first military draft since 1942 began; there was a huge (250,000+) antiwar demonstration in Washington DC, November 1969; also, in the summer, a huge rock-and-roll folk-hippie festival was held in Woodstock, NY; two US astronauts took their first step on the moon in July; Princeton University began admitting women as undergraduate students, and Golda Meir became the Prime Minister of Israel.

January: Thanksgivings were offered for Trinity Church (Wall Street), NY, [whose pattern since the 18th century had been to assist Episcopal churches and missions with financial backing] having hosted the first church-wide conference, with Presiding Bishop Hines, "to understand prayer in contemporary terms." Thanksgiving also greeted "the first American Indian priest at Good Shepherd Mission in AZ," and the formation of the National Committee of Black Churchmen. Petitions lifted up air pollution [a first ecological topic in the *IP*] and negotiations in Paris to end the Vietnam War.

A <u>Notice</u> to Companions on the last page: the SCHC ***Annual Report*** is unavoidably delayed.

---

28 Dec. *IP*, 7.

February brought petitions against capital punishment, for parents whose daughter is considering a mixed marriage, "may prejudice be healed, and with God's love, color not become a barrier," for those risking imprisonment due to protesting against the war, for the astronauts of Apollo 8, for a black family being welcomed into a white neighborhood, and for Lebanon and the Mid-East conflict. There were thanksgivings for the Peace Corps, for Agnes Sanford's leadership in healing ministries, and for the Spring Conference that Companion Alice Lewitin would chair.

March: Thanksgivings were offered for the *Memorials of Companions* printed in the **Annual Report,** so that Companions unable to attend Adelynrood could participate in that Society ritual; for St. Cyprian's (Roxbury, MA) hospitality, for a delay in the nation's production of expensive ABM and SST weapons, and for the Rev. Richard Gary's inner-city, multi-racial parish in upper Washington Heights, NYC. Also there were requests for the healing of Vietnam War wounded, American and Vietnamese. Prayers rejoiced that 8,000 had attended an Evangelism Conference in Minnesota.

April: Thanksgivings were offered for COCU (Council on Church Unity) talks, for the *ESCRU Newsletter* and Companion Carman Hunter's report in it, for parishes once again able to enjoy Evening Prayer liturgies after their long absence, for the needs of ethnic groups: Indians, Eskimos, and migrant workers, and for government-sponsored Community Action Programs that often met in church basements. Companions were praying about the unraveling of white middle class culture: one petition asked for the ability "to see good in the changes," another for support in realizing that "old" is not necessarily better or the best. There was a prayer "for parents watching in fear and dismay the changing customs and moral standards among young people."

May, when the *IP* carried only thanksgivings, Florence Humphries celebrated her years of association with Vida Scudder, and also honored Emily Morgan. There was a thanksgiving for an

Evelyn Underhill quote: "a real Christian is always a revolutionary, and belongs to a new race." There was rejoicing over the new organization *Clergy & Laity Concerned About Vietnam*, and for the organizations of the Fellowship of Reconciliation and the Episcopal Peace Fellowship.

June brought earnest prayers that today's consciousness no longer be divided by class, race, and nation, for Bishop Paul Moore, president of the Council of Churches in Washington DC, for an end to the compulsory draft, for a priest and his wife who are liberals in a reactionary Southern community, and that a black college (Voorhees) become accredited as a four-year college. Also a petition named Patsy, daughter of a Companion, who was starving herself on a fruit diet [the first *IP* appearance of anorexia]. **July-August**: Hearty thanksgivings were offered for Companion Esther Burgess and husband (the Rt. Rev.) John, and the new challenges opening to them by his election as a Black bishop in the Episcopal Church, for all newly graduated seminarians, black and white, and for the early childhood program Headstart. There were prayers for the Special Convention planned to meet at Notre Dame, Indiana in the fall, and that Episcopalians would acknowledge the need for black/poor people to have some decision-power over their own lives, also that the Episcopal Church not be known as "Rich and White."

NEWSLETTER **AUGUST 1969,** Theme: a changing world. Adelynrood (the house and grounds) itself has not escaped: the three cedars ("Marys") that have guarded our Great Cross since the House was built, had to go...the cross now stands bleak and austere, but little clumps of portulaca have a toehold on the gray rocks. In the Chapel: two priests who were retreat leaders asked for a free-standing altar, and served communion from a table in front of the altar that was against the wall. But already last summer, the impact of liturgical renewal had persuaded Council to alter the chapel, plans being drawn by a Philadelphia architect, the Rev. James Ludwig, husband of Companion Martha. The *House Committee* is relying on good old volunteers but in much need of new ones: Please Say "Yes" next time...More Companions are requesting 1st floor rooms; a TV was actually brought into the Adelynrood dining room for watching the astronauts land on the moon! Theme Conferences (on *Social Justice, Christian Unity,* and *Missions*) are now fifty years old; our first "psychedelic" church service at Adelynrood included dancing and singing. Companions report feeling "slightly shook up" but comforted that amid all the change, God remains.

Annual Report 1969, **Companion Conference,** Opening Paper, C-in-C Marion Rollings on the theme *Creative Power as given by God.*[29]

Over the past six years, Rollins' themes had all addressed "creative use of difference" in support of equal dignity and humans' deep commonality. Now she applied the opportunity for interaction to Womanpower, Racial power, and Ecumenical power. Racial: Today's theater, black and white, is full of ideas that adult whites must relearn. Please note visible changes in the American social order, e.g. racial integration of models in the Sears catalog, and at restaurant counters; black students creating their own organizations and programs at colleges like Barnard. Women: Usually portrayed in cartoons as stupid, silly, nearsighted, useless—why do *women* also laugh, especially at the woman-driver stereotype? Why do women devalue women's gifts such as intuition, or valuing an individual life, or holding a different conception of power [influence rather than force]? Women's courage is not expressed in combat but in endurance, in bearing pain rather than inflicting it. Ecumenism: Will the churches join hands soon enough to keep themselves from dying out? Can they attract young people?

The same Conference heard a presentation on *Race, Revolution & Women*, by Shirley Chisholm, the first Black woman elected to the U. S. House of Representative. (Companions perceived "a great coup" in obtaining a prominent Congresswoman as guest speaker).[30]

(Summarized for its historic import) The concept of *Revolution* raises paranoid fear and new, fearsome "labels": *Racial Polarization, Generation Gap, Virginia Slims, Vietnam,* and *Middle East*..."Campuses and ghettos are exploding fuses, causing revolutionary acne." Will we have a future?

Most women have never had a chance to measure the full extent of their

29 1969 *Annual Report*, Rollins, 12-13.
30 Chisholm, 1969 *Annual Report.*

own commitment to ending poverty, and racial discrimination—social injustice. Today, we now can.

The easiest course is giving the "most detachable extensions of ourselves, <u>money</u> and <u>sympathy.</u>" Some revolts are silly, some deadly. But the BLACK revolt is not solely black nor for blacks only, because it encompasses **all** aspects of human life. "Masters" aren't "free." Anti-feminism destroys both women and their bosses. Black Males are expected to be Supermasculine menials; the White Male is expected to be Omnipotent Administrator; and White women to be Super Feminine, while Black women are considered Sub-feminine.

White women ask, "What can we do?" under the assumption that THEY are in a position to help. The only answer? Free Yourselves! All must become revolutionaries, refuse old-tradition stereotypes. Start in your own homes, schools, and churches. Don't go home talking about integrated schools/churches/marriages or specifying institutions when what you really mean is <u>black/white integration.</u>

The Retreat *God Makes All Things New,* led by Bishop Charles Gilson, husband of Companion Dorothy, addressed the general task of adapting to change. The Rev. David Boulton (rector St. John's, Athol, MA) spoke about the new liturgical ritual—the renewal of baptismal vows—to be incorporated in the revised *Prayer Book.*

September, October, and **November** brought thanksgivings for newly elected C-in-C Alice Lewitin's talents and experience, for astronauts on the moon, for a Companion's half-way house for the mentally ill, for a new sense of brotherhood and concern for all colors and conditions of men. Thanksgivings were offered for the Group Dynamics movement that taught the value and contributions of small-group discussion in parish churches, for an increase in prayer groups everywhere, for Urban Renewal, and the new Volunteers In Mission program (Episcopal equivalent of the Peace Corps). A Companion's petition prayed: "Help us bring to life each intercession as if it were our own: behind the printed word are real people."

The **December** *IP* had on its cover a Christmas meditation by the Rev. Howard Thurman. There were thanksgivings for Founder EMM's birthday and her vision for SCHC, also for *Forward Move-*

ment leaflets on prayer written by Companion Cynthia Wedel and her husband Canon Theodore Wedel, Warden of the College of Preachers at the Washington (DC) Cathedral. Intercessions prayed that clergy will take time to read scripture and pray, that there be sympathetic acceptance of the plan for the Special General Convention, and courage for our Presiding Bishop and Executive Council. Petitions were offered that all troops be withdrawn from Vietnam, and for Strategic Arms Limitation talks.

An end-of-the-year prayer by Barbara Stockton read:

"May you be born on Christmas morning a Son of God, in the lowly stable of your soul, amidst the ox, asses, and sheep of your inner being, the animal part of you sanctified;

May your soul be nourished by Holy Mother Mary who dwells in your own breast, and may you grow in character, pleasing both God and man;

May the shafts of light from the daystar pierce the darkness of your soul, pierce the womb of darkness bearing seeds of creativity where waters are deep and no light filters through, yet where lie the beginnings of all beauty, music, and color of love, waiting to become fruits of the Holy Spirit.

May the angels bless you and raise you, with the Son, up to God for the benediction of peace."

1970—

A pop-art symbol, the word "LOVE" with its four letters blocked into a cube (created by artist Robert Indiana) was popularly available in commercials, paperweights, key rings and decor. The New Year began with thanksgivings for honors to Companion Cynthia Wedel; in February, for the Rev. George Webber of the New York inner city East Harlem Protestant Parish, appointed President of New York Theological Seminary, and for Vine Deloria (son of a Standing Rock Sioux Indian Episcopal priest) and his book *Custer Died For Your Sins*. Petitions asked for the spread of M.L.King's Christ-like teachings, and named one "who is deep in occult and meditation studies, that she may see that the only true light is in the Gospel." In **March**, there was a petition addressing a new social unrest: "that our young people will respect our laws, accept punishment, and try to understand the meaning of integrity."[31] In **April** there was a petition for a young man who had burned his draft card.

The **1970 Companion Conference** and Retreat theme was *And Be Thankful*. Alice Lewitin, C-in-C, recommended that Companions take the small-group experience at Adelynrood home to parishes, to see it as a useful format for discussing troublesome issues, for promoting openness and democratic participation. *Group dynamics training*, an empowering and liberating structure for uptight Episcopalians, has helped leaders "to free up" real human exchange and get rid of surface conformity. "The idea of listening to scholarly lectures devoid of personal contact has quickly become unacceptable," she noted, a "revolutionary" change that has established a new standard for conference meetings.[32]

The **Business Meeting** heard reports from all committees (in

---

31 *IP* 1970, March 20, 10,20.

32 Her Opening Paper chose to glorify God rather than present a "state of the Society" report. Beginning with our "controlling state" eighty-six years earlier, Change is as much a part of our Society as thankfulness. In 1920, Vida Scudder, "that mixture of saint and revolutionary," needed to save the world from itself and emphasized the "three great truths" of our Society: *Christian Unity* among branches of Christianity; *Social Justice* focused on industry and labor; and *Christian Mission*, our international focus. But today *Social Justice* must make room for a new triad: <u>Youth</u>, <u>Poverty</u>, and <u>Race</u>. Also church women need a new role: several dioceses have already dismantled ECW organizations. Bishop Paul Moore warned women <u>not</u> to give up that corporate entity, the source

Organization Chart, Appendix). Companions were changing the conception of program from one speaker to a room of listeners, to participation in both silence and praying, and much more discussion.

An interesting *Special Report* from an *ad hoc Committee on Public Corporate Stands* revisited the longstanding debate over an SCHC policy against public (and political) "stands" in the name of the Companionship. The Assembly Ruling on that issue, summarizing minutes of Council, Executive Board, and Annual Meeting Reports 1952-69, affirmed the policy which remains in effect today. The *Trial Liturgy* for the revised *Book of Common Prayer* was now in parishes, and had been "tried" at Spring Conference.

A remarkable 1970 companion paper, *"Be Black...and Be Thankful!"* presented by Companion Viola E. Pinder, (summarized) explained how the Black Power consciousness emerged. She had worried that her newness as a Companion (admitted that spring) might render her perspective unwelcome, but when her topic (White Christians, Heal Yourselves!) was presented to the Conference Committee they affirmed it as GOOD, and "packing a wallop."

> Pinder had always been able to be thankful for being "black," since her father had instilled great pride in their heritage—though she also grew up fearing that the Ku Klux Klan would kill her beloved father and brothers. She had never understood why she couldn't play on swings with other kids, or was forced off sidewalks by whites. "In my childish way, I thought blacks must be better in God's sight than whites, which made me glad I wasn't white." Citing post-Civil War documents, she read seven paragraphs in the legal and civic language of an 1865 petition to Congress by Tennessee Negroes and then asked: "Do these words sound like stereotyped-ignorant chattel slaves who should be kept in their place, lest they mongrelize the white race?"
>
> Next, she quoted Henry Turner, the Negro Representative from Bibb County, Georgia, elected to Congress Sept 3, 1868: "Am I A Man? If I am such, I claim the RIGHT OF A MAN. Am I not a man because I happen to be of a darker hue than the honorable men around me?" His religious self-affirmation ended by urging fellow Negroes to "never lift a finger... in defense of Georgia, unless Georgia acknowledges that YOU ARE

of their organizational clout. Similarly, Blacks should not give up their organizations (strength in numbers). Quoting Alice Lewitin's *Annual Report 1970*, 11,14.

MEN and invests you with THE RIGHTS PERTAINING TO MANHOOD."
Citizens' rights for "freemen" had turned out to be free in word only, a
terrible waste wrought by lynchings, bombings of black churches, dogs
attacking black children… it makes one ashamed to be an American!
White immigrants continually assimilate themselves into America, while
blacks are still in the mud.

Pinder then continued with a list of contributions by blacks: Dr. Charles
Drew who invented the Blood Bank (the Red Cross had formerly segregated
black-donor blood); Elijah Mc Coy, inventor of self-lubricating engines
and machines; Mary McLeod Bethune, educator and president of the
National Council of Negro Women; Paul Robeson, singer/actor/athlete
who was exiled for his communist sympathies; Benjamin Banneker,
mathematician and scientist who played a key role in selecting District of
Columbia sites for the White House, the U. S. Treasury, and the Capitol;
Matthew Hensen, the first man to locate and stand on the North Pole
while assisting Admiral Peary; and Lewis Latimer, noted scientific aide
to Edison. "Does America care? They were Black. Well, I care, because I
am black, and God cares, and I am thankful for their gifts…My people
could NOT hide their identity, as Jews, Italians, and Irish could. They
were [considered] 'white' and moving into WHITE POWER. The black
man remained powerless in his own country."

Those words BLACK POWER seem to frighten whites. Why? "We've
fought in every war, yet in WWII, German POWs were treated better
than black GIs." The white man gave us Jesus Christ who helped us
survive, but we did not equate our Christianity with the "white-man's
Christianity" that allowed him to exclude black people from his churches
and schools. A white man could leave his church and go beat a black man
just for the hell of it. Most Ku Klux Klan members are white Christians!
And I'm thankful for the Black Church, the first black institution in the
nation. Long before college studies about race, there were great black
saints and churches. The White man systematically killed our language
(African), culture (African), manhood (made us a matriarchal society),
and bodies—and tried to kill our souls, to blot us out…but our Christianity
freed us. Our religion had to mean more than that to us! We had to lose
ourselves in it—to emote, sing, shout, and praise for the strength to go
back to the fields, to janitor jobs, to Miss Ann's kitchens, to six more days
of being humiliated, insulted, given the status of a nothingness.

Once a white man I worked for asked: Are you not sorry that you're
not white? My emphatic NO astonished him. I was as surprised by the
question as he by my answer. Thank God I've lived to see this day when
blacks can become reconciled to the acceptance of their blackness. It
has broken the chain and freed us from the assumption that WHITE =
RIGHT. I am thrilled to see young blacks marching, smiling; I say in my

heart, welcome, soul sister. And I pray for those in ghettos, trapped by drugs and enslaved in hopelessness. <u>Pray with me for our oneness, one day,</u> when <u>there will be no need for a Companion paper with this title—</u> instead the title 'BE—and BE THANKFUL.' My hope is in the knowledge that God's purpose will never be defeated in His time.

Companions who heard Companion Pinder's passionate statement decided it should be printed and circulated to those who hadn't heard it. Separate copies still reside in the archives, and are available to 21st century eyes. It is possible that her paper confronted Companions with ideas and emotion then hard to assimilate, when the larger culture had not yet opened up its views about race. It sounds powerful even today.

Late-summer *IPs* prayed for the young Americans fighting in Vietnam, the dedicated work of Companion committees undergirding the Society's life in the Way of the Cross, for Christian hippies who carry Bibles with them in California, for the grape-pickers strike in California, and for the United Farm Workers labor union. A specific petition prayed for a girl who had experienced an abortion [a first time for that word in the *IP*] and prayed for "something good out of that tragic experience, that she can regain her spiritual values and capacity for affection."

1971—

IP petitions prayed for a ceasefire in Vietnam, for wisdom about the new legalization of abortion, for opposing the new Trans Alaska Pipeline, for better care of Juvenile Delinquents, and for the Society's re-evaluating its commitment to social justice issues. A Companion asked healing "for the many veterans of the Viet Nam war who are disturbed and guilt-laden over the role of the US and their part in the killing and destruction in that tragic country."

The **Companion Conference 1971** theme was *Sacrifice as Participation in Reality.* Three major Companion papers addressed it: *Toward a Theology of Sacrifice* by Marianne Micks, professor at General Seminary and later Virginia Episcopal Seminary [the concept "sacrifice" is now out of fashion but is actually a call to be more fully human]; *Therefore Let Us Keep the Feast,* by Elizabeth Randall-Mills [based on Evelyn Underhill's *The Mystery of Sacrifice*]; and *Sacrifice Today?* by Gloria Kehl [introducing the perspectives of Alvin Toffler's *Future Shock,* as well as newly published works by authors James Baldwin and Manual Chavez]. Bob Wagstaff, head of the Coca Cola Corporation and a prominent Episcopal lay leader, referring to the generation gap, had actually confessed, "I'm afraid of young people."

1972—

In the nation, the Watergate tapes were found to have an 18-minute erasure; the Arab Oil embargo produced long lines of cars idling their engines at the gas pumps; the Yom Kippur War in the Middle East ended, and there was a ceasefire in Vietnam. The *Roe v Wade* Supreme Court decision that legalized abortion, January 22, launched a divisive debate across the nation.

*IP*s gave thanks for the proliferation of Day Care centers to help young mothers who must work outside the home, for urban housing, and for steps toward peace in Ireland.

In **March**, seventeen parishes reported presenting *Faith Alive* programs. Petitions urged doing away with incarcerating juveniles, and prayed for minimal environmental damage from the new Trans-Alaska Pipeline.

In **April**, there were thanksgivings that the SCHC archives had been placed in safe storage at Diocese of Massachusetts headquarters [in Boston], Companion Ruth Leonard supervising their train ride from Northampton (MA).[33]

The ***Annual Report,*** **August 1972,** was 114 pages long. A startling challenge to the Society had been delivered at the Spring meeting of the SCHC Council by Companion Michelle W. Hawkins,

---

33 1972 *IPS,* Jan – May.

chair of the Social Justice Committee, and advisor to the C-in-C. In August, it was read to the entire Companionship. In a tone unusual at Companion gatherings, this young Companion questioned the Society's *corporate* life and commitment.[34] (excerpted and summarized)

> We are at a critical turning point in our corporate life, on the verge of losing (if we have not already lost) our Societal "direction." Statistics reveal the small number of Companions actually "participating" in the *IP*, in Social Justice and Mission conferences, and in general financial support of the Society. "Our self-assumptions about *being* Companions are not borne out by the facts." Organizationally, the "rigid territoriality of Committees" is a strangulating force, e.g. a decision about hanging a poster in the dining room involved the Chair of the Conference and 6 other people for an hour! Only 4% of the Companionship actually visits Adelynrood; even fewer spend the obligatory daily 15 minutes at the Chapel Intercession Desk. [In passing, she also mentioned the business practices of deficit budgeting and drawing from capital for operating expenses, significant threats to SCHC survival.]
>
> Two processes of renewal need to be "birthed" [an earnest '60s figure of speech]. First, re-determine our Society's function and relationships with each other, the Society, Adelynrood, the church, and the world... and examine our consciences about what that means *to the future*— to renewal at its best. Second, "Form follows Function"...let there be no committees again [a very 1960s ideal] thus evading personal responsibility. A Task Force can be a cadre of us, as loosely structured as possible, who then recommend an entire process for the Society. Task Force participants have to agree to the process and get an outside expert advisor to direct this self-evaluation. Each step must then be documented and evaluated as we go. Third, a moratorium is declared on Theme Committee conferences in summer 1973, giving that time to Task Force work. These meetings must take place at Adelynrood, in winter and spring, to present Council with a report in 1973.

The last two pages of her challenge proposed a Time Sequence and a Questionnaire to be sent to the entire membership and returned, filled out, to Companion Rowena Thompson by the end of 1972. For Companions living at a distance, perhaps less aware of the true financial situation and inexperienced with internal Retreat House administrative practices, reading this could have been puzzling.

---

34 Hawkins, 1972.

The **1972 Companion Conference** (the 76th *Annual Meeting*) whose theme was *Saints and Sainthood*, featured Episcopal Theological School (Cambridge MA) Dean John Coburn, as retreat conductor, Janet Morgan as Conference Chairman, and Cynthia Wedel leading the Bible Study. Three Companion papers examined saints and sainthood: Cynthia Wedel's *"I want to be one too!"* and Elizabeth Falck's *"Climbing the Saint's Stair."* Companion Lee Beaty, a recent Yale PhD in early English literature, delivered *"To Walk in Measure Below"*—the story of the first (15th c.) lay Anglican religious community, Little Gidding (the predecessor model for Adelynrood, in some ways, according to EMM[35]), and its leader, Nicholas Ferrar [immortalized in a poetry cycle with that title by T. S. Eliot]— summarized below. Reclaiming both the Church of England spiritual heritage and SCHC's religious community ideal, Beaty concluded that SCHC was indeed a Christian commune in principle, improved by the rich sacramentalism available in our chapel. "Here is the Banquet, the contrapuntal Gloria, the sensitive Dance, moving in measure toward his Kingdom."

> Nicholas Ferrar, its founder, reportedly said that great saints are of little value because they are so discouraging to the average Christian! Thus the family Household at Little Gidding concentrated on "ordinary" saints. Ferrar was then 33 years old, intelligent, sensitive. In England, the Civil War was rampaging; popish plots suspected everywhere—"Jesuits behind every bush." The socioeconomic conditions were even worse: the landed upper class reeked of conspicuous consumption and the poor were ignored. The education system was somewhat better, though the great universities (Oxford and Cambridge) were politicized. John Milton was suspended from his congregation, Shakespeare was writing his plays. Added to that was the outbreak of bubonic plague that took 1/6th of the London population, which Christians understandably viewed as God's wrath. Ferrar, a humanist gentleman, merchant, democrat, and pleader for "practical piety," had decided to "withdraw" to the country. Having graduated from school in 1610, Ferrar was the very "Model of a Modern Commune Leader," a kind of charismatic man suffering ill health (too bookish). He'd taught, traveled all over Europe, and grown up reading Foxe's *Book of Martyrs*. The really big gift of the Counter Reformation, the true fruits of 16th c. Europe, was rediscovery of the interior life of

---

prayer—after the total Protestant-reformed emphasis on doctrine and theology, intellectual thought rather than prayer. He read St. Ignatius, St. Theresa, St. John of the Cross, and Francis de Sales; his friend was poet and priest George Herbert. He focused on laymen instead of priests— and while still in the commercial world, had tried to rescue the Virginia Company experiment in the New World. [Here "in-house" humor led Lee to note that he'd served on some 25 *ad hoc* committees, and was therefore probably guardian saint of Companion Irma Titus.]

Ferrar's decision to leave London's corruption for the country house called Little Gidding was an experiment of a Protestant family living as a Christian community—some thirty human beings of all ages, with all the usual human problems. How did they survive? By adopting a rule, *The Way of Little Gidding*; their plan had a routine of work and worship as its warp and woof. In one sense, they were "doing the Lord's work without ceasing." There could be no spontaneity, but also no monotony. Daily life was segmented into small units, as in a convent, with big feasts used to centralize and celebrate the internal Community by inviting in the surrounding community. Shakespeare's plays, Milton's poetry, Bach's *Oratorio* were part of their communal experience. Each member had to "walk" in unhurried self-control in his/her role and tasks, like a dancer. A daily Liturgy set the schedule—family prayers, Bible study, prayer. The family members' community product or work was writing out "Harmonies" [concordances of the four gospels]. The household, in pairs, read aloud the entire Psalter each day, praying it around the clock. But the Protestant slant of their Anglicanism allowed them to celebrate Eucharist only once a month. Even so, this "earliest Anglican experiment in Christian communal living gave SCHC our clear heritage."

Like us, they had three set "Offices" each day, with individual members taking leadership in praise, thanksgivings and intercession. They set aside an oratory for private devotion, placed high value on huge acts of charitable hospitality (among their desperately poor neighbors), and functioned under a governing structure that demanded strong leadership and required the self-discipline of individual members. Our Sponsor-Probationer relationship incorporates some of these "family" overtones, Lee noted, along with the same longstanding emphasis on reading widely, "keeping open the casement windows of our minds and spirits," and worshiping God with our brains as well as heart, soul and strength.

We, SCHC, improve on Little Gidding by the rich sacramentalism of our life at Adelynrood; "HERE is the Banquet, the contrapuntal Gloria, the sensitive Dance, moving in measure toward his Kingdom."[36]

C-in-C Lewitin's Opening Paper set the stage for Society re-

---

36 1972 *Annual Report,* 10, 12-14, 22.

newal by recalling historical precedents from SCHC's genesis: the *monastic movement* (a source of peace movements, sanctuary creation, care for refugees, and hospice/hospitals). Each spin-off at some point slipped from its original aspirations and required a process of renewal. From that review her question was: "Is it right for us to keep this luxurious place [Adelynrood] for *our* sole enjoyment?" And adding a financial element to the rationale for renewal, she said: "increasing practicality [about finances] can be a sign of developing sanctity: progress in holiness is not marked by dreaminess but by greater shrewdness, more common sense, e.g. St. Paul, St. Benedict, St. Teresa."[37]

The C-in-C's **1972 Annual Report** then asked: Why do we emphasize Chapters so much? Because they are the locus of our first prayer bond, personally and symbolically. EMM did not want a "prayer-group by correspondence," but rather one bonded through praying and struggling with competing ideas, laughter, and fellowship. Companions who've never been to Adelynrood have less idea of what the Society really is—its understanding and experience of community. Sponsors carry the responsibility of making that clear to Probationers preparing for their vow. Huge financial worries had been responsible for the budget deficit: the danger of losing the IRS Tax Exemption status, and the very minimal return from the investing of the Ruth Mary Wilson Bequest. [See Nan Clarkson's *An SCHC Autobiography of Money, Imagined and from the Archive and Records, 1985.* This was the first and only analysis of the Society's financial history, up to the year 2000.]

The usual Committee Reports included a proposal from *Artistic Planning* that Miss Morgan's Plaster-of-Paris bust be cast in bronze. The *Grounds Committee* was looking into mosquito control; and the *House Committee* pointed out that the greater numbers fed in a summer season, the better off the Society, financially. Again, the idea of an Associate Companions category was considered to raise income.

---

37 *Annual Report* 1972.

IP petitions for the rest of that year named many Social Justice concerns. A Companion asked "for wider understanding of those forced to live in slums, and more concern from leaders, more help from concerned Christians." Another set of petitions focused on gang war, troubled youth, Community Action Program training centers in Spanish-speaking neighborhoods, state care for those with mental retardation, prevention of further strip mining, and aid for migrant laborers. A petition urged support for the Havasupi Indians' grazing rights in the Grand Canyon, and for saving the land, air and water of the Southwest US from the pollution of hydroelectric plants and off-shore oil drilling. A special prayer asked that "welfare and education funds intended for the rural poor be restored as long as farm owners and corporation heads still enjoy generous tax deductions."

1973—

The **February** *IP* requested prayers for all the new learnings: "may insights gained through studies for the Task Force show fruit in our personal lives as well as in the SCHC." In **May**, thanksgivings were offered for the great thinkers of the Society, especially V. Scudder and V. Huntington, whose writings inspire action even today! Also there were thanksgivings for (Bishop) John and (Companion) Esther Burgess. One of the liturgical "innovations" in the experimental ecclesiastical 1970s generated the following lament: "for those of us who weep in our hearts at the seeming irreverence of burlap dossals [for the altar], guitars, and pop music on the organ, the informal atmosphere, and chatter before the worship service."[38]

The theme of the 77th **Companion Conference, August 1973**, was *Simplicity & the Environment*. Alice Lewitin's Opening Paper (excerpted) noted that this topic of simplicity had been addressed seven times in 77 years (Intercession had appeared 6 times, Thanksgivings only 3).[39]

---

38 *June 1973 IP.*

39 Lewitin, 1973: *IPs* 1973; Feb., 14 May, 8.

In 1896, the first-ever Companion Conference, the topic *Simplicity of Heart* cited Browning and St. Francis for a simplicity that is *joyous*, not ascetic; Lewitin's update described that as instinctive rejection of "baubles" in favor of that Glory "for which the world is well lost." In 1904 *Simplicity in Religious Life* cited St. Francis, the spare elegance of Japanese art, New England Transcendentalists (the first back-to-the-land group), and Tolstoy in Russia. In 1928, *Simplicity in Mental Attitude*, EMM had looked back to 1904 at the "simplicity" of one Companion who had several children: she adopted another the same age as each, to provide them with company, and dressed them all like boys! Simplicity really can't be *consciously* cultivated; when it is, self-consciousness corrupts it.

In 1940, Lewitin's godmother Companion Josephine January equated *Simplicity* with kindness: doing for others leaves no time to elaborate one's own life. In 1956, Virginia Huntington defined Simplicity as the absence of complexity, to be achieved in the midst of complexity; and in 1961, she called it "simply the Way of the Cross," a beautiful quality rather than a burden. Lewitin also quoted Mrs. Nelson Rockefeller on the qualities of modern art; she called *Simplicity* "freedom within a framework," a perfect description of SCHC. In the Society we are free to pray, interpret, and act in the various circumstances in which our lives are cast—according to and within the six rules that Companions keep.

In her **Annual Report**,[40] the Companion-in-Charge observed: "The shadow of Task Forces, *refreshing shade and menacing cloud*, dominated this past year." Beginning with the Enabling Action passed in August 1972, by the Council, fifteen appointed volunteers created the Task Force I report...and now bring it back: Rita Abbott, Lucy Acock, Doris Boyd, Ethel Colt, Edna Keating, Harriet Kellemen, Janet Morgan, Isabel Pifer, Ethel C. Roberts, Dorothea Shedden, Margaret Sheets, Rowena R. Thompson, Polly Wiley, and *ex-officio* Alice Lewitin C-in-C, and associate Michelle W. Hawkins. Two male clergy served as professional consultants, and the questionnaire returned by Companions had been analyzed.

The Task Force I Report was accepted, and an Ad Hoc *Committee on Bylaws Revision*, necessary for its implementation, created. "Job Descriptions," the modern organizational term, should henceforth specify the responsibilities of both officers and those in

---

40 *Annual Report* 1973, 105-115, 107.

appointed positions. SCHC must employ a Secretary, the first paid SCHC employee. Companion Michelle Hawkins was appointed Chair of the **1974 Companion Conference**, whose theme would be *Renewal*, at which reports from the newly constituted teams in Task Force II would be received and enacted. Under Task Force I were the general topics of programming and communications.

Program was the major renewal focus. Since it was the public "face" of Companionship, strengthening and revitalizing Program (in chapters, in national regions, and at Adelynrood) was basic. It was to be in the "women's-meeting format," valued and taken for granted in this era, rather than emphasizing meditation and silent prayer as in earlier eras. This cultural assumption said that *"programs focus attention on where most Companions find themselves [thoughts, puzzles, concerns]."* The late 20th c. rediscovery of "spirituality" and group silence still lay several decades ahead.

A service of recommitment [supported by a regime of Corporate Prayer in which all Companions could join wherever they were] would be planned for Companion Day 1974, to enlist the participation of the entire Companionship. A sub-task force group would examine expanding the uses of Adelynrood and its programs, as well as means of additional use by chapters. "Training programs" for paying customers would be considered. It would also rethink summer programs sponsored by the Theme Committees, in light of their lack of drawing power. At this point, an "inhospitable" atmosphere at Adelynrood had been experienced by both non-Companions and Companions. This was reflexively affirmed by task force veterans though not named, only implied.

Serious attention would be given to Communications—newsletters & action sheets from various committees, especially Social Justice. Also Companions' biographical records should be carefully monitored and kept up-to-date. A proposed structure-chart was appended. A serious organizational step of employing a Secretary of the Society to keep financial records, handle mailings, proofread reports, and act as House Secretary was approved. The **Business**

Meeting presented farewells to long-term officials, including a graceful and witty poetic tribute to Frances Hepburn by Lee Beaty for her 40 years assistance to ten Cs-in-C of Probationers, also Alice Bartlett's four decades as Treasurer, and housekeeper Mary Evans' retirement after 25 years.

The **1973** *Annual Report* (p. 82ff) included a special report (paraphrased] from Companion Caroline A. Rose, describing her experience on the national committee responsible for *Prayer Book* revision. From the 1960s on, churchwomen had agitated against the pervasive all-masculine language of the *Prayer Book*, a specific case in point being the outmoded theology and language of a Victorian Church of England service known as the "Churching of Women" to follow childbirth.[41] The Revision Committee authorized by General Convention involved about thirty women participants among the fourteen working groups; her assignment was the section called Occasional Prayers and Thanksgivings. Every word, every phrase of every suggestion is weighed and scrutinized, she wrote; the results will first be published as *Prayers For Trial Use, Prayer Book Studies* 25. She believed the whole process was producing a wonderful groundswell of renewal in Anglicanism. Our "space age" appreciates shortened, up-to-date language that is welcoming to newcomers, encourages participants, and has flexibility. The Rev. Dr. Massey Shepherd from CDSP Episcopal Seminary in Berkeley CA is our inspiring and hardworking leader.

The first and major problem confronting all revision workers involved substituting "YOU" for "THOU." If and when that is changed, it requires changing verb forms; would we want to retain "du bist" if we were German? As we work, we realize that too-complex language makes us tongue-tied; our goal is to return the liturgies to common speech, e.g. removing the "est" on words like "reignest, ordainest." We are also leaning toward translating the Lord's Prayer to the same version used by Roman Catholics, Lutherans, and Presbyterians: e.g. "do not bring us to the test," which is apparently closer to our Lord's actual words.

The Bible readings reflecting modern scholarship are not yet printed out because different versions appear in Years A, B, and C. There will be new translations for the Psalms. A recommendation will suggest substituting the O. T. lesson as an alternative to the Epistle. Her contagious enthusiasm for being involved in this important process concludes: "At no time [within our national church structure] have channels to receive personal [women's] suggestions and comments been so wide open."

---

41 Nancy Shepherd, *The Oxford American Prayer Book Commentary*, NY, Oxford Press, 1959, 305.

· Like other Companions in this era, women felt honored to be involved in national church actions and decision-making, of finally being taken seriously in policy and planning matters. This was a key example of attitude-change within the institution, presaging the even-more-major step of women's ordination.

The **September 1973** *IP* carried prayers that each Companion take the Task Force I recommendations to heart. Also acknowledging ruffled relationships, Companions prayed for guidance in what to say and when to say it in all situations, as well as <u>how</u>— endeavoring not to hurt the feelings or sensitivities of others. The **December** *IP* added extra pages detailing the seriousness of the Society's financial and vocational concerns, and asked special prayers for C-in-C Lewitin, "that she may be sustained and empowered during this critical time," also for "the Executive Board, the Coordinator of the Task Forces, and all Companions with special responsibilities" and their "concern for the future of SCHC" in the wake of canceling the 1974 Adelynrood Summer Programs (the step reported below).

Please PRAY for the following Task Forces meeting in January 1974 (volunteers still welcome in each): <u>Sponsors and Probationers</u>, Kay Merigold chairing; <u>Communications</u>, Ruth Leonard; <u>Adelynrood-Program,</u> Elsa Walberg; <u>Adelynrood-Management,</u> Isabel Phisterer; <u>Chapters</u>, Rowena Thompson; and <u>Coordinating Committee</u>, Ethel Colt, Michelle Hawkins and Rowena Thompson. Names of all Task Force volunteers were to be listed in the *February IP*, plus financial contributions underwriting the expenses of this self-analysis.[42] That itself was an indication of crisis mentality in the Society.

1974—

In the world context, there were inflation anxieties, President Nixon's resignation, the A-bomb developed in India, Solzhenitzyn exiled from USSR to Vermont, and the kidnapping of Patricia Hearst.

---

42 Dec 1973 *IP*, 16,18.

The Executive Committee of the SCHC moved the Summer Conference to a Roman Catholic facility in Natick, MA to save the money it would cost to open Adelynrood, and to focus all Companion energies on the Task Forces. The Executive Board, having met March 31, 1974, adopted Guidelines for the Financial Goals of the Society that *for the first time* established a distinction between investment funds for income, and those set aside for future needs of Society. The lesson spelled out? *SCHC must try to live within its own income; annual dues must be readjusted realistically! No more bequest capital eaten up by operating expenses.* Companions on the Social Justice Committee, deeply concerned over the present investment policies, voted to change the name "Committee on Social Responsibilities" to "Committee on Financial and Social Responsibilities in SCHC Investments."[43]

As promised the **February** *IP* contained a *Supplement* listing all Companions in each Task Force—averaging eighteen per team. The chaplain of the Society, the Rev. David W. Boulton, submitted a four-paragraph meditation titled "Sentimentality And The Way Of The Cross," his spiritual prescription supporting Companions confronting change. He warned against sentimentalizing the Cross, against seeing it only as "splendid, noble and heroic." Rather, it must be seen as a challenge to the "stereotype of happiness" that reduces the resurrection to a mere symbol. His concluding collect was a 1938 prayer by British writer Charles Williams: Help us recognize "the exchanges of Thy love, and redeem us from the common agony of our lives" to the "universal joy in Jesus Christ our Lord and Savior..."[44]

The 78th **Companion Conference 1974,** held at the Oblate College and Seminary's Center, Natick, MA, had the theme of *Renewal.* On the cover of the *Annual Report* was a <u>prayer of intent</u> adapted from the 1968 World Council of Churches gathering at Uppsala, Sweden. *"God, you make all things new. We commit ourselves to you:*

43 *Annual Report 1974*, 59, 61.
44 Feb 74 *IP*, 22.

to live for others, to seek those truths we have not yet seen, obey your Commands we have not yet obeyed, and trust each other in the Companionship you've given to us... Amen."

C-in-C Alice Lewitin's Opening Paper chose the prophet Joel as her symbolic voice: "your old men shall dream dreams, your young men see visions." Recalling M. L. King Jr.'s incantation, *"I have a dream,"* she pondered *dream* and *vision*. The rest of the week will be spent inwardly digesting the work of 45 people on 5 task forces who have developed a renewed SCHC "vision"—all supported by a 6th force (the strongest of all, the one undergirding everything with prayer), and a 7th, the financial generosity making these meetings physically possible.[45]

(excerpted) Asking *why* the Society needs renewal confirms it: some Companions say, "It's about time!" others say, "Are there <u>any</u> possible answers?" The church that lives to itself will die by itself... Jesus' words were: "let the dead bury the dead," meaning that God is always *before* us, not behind or calling us back to yesterday... "Some Companions have erroneously labeled me as wanting SCHC to become an activist group, confusing 'action' and 'activism.' Action doesn't have to mean physical movement. The SCHC reason for being is prayer, concern for the lives of those for whom we pray." She quoted Miss Morgan for a possible first step: What we must try to understand is our <u>own vocation</u>: women living in the world, making our own individual influences, social or other, [but also] banded together to meet the serious religious, educational, social problems of our age, **first by prayer and then by battle.** Our calling is not so much to *change* (an idea that threatens many) as to *re-examination*, renewing our commitment to Christ, daily." Being a Companion, and the quality of Companionship, requires acknowledging the 'blocks' that get in the way, and removing them. "God lets death come to institutions and societies when they put up blocks while He moves on!" She cited several blocks:

1) <u>Self Satisfaction</u>—"everything is fine the way it is." We tend to "take refuge" in SCHC, enjoying a certain elitism nurtured by secrecy and the process of membership through invitation: we're "special, we've arrived." Words about Companions that are truly frightening: "likeminded," "compatible," WASP. Our "only commonality" should be *OUR CALLING.* We seem to think <u>we</u> determine who joins us. God help us if that is true! God is the one who determines, designs, leads; ours is <u>response</u>. Probation and Admission are a testing of vocation otherwise

45 Lewitin's *Opening Paper, Annual Report 1974*, 7-8.

we are a club, not a community of religious. A proprietary feeling about SCHC is a weakness; it is not "our" society, but God's, who called it into being in 1884, via EMMorgan and Harriet Hastings.

2) The <u>Inability to Face Conflict,</u> let alone resolve it.—Jesus' kindness toward the Samaritan community is a model (he didn't call down "fire" on his enemies); we all know that *hostility between* and *within* families and communities is much worse than toward strangers. The era of Machiavelli is past; we should be ashamed of using 16th c. tactics: being silent, ladylike, afraid of "exposure, hiding behind being Companionly," spreading rumors that "love has left the Society." There have *always been and always will be conflicts.*

3) <u>Differences Regarding Prayer:</u> do we truly understand what Intercession is, and means? To read a prayer is not enough. <u>We</u> have to *expect to be used, to do* something in connection with it. "Holding her in my thoughts" is action, not just pious mumbled words. It is a privilege to be Companions with not only the likeminded. "Where action reveals the difference Christianity makes, the message is actually being heard" (quoted from Charles W.B. Smith, Companion Ivy Smith's husband, in <u>Response</u> May-June '74)

4) <u>Her closing prayer:</u> "Quicken all members of our Companionship that they be alive to the opportunities and responsibilities of these times. Save us from complacency and the fear of new ways; inspire and stir our wills, to pray and work until your will is done. Amen."[46]

Companion Papers at the **1974** Conference were presented by Priscilla Martin, *Simplicity & Environment* (not a "simple" life but rather wholeness; Companions share the American tradition of "adoration of nature" alongside our historic exploitation of nature); Madeleine L'Engle Franklin, *Under the Fig Tree* (parable of Nathaniel: each must find her own fig tree or "peace." We mourn the death of pelicans in the Gulf of Mexico due to pesticides in the Iowa wheat fields); and Angela Williams, *Simplicity: Opting Out vs. Involvement.* (Today's problem is <u>overchoice</u>, Alvin Toffler's word; limitations are the very meat of creativity! "Do your own thing" is good advice because doing anyone else's thing is phony. Citing EMM's "simplicity," she urged, don't let it become "that most unsimple of all things, a pose.")[47]

---

46 *op cit*, Lewitin.

47 Ibid. 34, 23.

Five sessions of the Executive Council, meeting at the end of **Companion Conference August 1974**, produced pages of votes on varying steps and policies, among them:

1) An *Evaluating Committee* to report in Summer 1975; Michele Hawkins, Chair; Council-appointed members-at-large were Marion Rollins, Isabelle Ackerman, Helen Turnbull; and five from the Prayer Task Force (or others attending the 1974 Conference).

2) A *Communication Committee* and a *Program Committee* to be appointed, plus a part-time Program Coordinator to be employed. Numerous changes in the House must make it more accessible for "people with special needs." New guidelines will be written for the *IP Committee* and the *Summer Calendar Committee*; an *Ad Hoc SCHC Centennial 1984 Committee* must begin planning.

3) The Task Force recommendations will become a *guidebook* for ACs-in-C to use during their 1974-75 program year, accompanied by an evaluation sheet for ranking the various suggestions and recommendations. Also: there is now a new organizational requirement: *six Companions are essential for establishing a new chapter.*

Executive Board and Council Meeting. The Money Report: fiscal 1973-74 ended with a net deficit of $2,598 for the Society, and $41,545 for Adelynrood. How to face it? Increase charges for Adelynrood, use $12,000 in capital funds to implement the necessary improvements recommended by the Task Forces; apply to foundations for grants; and by October 1974, employ a Program Coordinator. An accounting of Task Force expenses and extra meetings, November 30, '73 to August 12, '74 amounted to "about $12,000, much of it contributed by members."[48]

Can stolid black-and-white print possibly evoke the profound excitement and pain generated by the words in this process? Each

---

48 1974 *Annual Report* 97, 88; task-force expenses, 114-115.

Companion recalling 1972-74 mentioned the tremendous energies expended, the hopes and hurts revealed, and an awakening commitment to real financial responsibility—toward making the label "financially naïve" no longer applicable to Companions in the SCHC.

In the **1974** *Annual Meeting*, C-in-C Alice Lewitin filled in (retrospectively) how this historic meeting had come about: 1973 was its preparation. She credited the Executive Board's willingness to stop, listen, and act in accord with what God seemed to say. *The only way to renewal is through two decisions, one painful to all, another hurting a few.* What was painful to all was the November 1973 Executive Board decision not to open Adelynrood. That created "a stabbing pain that became a prolonged ache," and was relieved only by the realization "that SCHC is people, not just a place." Spring Conference that year, also held at the Oblate Center, proved it. "I believe that history will prove the decision essential, also one of the most inspired in our ninety years of life."

Here is what was painful to some: her letter had not made it clear that the Adelynrood closing was only for summer 1974. As the C-in-C interpreted it, there was to be "a year off" for a good, hard look at how to improve the physical plant, our Program, community life, and accept a deficit budget. Now that we've caught our breath, she exulted, there is no deficit for fiscal '74-75, and we've made the decision to be morally responsible about funds and investing. "We start the new era, '75-76, fiscally even, and have put our funds in a bank [that has] a printed statement of social responsibility. We may in future have to operate again on a deficit budget, or obtain a foundation grant, but from now on, we will do it knowingly—not subconsciously."[49]

---

49 *Annual Report* 1974, 47, 28, 49, 50. In the exciting recommendations at Natick, 1974, small groups had listed what they wanted in a paid Program Staff person, and Elsa Walberg (chair of that Task Force) was elected to that position by a large majority.

TASK FORCE RECOMMENDATIONS (summary overview)

1) <u>Task Force on Adelynrood-Program</u>, Elsa Walberg chairing, Michelle Hawkins reporting: hire a Program Coordinator. Plan mini-conferences on special topics.

2) <u>Task Force on Adelynrood-Management</u>, Michelle Hawkins reporting: SCHC must charge more for room &-board, serve meals family-style (no more waitresses), substitute the term "Evening Office" for "Compline," and install a vending machine! San Damiano bedrooms (all on the first floor) should be reserved primarily for Companions, the Refectory ceiling should be soundproofed to reduce dining clamor, and fourteen tables should be purchased. The New York room should be equipped for audio-visual showings, the Della Robbia porch fitted with sliding glass windows. Rooms 33, 34, 35, and 36 should be made useful for couples in residence, and a bathroom established opposite the upstairs library room, Hilda's Rest (adjacent to the existing bathroom), by enlarging the broom closet. "A year-round facility should be created out of part of Adelynrood, or one of cottages."

3) <u>Task Force on Communication</u>, Ruth Leonard chairing: systematizing the print materials of the Society meant specifying what the printed *Annual Reports* should include, also storing archived information carefully. A Members Directory should be issued every two years, including phone numbers and geographical index. *Corporate Devotions* would continue to be a summer publication only. *IP* items should be expanded to carry both program ideas <u>and</u> prayers, *Theme Committees* should be responsible for *IP* theme pages; both names should appear in an *IP* petition unless otherwise requested, and new forms of bills and business documents should be designed. An emergency prayer chain should function by telephone between *IP*s, and notices of chapter

meetings should be published in each month's *IP*. An Archivist must be appointed, and reports from the Task Forces sent to the entire SCHC membership. Telephone prayer chains should continue, as should the quarterly publication of (newsletter) *Companions Along the Way*. Also this group recommended forming an Ad Hoc Committee to plan for the 1984 centennial.

4) <u>Task Force on Chapters</u>, Rowena Thompson chairing: a strong emphasis on strengthening chapters included the suggestion that each chapter re-read and discuss the Rule annually. All chapters should participate in sending nominations for offices local and national, and inform themselves about the tasks and roles to be filled. It was recommended that *Sister Chapters* be inaugurated, a lateral focus intended to broaden loyalty and community among Companions beyond one's own chapter. [This recommendation was similar to the the early 21st c. effort toward Cross-Chapter Companionship. It apparently met the same lack of interest and response as the more recent attempt.][50]

5) <u>Task Force on Sponsors / Probationers</u>, Katharine Merigold chairing: a printed booklet of guidelines for both roles (non-existent before) was mandated. The debate continued over whether the probationary period before admission should be two years or three.

At the **Executive Board** meeting, a <u>Management Task Force</u> was appointed for implementing the changes in buildings and arrangements; the costs for printing the *Blue Book* [Companion Directory], quarterly publications, and selected Conference papers were entered in the budget; a professionally designed brochure was recommended. "Let's get going on hiring a Secretary for the Society to keep the official records of membership and dues." (Four of the five Task Forces had recommended this expenditure as a step toward

---

50 Ibid. 82, 84-89.

regularizing and coordinating the Society's business and administrative records.) Ruth Leonard was appointed archivist; IRS had resolved the Tax issue so the Society was no longer in danger of

losing its exempt status; the earnings of the RMWilson bequest were to be invested, since SCHC had become free to change or reinvest capital funds. Finally, a use had been found for no-longer-needed enamel washbasins, pitchers, and pails with covers: they could be sent to a hospital in Thailand!

A summary report on this historic Conference, by Susanna Cockrell, C-in-C Elect, acknowledged the very human fear of new ways, and the huge need for <u>workers</u> in the church and our Society: "our symbol should be a packed suitcase." Also a plea for flexibility in the process of changing: "Let's not be encumbered by strangling regulations."[51]

Companion Mary Morrison led a remarkable Bible study; in her oral history she recalled planning it in the awareness that all "the possible stuffinesses" of which we are capable "might coalesce around the question 'do we change, or don't we?'" [This may well have been one of her scriptural studies later printed as a pamphlet by Pendle Hill, the Quaker Retreat Center in Philadelphia, titled "Re-Conciliation, the Hidden Hyphen."] Her focus was Biblical warnings against destructive religious attitudes such as "Phariseeism"—the danger of falling into legalisms that an organization confronting an unknown, fearsome future might fall into. She wanted Companions to see that Jesus' paradoxical statements offer a new dimension on the subject of conflict. Afterwards, a Companion said to her,

---

51 *Annual Report* 1974, 133-4.

"the Holy Spirit was speaking through you. I know it because I was borne up."[52]

On the final evening, the Executive Council viewed a film *The Supper*, dramatizing ways of dealing with the first two "blocks" (self-satisfaction and inability to handle conflict) in C-in-C Lewitin's Opening Paper. She dismissed the conference, saying: "all things are possible with faith...but most of us are too scared to try, most of the time."

"In the closing (August) moments, we sat quietly listening to a brief, much needed rain, a report on disposition of the young cat sent to the Oblate Center by happy chance, and Florence Risley's suspense-filled letter regarding Adelynrood mosquitoes...Through these long two days in the Oblate chapel, the Council has been uplifted by the prayer vigil other Companions were holding... [signed] Margaret Sheets, Recording Secretary."

Companion Evening featured Janet Morgan's rhymed parody titled "Got a Little List," drawn from Gilbert and Sullivan's *The Mikado*. It was a witty allusion to the list that had been delivered to the new C-in-C at this meeting—names already decided on by the outgoing leadership team that they wanted her to appoint. The lyrics convey an implicit "we" vs. "they" stance, a disquieting portent.

> We had to have a list—
> of Companions so endearing
> Of theology so sound,
> They simply must be kissed!
> Who ever could resist.

Then a more direct verse:

> There's Jan and Ethel everywhere attending to our needs;
> And if they sometimes o-so-gently slap us on the wrist,
> They still are on the list
> of Companions to be kissed.
> We'll keep them on the list,
> velvet glove in iron fist!
> They will all of them be kissed,

52 JBG, Oral History of Mary Morrison, 1996, 61-63.

Each <u>one</u> of them be kissed.
(An obvious rhyme from a different mindset might substitute the word "kissed" with "missed.")

Second verse:

Our So-ci-e-ty was founded
By a gal named Em-i-ly;
A fervent feminist,
She heads our little list!
And we hope that up in Paradise
She's happy now to see—her principles persist...
Oh Boy (whoops, we mean), O GIRLS, do they persist...

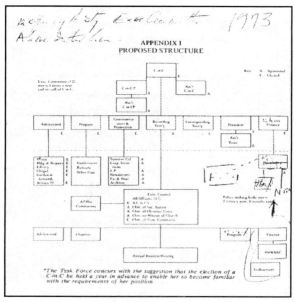

Draft of Reorganization

(top) 1982 Admissions;
(center and bottom)
candids of various
Companions.

Chapter 7

1975–1984
SCHC's 100th Birthday

**"[Let us] march breast-forward,
praying to be flexible in adapting."**

EMM 1904 quote, cited by Lewitin in 1973 Opening Paper[1]

Socio-Historical Overview and Background

The crisis summer of 1974 launched the process of Society renewal from within. And, as with any spiritual triumph, the immediate aftermath brought trouble and temptation—as surely as Jesus' 40 days in the wilderness followed his Baptism. The human drama among Companions at the 1975 Adelynrood summer program was the organizational arena where signs of strain appeared. Deep intra-Societal preoccupation was evident in several ways; there were fewer invocations of Vida Scudder's name and influence, and there were beginning plans for the Centennial Observance.[2] Scudder's name appeared rarely in *Annual Reports* or *IP*s until **1984**, when the selection of her autobiographical title *On Journey* was chosen as the fitting theme for Centennial. And C-in-C Margaret Ann Young would invoke VDS's name in connection with the outreach fund

---

1 *Annual Report* 1973, 9.

2 Unless I have missed it, Scudder's name was hardly visible until the 1986 Companion Conference Opening Paper by C-in-C Nan Clarkson, who contrasted the outreach stances of EMM and VDS. She cited VDS as saying: "Social Intercession may be the mightiest force in the world." And herself added, "To which EMM would have said 'Amen.'" *Annual Report* 1986, 13.

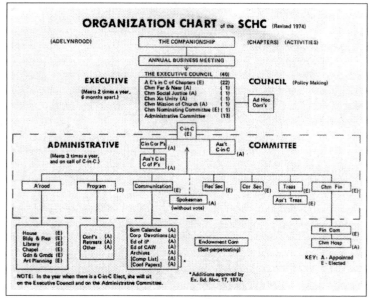

Reorganization

named for her at the **1984 Companion Conference**.[3] By 1986, Vida Scudder would again be referred to as co-founder. Organizational anxiety and determination to put the Society's house in order (in both senses of that phrase) seemed to assume dominance in the Society at this juncture.

During this organizational reshaping, the Society's internal operations were "at once graced by God and tormented by the evil one," to quote a figure of speech from a veteran Companion. Companion Day processions and other Adelynrood rituals continued seamlessly, partially masking the tensions surrounding Susanna Cockrell, elected C-in-C from 1975-79, and her successor, Helen Turnbull, 1980-84. "In memory at least, it seemed there was an awful battle of wills, though conducted mostly out of public view," observed another veteran of the 1974 Task Forces. "We saw individual Companions at their best and at their worst, almost simultaneously."[4]

---

3 *Annual Report* 1984, 11,34.

4 Companions interviewed are, in alphabetical order, Nan Clarkson, Susanna Cockrell, Dorothy Pillsbury, Violet Porter, Joan Russell, Betty Sawyer, Eleanor Spinney, Peg Tyson, Helen White, plus others in general conversation. Any omitted names are unintentional. No comment is identified by

Yet any perspective on this historical breakpoint must begin with acknowledging the power of that decision. Keeping Adelynrood closed the summer of 1974 was an essential step in the Society's history. Interrupting routine, especially one that is spiritually grounded, strikes deeply. During the 1974-84 decade, many Companions had recently emerged from their domestic lives into weekday jobs, and were inexperienced in hardheaded organizational actions, although they could see the merits of a summer's self examination toward renewal. Thus the actual shutting down of Adelynrood "registered 14.9 on the Richter scale," one Companion recalled. The leaders' preemptive strike had plunged the Society into revitalization, ready or not.

The succeeding leadership team found itself pinned between those eager to implement the new plans for the Society, and those who would cling to their former influence in the reconstruction.

A graph of the Society's first century reveals the usual peaks and valleys. The first peak, after the uncertainty following Emily's death, came in Companion-in-Charge Virginia Huntington's 1959 restatement of SCHC meaning and vow, during the 75th **Companion Conference**. From there, the organization gradually seemed to head downward toward what would be the 1974 crisis. After 1974, the momentum reversed and headed generally upward during the rest of the 20th century. This study began in response to C-in-C Joan Melvin's 1990s request that lessons gleaned from the 1974 crisis be investigated. The Society's halting steps toward financial independence and 20th century business practices were an important element in this revitalization. Nan Clarkson's analysis of the SCHC financial evolution (*The SCHC's Spiritual Autobiography of Money*, unpublished paper 1995) was the indispensable building block for this understanding.

Tracing the internal evolution of SCHC amid the external events surrounding and shaping it appears to locate the Society's hybrid

name for Companionly reasons.

organizational structure as its major gift and challenge. Its two organizational imperatives—human relationships committed to a spiritually-bonded community while continuing to live in a complex day-to-day world, and preserving the intercessory prayer vow amid evolving attitudes toward organizational authority and women's self-expectations—required, continues to require, constant adaptation. The ideal of intercession, a focus on others and on societal ills, was a perfect fit for churchwomen craving a serious religious role at the end of the 1800s. It offered a spiritual means of protesting the exploitative arrangements in their urban New England context, and gave them permission to reach into others' lives in the "real world." It also gave them an organized community or sisterhood from which to prod their church (and other Christians) toward realizing God's promises in the here-and-now.

At the beginning of the 20th c., those original Companion retreats and study conferences had been groundbreaking, life-giving, radical. But keeping that framework static through the 20th century inevitably allowed personality issues to emerge and become predominant, over and through any *organizational* issues. In the mid-1950s, intense exploration of the psychology of religious experience led Companions toward a new angle of vision and a more intense focus on spiritual practices, diverting some of the energy formerly focused on the external social issues. For example, liturgical additions included once again having a holy water basin for crossing one's self at the entrance to chapel for symbolic cleansing and gesture of devotion. The sanctuary had been renovated to feature a free-standing altar. Without consciously downgrading emphasis on external-world problems, cultivating the personal "internal" spiritual ground assumed prominence in Companion programs and intercessions, perhaps serving as a refuge from those complex world problems.

With the highest of motives, the 1950-60s Companionship unwittingly prepared the ground for the 1974 crisis by embracing the preoccupation with psychology and the internal self-analysis of white, middle class, educated Episcopalians. In part this may well have been a factor in Companions' lack of attendance at Social Justice conferences. Also, the former view of foreign missions, earlier a vital enlarging force in Companions thinking, had changed. It began to reflect the new, anthropologically enlightened lens on distant peoples and their cultures, allowing the powerful vocation of foreign mission work to shift from center stage. At the same time, the former objects of Anglo foreign missions, countries in Africa and Asia, were impatiently freeing themselves from European and American colonial ties. Some Episcopalians and the SCHC itself would see the Peace Corps and Vista as updated versions of what once was heroized as missionary work.

Meanwhile, outside the Society, processes of rule breaking, barrier dropping, and shifts in meaning permeated the American 1960s culture. The Society's organizational fabric, congealed in internal practices, had remained inelastic despite the ever-widening horizons brought into the Society through Companion intercessions. A key symbol of Adelynrood rigidity, particularly disconcerting to new Companions initially visiting the "motherhouse," was the arbitrary dining-room arrangement that had its origins in the

The Dining Room at Adelynrood, 1950s.

monastic tradition. Adelynrood dining room tables were arranged in a horseshoe. On either side of the C-in-C, seated in the center, chairs were assigned according to hierarchy in the administrative team. Food was formally served by waitresses; there were no unassigned chairs, implying unwelcome to newcomers. This physical pattern alone was sharply out of sync with the mood in their exterior world: it was a visible expression of restrictive norms for Companionship. That message projected through furniture arrangement sounds ludicrous in the early 21ˢᵗ century, but its impact on the spiritual and emotional landscape of SCHC in post-1960s culture was profound, even destructive.

The crisis of 1974 broke open this outmoded "asymmetry." In her final ***Annual Report* (1975)**, C-in-C Lewitin suggested "keeping Adelynrood closed during '74 was likely the most important decision the Society had <u>ever</u> taken."[5] Whether or not hindsight can affirm that assessment, she and her administrative team had not reckoned on their personal and psychic investment in the revolutionary movement they had loosed. Though subsequent organizational adjustments were incremental rather than dramatic, there could be no turning back. Change itself felt explosive.

By the 1970s, the larger US culture and the Society's expectations of its members had absorbed the ideal of "participatory democracy," as it was then called, a phrase emerging from President Lyndon Johnson's "war on poverty" conducted through neighborhood groups. Participants in such groups were encouraged to, and began to expect, speaking out in discussions and voting on decisions. This produced a range of voices expressing previously unheard or ignored views. The "monarchical" tone, an adjective several Companions invoked, of the pre-1974 leadership in the SCHC and other organizations would no longer be possible, or desirable. What today would be called "high-handed" had been unconstrained in pre-1974 administrative custom. One Companion repeated, over

---

5 *Annual Report* 1975, 71.

and over, that the early 1970s Society was "just very different from today's—it was a whole different world." Several Companions recalled struggling to accept the reigning assumption that administrative authority was the rightful property of the executive team, the Society's "central nervous system." Outside the circle of Companions immediately involved in Adelynrood, the majority of Companions were left to observe and wonder at internal relations "where all the action was." There was obsessive interest in "who was appointed to what role, and by whom."[6]

A financial factor had indeed been part of the 1974 crisis. An audit had found "the wrong box had been checked on an IRS statement," a mistake threatening SCHC's tax-exempt status. Several years of legal fees to untangle this issue exacted a frightening toll on the Society's finances. Fortunately, after several years, the tax status was clarified. But worries about money—that the Society would slip into insolvency—gave concrete weight to members' general disquiet, and fueled the sense of disjunction between Companion aspiration and Adelynrood community life.

The 1972 challenge delivered to the Companion Council (launching the 1973 Task Force I analysis) had accused Companions of "hypocrisy in the area of race." Companions were resting on their founders' laurels, it appeared: what was the Society's contribution to the blatant racial injustice that "good women" had allowed to exist in our cities, churches, and nation? In the published (*Annual Report*) version of this challenge, the lament about financial fears was distinctly secondary. One long-time Companion explained that inner-circle management then edited all printed reports, the public face of the Society: "Of course it [financial inadequacy] had to be cleaned-up for the *Annual Report*!" Companions in that era, thinking of themselves as dutiful churchwomen, were expected to accept the charge of moral hypocrisy about race more readily than the charge of financial irresponsibility. The "women's movement"

---

6 Companion interviews, 2002-3.

consciousness just penetrating the external culture had not yet assimilated the idea that women could or should be as financially sophisticated as men.

Any organizational change that releases positive energies also frees vigorous negative dynamics. Temptation immediately challenges a spiritual or secular victory. One chaplain to the Society employed the harsh word "demonic" when describing internal Society responses in the immediate post-crisis years. Hurtful verbal exchanges, open rudeness in the dining room, unapologetic cold-shouldering of a Companion, and other "un-Companionly" actions were recalled. Bruised relationships proliferated.

Companions who lived through the post-Task Force era between 1974-1978 wonder, today, why so few of them had felt free to address "un-Companionly" actions. One likely factor was the less-democratic ethos that had prevailed before 1974. After all, as one Companion noted, when a Society has had *one* C-in-C who, "for all her graciousness and generosity, ruled pretty much single-handed during its first forty years," the pattern of autocratic governing was something that had to be "gotten beyond." And this involved sweeping out ingrained assumption—"how WE do things." A second factor was an opposite, mediating influence: group-dynamics concepts, widely disseminated in the 1970s, helped accredit evolutionary change instead of arbitrary rule. Group conflict could be talked out, negotiated, made less destructive. Companions could learn to be "forthright" instead of inhibited and ostensibly "nice." In that light, the leaders of the 1974 crisis were beacons of the ongoing cultural evolution. They saw themselves as (and were) invigorators, explorers, re-directers, and boundary-stretchers. Historically and theologically, their actions were the hand of God in SCHC organizational history.

The image of themselves as God's handmaidens played into the departing team's unwillingness to relinquish leadership to their successors. Despite its essential, reviving effect, the aftermath of the

1974 crisis dramatized the personal attempting to overrule the organizational process. Formerly elected authority, cloaked in a language of spirituality and prayer, was caught in its own "iron cage," the brilliant metaphor of bureaucratic inflexibility and implacable leadership coined by early 20th century sociologist Max Weber.

The field of organizational dynamics offers another illuminating perspective on this tense time in SCHC organizational history. "A tradition is often most successfully sustained by those who appear to be trying to attack or destroy it." In Western religious history, for example, one can argue that Saints Francis and Dominic were rescuers of institutional Christianity at a time when the Christian movement's expansive potential seemed exhausted, "all but beyond renewal." But an appeal to the monastic movement's founding ethos and traditions—or in the case of SCHC, the 1972 call to revitalize social justice activism and membership responsibility—contained both the power to renew the Society, or to pull it apart. Fortunately, "tradition" as lodged in human memory is malleable rather than fixed; a return to (or rediscovery of) "origins" at a crisis point may alter and reinvigorate the dynamic that originally inspired those origins. In effect, a challenge that threatens potential destruction may be the very "attack" that transforms and updates the past, producing new hope. And the outcome, in the medieval monastic movement as well as in this late-20th century Companionship, honors the "attackers," articulators of dissatisfaction and challenge. They turn out to be crucial agents of change.[7]

When the Society's 1975-79 leadership team began implementing the 1974 Task Force recommendations, the major organizational step involved hiring, for the first time, two paid part-time staff: Companions to serve as Adelynrood Director combined with Program Coordinator, [and later] a Secretary of the Society. The first goal was to present a new external face of the Society supported by a new administrative cohesion—a step rife with possi-

---

7   "Culture on the Market," by Charles Rosen, NY Review of Books, Nov 6, 2003, 70.

bilities for disagreement. Various tense encounters between the former and newly elected leaders attempted to shape those official acts. "Susanna [Cockrell, Companion-in-Charge] hung on that cross a long time," one Task Force member said, "alongside Elsa [Walberg], Dottie [Guild], and Victoria [Wells]" the first Society-paid staff. "As I have come to see it, Susanna's courage and faithfulness served SCHC crucially."[8] In historic overview, acknowledging that Companions were capable of unCompanionly behavior toward each other seems an essential step in any conflict resolution. Yet, another Companion disagreed; she wanted to overlook "personality issues" and minimize recollected tensions; "why bring up that old stuff?" Preserving a surface of organizational harmony, retrospectively, could mask the competitiveness that had burdened the Society's central management.

Today this period of anxious confrontation can be recognized as the very seed-bed of the Society's late-20th c. growth. In the edited *Letters* of EMM, the word "reconciliation" was indexed only in relation to the 1920s-30s social class inequities: economic injustice. In the last two decades of the 20th century, the reconciliation preoccupying the Society was internal: adjustments to organizational and personnel displacement, defining and assimilating what was "new," integrating differing ideas of how Companions thought of themselves and relations with their church, and finally, facing how *"financially naïve"* the Society had allowed itself to be—the exasperated expression of a veteran Companion. None of those elements could be changed until they were exposed and confronted. In the late 1970s, Companion Elsa Walberg arranged a face-to-face meeting of past and present leaders with the goal of reconciliation. A Companion named it the contemporary version of Jacob-wres-

---

8 Interpretation: Those three Companions were (sequentially) the initiators (some called them "sacrificial lambs") beginning to develop the first paid positions--at a time when the Society's own expectations of those roles was just emerging, when finances were uncertain, and when undermining the new leadership was not fully repressed. (The quote expressing that confusion was "the Queen is dead! Long Live the Queen!") Societal agony in the racial desegregation struggle and the dispute over women's ordination were also profound crises converging on all church members, not just Companions.

tling-with-the-Angel, when Jacob finally "wrested" a sacramental blessing from that encounter. That, and a reinvigorated social justice outreach, began to move SCHC toward the millennium; by the year 2000, the Society would look back to see itself fully entered into the Computer Age.

With Adelynrood "hospitality" (in the larger sense) freed from its former rigidity, and with a Program Committee that combined the former Program Coordination and Summer Calendar tasks, the administrative role and influence of the Companion-in-Charge within the Society was naturally reconfigured more democratically. The decade from 1974-1984 would see SCHC concentrate on deepening and developing the structural changes initiated in the "crisis summer" and building renewed Companion optimism about its future.

Chronological Overview from Newsletters and Intercession Papers

1975—

The 1975 Spring Conference, consciously planned by the Washington (DC) Chapter to "bridge" the Companionship into new expectations, was a first step in reconciliation. Two stunning Conference papers addressed the ethos emerging within the Society and in the larger church. African-American lay leader Verna Dozier presented "In Search of a Theology of Liberation, " and Companion Marianne Micks, "Jesus Means Freedom." (summarized)

Dozier began by locating Christianity's roots in slavery, even though Christ's salvation is freedom *from* slavery.

> The history of institutional Christianity is "a dreary record of the flight *from* freedom"...The church, often the handmaiden of the culture rather than its prophet, rears up in resistance to anything new. "Even so, there is a new Reformation breaking all around us!" And "the oppressed are always the Chosen."

> Her readings from the theology of liberation brought new voices into Companion consciousness: African-American professor James Cone (Union Theological Seminary in NYC), Martin Luther King Jr., Frederick Herzog's study of the Gospel of John titled *Liberation Theology*, and

Professor Letty Russell (Yale Divinity School) whose exciting *Human Liberation in a Feminist Perspective - A Theology* introduced that topic. Freedom means journeying with others toward God's future, Dozier commended. She aimed to arm Companions for their own changes. "God is ahead of us, sisters; yesterday's manna is no food today. The liberation theologians promise that life won't be less difficult, but it will become more meaningful."[9]

Micks' opening image was the colossal, deep muscle stre-e-e-tch of a prisoner just released from his handcuffs—the very image appropriate for Companions at this juncture.

What does Jesus free us from? from the law, conformity, being automatons, sin, and from death. British poet and priest John Donne chose to have his last portrait painted in his actual coffin and "winding sheet," which evokes for Companions the phrase from our official prayer, "fashioned after His life-giving death." Each of us is given "New Being as an Easter gift." But none can be free until my sister, generically speaking, has the circumstantial freedom to be both airplane pilot and stewardess, to be ordained and lay, till black mothers have equal opportunities with white mothers. We can't "go home" till then. Thirty years ago that very week, German anti-Nazi theologian Dietrich Bonhoeffer had been martyred. Micks quoted from a translation of his last poem, "Stations on the Way to Freedom"—

"Bravely take hold of the real, not dallying with what might be.
Not in the flight of ideas but only in action, is freedom.
Make up your mind and come out into the tempest of living."[10]

At C-in-C Lewitin's final **Companion Conference (1975)** (theme: *Renewal*), she noted that having held the **1974 Companion Conference** in a different setting proved that Companionship was a *community of relationships* rather than only a *place*. And the Society's joy in returning to the beloved retreat house was more than multiplied. Summarizing the Task Force recommendations, she warned that SCHC could not continue to exist without more realistic money management and better social justice outreach. However, she also quoted a recent clergy visitor at Adelynrood who had made an observation typifying the religious climate in the church at large

---

9 *Annual Report* 1975.

10 *Annual Report* 1975.

Companion Day Procession

during the 1970's: "[Companions] are exciting. They make no bones about their prayer life, they're anything but embarrassed about it... it is the source of their electricity about involvement in Social Justice."[11] In 2005 it seems surprising that, as recently as 1975, women's public praying and spiritual leadership at a retreat house could be thought of as "embarrassing."[12]

Modernized communications were essential, first the use of bulk mail rates, then creating a slide-and-tape presentation of the Task Force recommendation for chapters, and a telephone Emergency Prayer Chain to function between *IP*s. The Program employee would be paid full-time for 6 months, and halftime for 6 months; program fees at Adelynrood would be raised to $16 per day. A newsletter to be titled *Companions Along the Way* would henceforth be published quarterly, two annual issues as "action sheets" (reporting Society activities), and two filled with personal and chapter news of Companions. Lewitin concluded with a typically wry observation about clothing styles of the day: the pattern of men dressing like women, during Jesus' time, was being reversed. Women today were beginning to dress like men. (Wearing slacks to the evening meal at Adelynrood was still a new trend.)[13] A major step toward solid organization and SCHC administration saw Companion Joan Russell hired as paid Secretary of the Society.

In the *IP*s of 1975, while organizational retooling proceeded,

concerns outside the Society named the miseries of unemployment due to closed factories and businesses, food stamp injustices
in the Texas Department of Public Welfare, Medicare funding, and
the establishment of a National Center for Child Abuse. Petitions
were offered opposing the harassment of American Indians by
removing their children to government schools, for the Boston
school desegregation conflict, and the Fresh Air Program sending
inner city children to families in the countryside for two weeks.
Thanksgivings were offered for women peacemakers in Ireland
and Lebanon, and for captioned television programs to assist the
deaf. Petitions were offered about the Attica prison riot and more
enlightened prison management generally, plus restraining po-
lice violence against black citizens in Detroit. Gradually expanding ecological awareness produced petitions for protecting public
"green places," Alaska's unspoiled wilderness, the Heritage Trust
of national cultural and historical resources, and special concern
over water, air, and soil pollution.

A combination of social-class and ecological consciousness
produced this vivid petition: "stab our consciences awake regarding strip mining and bare hills," and the consequent destruction of
underground aquifers.

1976—

The **Companion Conference** theme was *Building Community.*
Margaret Ann Young, chairman of the *Finance Committee*, "delivered a message of great seriousness" concerning the '75-76 budget.
Her expressed determination was to make ALL Companions aware
of their financial responsibility. She reported the need to generate
$50,000 more each year, and called on Companions to face that re-
ality. The idea that SCHC was "wealthy," which had been allowed
to take root during EMM's years of underwriting Society expenses,
must be dispelled! The newly hired part-time Program Coordinator,
Companion Dottie Guild, was familiarizing adjacent dioceses and

clergy with the Society and Adelynrood through her visits to ECW and YWCA meetings, with the goal of creating a new base of potential visitors and facility-renters.[14]

In the *IP*s, there were many social justice issues. Special petitions were offered for "a change of heart" in South African apartheid, as well as for relief in the desperate lives of those still enslaved by conditions throughout Africa; another petition prayed that native Indians and Eskimos be exempt from the ban on whaling because of food needs, another that intolerance toward homosexuality begin to yield. Companion prayers protested the costs of "hyper-expensive weapons development" such as the B1 Bomber, the wrongs of drug companies trying to unload defective products on third-world countries, and that the national "Trade Commission [would] support restrictive legislation against the 25,000 annual television commercials aimed at kids." A petition also urged a "sunshine" law allowing oversight of legislation in the making. Further ecological concerns brought petitions for more responsible stewardship of public parks, and protecting Alaska's unspoiled wilderness from roads and exploratory oil drilling.

During the nation's Bicentennial celebrations, Elsa Walberg chaired the **Companion Conference** and Mary Morrison led one of her renowned Bible Studies on surrendering hypocrisy, promoting intra-Society healing and reconciliation. Companion-in-Charge Susanna Cockrell's Opening Paper suggested the Rule of St. Benedict for Companions' guidebook in rebuilding community within the Society. Priscilla Martin accepted editing of *Companions Along the Way* (later called *Newsletter*). A long poem by Ann Weems celebrated the institutional Church in glowing tones that reflected the optimism generated through liturgical renewal and changes in the *Book of Common Prayer*.

---

14 Organization Chart, 1975 *Annual Report*, 162.

1977—

In the **Spring** *Companions Along the Way*, (Vol. 3 #4), the Virginia Chapter reported educating themselves in the legislative processes necessary to pass laws for social issues. The Rev. Fletcher Lower, with the Ecumenical Social Concerns Alliance in Richmond, led them through the process of revising the juvenile code to handle problems brought before the courts affecting children and families. The *Committee on Missions* announced its first conference on the topic of Aging.

In the article "Is the SCHC Exclusive?" a self-analytic concern was addressed. This topic had not appeared in the print record since the 1950s, an indication that the Task Force mandate to "open up" the Society was being taken seriously. Should an unrestricted number of Probationers be in the works at one time? Should anyone interested in SCHC be welcomed into Companionship? Would either or both of these policies endanger or "dilute" the Companionship? Is it exclusive, even perhaps unchristian, to limit the growth of SCHC? AND what is the Society's mission? Acknowledging an earlier time when Companions did not "talk" openly about SCHC, Companion Peg Davison wrote that SCHC was no more a "secret society" in the past than it is now.

However, Companionship is a vocation, a commitment beyond and separate from all other involvements. It is a commitment to prayer, especially to thanksgiving and intercession, plus to Social Justice, Mission, and Ecumenism. Beyond those vows and aims, it is far more a commitment in Christ to each other in a special way, so that each is strengthened by the whole to do her individual work for God, better than she might otherwise be able to do it. The customary caution recalled from EMM warned 20th century Companions and the Society against trying to be "avant garde" and getting caught in each passing wave of excitement. At the same time the Society must make sure not to get caught in mere "comfortable repetition." The Task Force years "forced us to tear apart, look, and consider how we were made. The reconciliation now in progress should allow us to fulfill our mission, reconciled. By loving [each other], and living the Companion prayer each day, we [will] lose the need to be self-conscious."[15]

In the published *Annual Report*, the **Companion Conference** theme *Ecumenical Awareness* also promoted openness within the SCHC. Companion-in-Charge Susanna Cockrell's Opening Paper highlighted the danger of "denominational idolatry," a phrase coined by Companion Cynthia Wedel from her experience as the

---

15 Spring *Newsletter* 1977,7

first woman president of the World Council of Churches. Also, Cockrell enlisted various Companions to offer a paragraph about the Society that would complete the phrase "I celebrate"... Kay Whittier, Helen Heers, Frances Young, Fran Sydnor, Lucy Acock, Alice Lewitin, Hilda Davis, Aileen Rucker, Joan Russell, Keyo Russell, Ruth Leonard, Polly Wiley, and Phebe Hoff—five of these Companions are still living, at this writing.

Seminar topics were: *Unity, Relations between Anglicans/Roman Catholics/the Orthodox; Unity and Social Justice; Unity and the Mission of the Church; Christian Unity in the World;* and *Jewish-Christian Relations.* The Rev. Dr. Tom Govan, a college chaplain, presented "The Rejection of Denominational Idolatry."

The Treasurer's Report was another shared presentation, Rowena Thompson having enlisted eight Companions, all voices from various geographical locations and representing different lengths of time in the Society, to say briefly what <u>they</u> valued about the Companionship: Jo Bishop, Nan Clarkson, Peg Davison, Priscilla Howe, Edith Neide, Nicki Nielsen, Alma Paradise, Isabel Phisterer, Dorothy

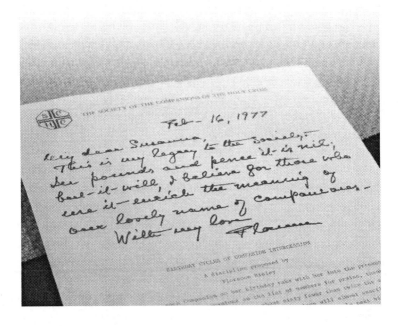

Pillsbury, and Dorothy Worrell. The former lecture-style Companion presentations were definitely changing.

Companion Day brought the delight of singing Florence Converse's hymn saluting Founders "Ad-el-lyn, Em-i-ly" to the familiar tune *O Quanta Qualia*. Florence Risley introduced her "birthday-prayer round," a simple, profound means of connecting Companions throughout the Society. Starting on one's own birthday, a Companion prays for two Companions each day, following the alphabetic listing in the Blue Book [membership directory] "[This is] my legacy to the Society: in pounds and pence it is nil," she wrote C-in-C Cockrell. "But it will, I believe, for those who use it, enrich the meaning of our lovely name 'Companions'...[a name] by now fairly widely used [known], and appreciated."[16] The **Business Meeting** ratified a policy statement about the new phenomenon of women-clergy Companions: they were to be treated the same as any other clergy, no special rates; it also affirmed a balance be maintained between women and men celebrants of Eucharist in Adelynrood chapel.[17]

The *Finance Committee* reported only a $6,000 deficit, and departing Finance Chairman Margaret Ann Young said: "In spite of ever-increasing costs in House maintenance and in carrying out the Society's enlarged activities, the year ended with a positive balance. And SCHC stock holdings are now being evaluated in terms of 'socially-responsible guidelines.'" There was a conference on *Healing*, one on *Aging*, and one on *Intensive Journaling*, plus a seminar on CG Jung's psychology, "*The Unconscious as a Source of Religious Experience*," topics reflecting the cultural as well as Societal consciousness.

IP petitions focused on the victims of Jim Jones and the Jonestown massacre in Guyana, the revolt in Iran, the "boat people" from Cambodia and Vietnam, promoting a ban on handguns, and Muslim fanaticism against Christians. A petition asked "that objections to the Clean Air Act and the Environmental Protection Agency

---

16 Archive, Companion Risley to C-in-C Cockrell.
17 *Annual Report* 1977, 57.

be seen as phony," and that the family continue to be held up as "the pillar of American Society." There were thanksgivings for a book on jailed juveniles *(Weeping in the Playtime of Others,* by Kenneth Wooden), efforts to solve the Boston school desegregation conflict, and for the work of Roman Catholic inner city missions rescuing street kids and addicts. One petition prayed that elections should be publicly funded in order to close off the undue influence of huge donors! Petitions were offered for the Job Corps, for a peace treaty between Israel and Egypt, for the *Bread for the World* program, and the *Fortune Society* working in New York City prisons, and that the New York City public school teachers would not go on strike.

1978—

The **Winter** *Companions Along the Way* (Vol. 4 #2) contained several items explaining new procedures emanating from the 1974 structural revisions, in particular the function of a "Companion–in–Charge Elect" while the current Companion–in–Charge had another year left in her term. The reasoning behind that change, quoted from the **Annual Report 1973**, was to provide the incoming C-in-C a time of "becoming acquainted with the situation in which she will function"—a common practice in many organizations and one intended to reduce friction between leadership teams in the SCHC. The *Library Committee,* Lee Beaty chairman, announced the purchase of "more than twenty new books not dependent for their appeal upon sex, scatology, or simmering scandal."

In the **1978 Companion Conference** (theme *Discipleship: Called to Become*), C-in-C Susanna Cockrell's Opening Paper acknowledged a climate of "rough feelings and torn loyalties in the years since 1974," and nominated compassion for the "active ingredient in the Society's new solidarity." In a Society like SCHC, she said, any belief that "everything should be *just fine* could only be illusion." Some Companions worried that Probationers ought not be exposed to intra-Society tensions and hurt feelings, lest it dampen their enthusiasm. Others were saying that spiritual growth is dependent on the grace to know and face reality honestly.

Henri Nouwen, a new spiritual authority among the male voices being cited by Companions in their thinking and writings, was recommended as Companions tried to reexamine their vocation around the mandate of "leadership." In this year of "tremendous learnings," a first conference openly named the topic of sexuality: "The Church Addresses Issues of Human Sexuality," led by the Rev. Bill Doubleday. And a complete list of Committees in the newly revised organizational structure filled the final pages (119-121) of the **Annual Report**. A new financial policy established the Society's responsibility to cover costs incurred by Companions fulfilling Society jobs: money must be no barrier to accepting leadership roles in the Society. Of course, tight budgets made voluntary reimbursement of their expenses by individual Companions very welcome. Before 1975, Companions had been expected to pay their own way.[18]

In the *Committee Reports* section, Companion Fi Mithoefer submitted a tidy summary of the concrete changes in custom and practice that she had experienced during her time of being a Companion. Since her 1970 entry into the Society, the authoritative, rule-bound culture at Adelynrood was consciously giving way to more informality and an open, welcoming attitude toward outsiders, visitors, and newcomers...quoted in its entirety.

-*from* meals with cloth napkins, and neat young table-service maids in white uniforms, *to* buffet style, the tables unset, no place mats;

-*from* Companions being expected to keep their own rooms clean for the next resident, *to* a hired cleaning service;

-*from* having one Adelynrood Hostess for an entire month, *to* three per week, allowing for a relaxed work schedule;

-*from* trying to serve as servants to incoming conferees, *to* allowing them "to take care of themselves" [giving them more freedom of space, choice, and movement];

-*from* a single House chairperson in charge of housekeeping arrangements for all five months, *to* allowing others to help by filling in during various parts of summer;

---

18 *Annual Report* 1978, upset feelings, 26; compassion, 76; sexuality, 119-121.

-from volunteers expected to work seven days per week, *to* a 6-day week with the House closed each Monday, allowing for rest and preparation for incoming conferences;

-from the ritual of daily tea at 4 p.m., after which Companions scurried to their rooms for a quick [alcoholic] drink, *to* a pleasant 5 p.m. gathering that includes wine, juice, etc.— This was <u>the</u> hottest issue I faced, when I became Chair of the House Committee.

(signed) Fi Mithoefer, *Chairperson, House Committee*

To her *Before and After* list, she added this reflection: "When I entered the SCHC in 1970, I was scared stiff the whole weekend; women in little white caps [prayer head-coverings to be worn in chapel in place of then-still-required hats in church] seemed more eager to point out my deviations from the rule than in welcoming me. I didn't even notice the beautiful pictures, the brass candlesticks!

"We've become friendlier: now we let guests open a window, or close it; whereas I was told that only the Chair of the House Committee could open or close a window! We let them choose their own seat at meals, and I sat in a wrong seat at the horseshoe table!" She concluded with a philosophical sentence: "Change is always going on: it will never be like the past, but there will always indeed be peace, quiet, prayer, and play here...we who work here give it *'our whole hearts' best'* [a phrase from the Adelynrood grace sung at mealtimes]."[19]

IP petitions that year included a prayer for a racially quiet summer, and the international relief program OXFAM. Petitions also asked that racism in the USA, on the rise, "be reversed through educational progress and changed prejudicial thought patterns." There were prayers for President Carter's visit to local anti-poverty programs, for more research into non-petroleum-based energy supplies, for Middle East peace talks between Begin and Sadat,

---

19 Ibid, 37-38.

and against subsidies for tobacco growers. Petitions were also offered for the murdered Archbishop Romero, the inner city ministry of Catholic worker Dorothy Day, and for the international disarmament movement. There was a prayer for the Diocese of Southwest Florida as it dealt with Cuban refugees, for a treaty against genocide, and against the brutality and mistreatment rampant in Central America. Thanksgivings were offered for honors awarded the late Martin Luther King Jr.

1979—

In the **Spring Companions Along the Way**, the lead article announced a Social Justice conference for the coming summer, its goal to equip Companions for practical involvement. EMM's words from a 1909 conference on the same topic cited her caution against denominational idolatry and spiritual pride: "The longer space [here allotted] to...the work of the Protestant Episcopal Church [in this report] is due to no claim that such work has greater intrinsic importance than that of other communions, but...that the first duty of the Society is [was] to know in detail what is going on in its own body." A special focus on world hunger was announced, plus The International Year of the Child.

The *Annual Report* announced that Helen Turnbull, an experienced educational administrator who had directed the Windham House Program in N.Y. City [for women graduate students entering church professions], was elected to succeed Susanna Cockrell. Victoria Wells left the paid job as SCHC Program Coordinator to seek ordination. C-in-C Cockrell's Opening Paper used the image of *forced growth* as the metaphor for the Society's recent past. *'The Society crossed a threshold when we started over in 1975, after the Task Forces* [italics added]. SCHC had to confront both "a challenging new concept of our broader ministry," and the "financial crunch" forced us to look at who our neighbors <u>were</u> and <u>are</u>, to make our facility and ourselves more appealing to non-Companion "user groups." Her concluding comment: "Community helped us give thanks in the midst of breaking [the Society] out of its shell, and believe me, we've been in some 'midsts'!"

The Society's annual income in 1978 had been approximately $172,000. Now five years after the Task Forces, Treasurer Ethel Colt requested that House construction be "sufficiently altered" to allow space for hosting more than one small group at the same time. However, because of urgency about reducing the SCHC deficit, no plans for House structure or equipment could be undertaken at this time, only necessary maintenance. An *Archives Committee* was formally created.[20]

Companion papers addressed the uses of psychotherapy in religion and mental health: Cynthia Wedel, PhD in psychology and religion, explained that the quality of a person's inner life allows clergy to distinguish between a chronic "complainer" and one who is seriously mentally ill. Mona Hull presented the Centerpoint (St. Louis, Missouri) Institute's program of Jungian studies, her title *Centering Down, Reaching Out: Christian Perspectives in a Psychological Society*. From her Family Studies and teaching in Gerontology, Mimi Simson discussed *stress* in various life situations. And Myra Jewett addressed the state of "becoming aware," from Frances Wicke (a Jungian psycho-analyst) *Inner World of Choice*.

Leading the Bible Study, the Rev. Peter Burrows spoke in modern idiom, "shaking us loose from cherished banalities." The Hebrew word *love* for example is not used to express an emotion but rather commitment. "The wedding service statement 'to love and to cherish' means commitment from A to Z, and the whole alphabet between." On Companion Evening a witty parody of *Carry Me Back to Old Virginny* by Janet Morgan capped the entertainment with rhymes capturing the current preoccupation with psychological language.

> Carry me back to Old Vienna
> That's where my Super Ego really wants to go.
> That's where the Ids warble sweet in the springtime,
> And in those couches rock me gently to and fro.
> That's where my dreams bloom in colors fantastic

---

20 1979 *Annual Report,* 19 and 37.

That's where my psyche expands in fancy free.
Carry me back to Old Vienna,
That is the only place to find the real true ME.[21]

The *Annual Meeting*, the Society's "ritual action in our corporate home," formally designated SCHC structural arenas as major: *Program* (everything we do); *Adelynrood* (the House, and the Society); *Communications* (Newsletter, *IP*, Companion Membership Lists), and *Finances,* now including socially responsible investment. New thinking about "probationship" led to formalizing the status of Visitor-Inquirer. The question was again raised as to why Social Justice conferences must so often be cancelled for lack of registration. One explanation suggested that social-action information and presentations were often available in Companions' local area and churches, whereas spiritual nurture and growth were not. "Companions come to Adelynrood for that which is NOT available—for a spiritual recharging [to enable] action out in the world."[22]

A big report on Society finances projected a deficit of $25,000 and called for strenuous economies. Only 212 Companions had paid dues in the past year, while the previous year 355 had. The Equal Rights Amendment came up in planning the next Spring Conference—should SCHC gather in a state that had not ratified ERA? A Friday night feast honored retiring C-in-C Susanna and her husband Jim Cockrell.[23]

The **Fall** *Companions Along the Way* announced the installation of a public address system that would enable many Companions to hear and understand worship services and conference presentations for the first time in years. A gift of audio-visual equipment including a Sony tape recorder could now enable a Probationer who is blind to read the books on the Probationer's reading list, recorded by her Sponsor.

The **Winter 1979** *Companions Along the Way* (vol. 4 #2) filled with Chapter news included a special reminiscence of EMM by Companion Mary Edgerly, New Hampshire-Vermont Chapter. "The queen of dowagers was, without question, Emily Morgan. While at Adelynrood she wore white all the time, and it may have been her long white cape that gave rise to the affectionate cognomen, 'The Lady Abbess.' Her proportions were generous, her bearing regal, her laughter frequent and unrestrained. She had an inexhaustible fund of anecdotes and delighted in telling jokes on herself. Although she admitted to being a little fearful when the number of Companions climbed into the 400s, I believe she would be pleased if she could know how the Society is reaching out into ever widening circles of concern. Perhaps she can."

IP petitions were offered for a nuclear freeze, for the more than 100 million agricultural workers who have little or no land of their own, for the anti-war witness of the Berrigan brothers, for the murdered Roman Catholic nuns in El Salvador, for Operation Stewpot in Jackson, Mississippi, that provides meals for the needy, and for peace over the bloody battlefields in the demilitarized zone in Vietnam. A special prayer pleaded for an end to the exploitation of mixed-race children.

1980—

The **Companion Conference** theme was *Come as a Child*, Helen Turnbull C-in-C and the Rev. Frank Griswold, retreat leader.

The **Fall** *Companions Along the Way* (Vol. 7 #1) reported a training program presented by the Massachusetts Coalition for Basic Human Needs, to help Companions learn how to work effectively and humanely with welfare recipients. That use of Adelynrood by an outside community organization promised to open new ways of fulfilling the Companion vow of social justice. Twenty-five children (of the five Conference participants presenting their stories) accompanied their mothers. Extensive reports from Companion work in the Middle East, Lucy Acock in Jerusalem, and Priscilla Howe in Saudi Arabia, explained their culture shock, and urged deeper involvement in and education about that part of the world.

In the **Business Meeting,** the ad-hoc *Centennial Planning Committee* suggested creating a book of stories from 100 Companions edited by Lee Beaty, to be titled "Well Tuned Hearts." Other suggestions: specially written prayers, plus collecting oral history tapes

of older Companions, "Graceful Graffiti" (ditties, limericks) and in-house merriment. The *Finance Committee* decided that two major expense items, insurance and remissions, should be included in the budget, along with a clearer treasurer's report. Salaries now had to take into account the cost of living increase, retirement, and medical benefits. Extra financial gifts were making a huge difference. A travel fund for hospitality was established, named for Emilie Hurd (the C-in-C who had immediately succeeded Emily Morgan). The newly constituted *Program Committee*, responsible for Adelynrood summer workshop and retreat programs, was working toward a better balance among Companion-sponsored conferences, non-Companion groups, and outreach gatherings.

Future goals included: better channels of communication between major committees, and the delineation of "reasonably precise" areas of authority, a delicate reference to previous disputes over terrain. There was also an oblique reference to "delegated responsibility:" a committee or individual requires the "authority to act" be delegated at the same time as the task assigned. The *Annual Report* admitted in print that "periods of sweetness and light" had been painfully "few," but that one could always count on "lots of dynamism" in Companionship workings. A chart showed that 499 Companions paid dues in 1979.[24] A major step toward making Society's business procedures more systematic bestowed the title *Director of Adelynrood* on Joan Russell, and *Program Developer* on Eleanor Spinney. Chapters were urged to have at least one program per year on

---

24 *Annual Report* 1980, 3, 19, 25, 26, chart 29.

Social Justice topics, a Task Force recommendation. And for the first time, a short-lived Promotion/Publicity chairman was appointed.

IP Petitions were offered for civil rights workers in Alabama, for imprisoned Buddhist monks who protested the war, for Church World Service and for organized CROP walks, for the work of the Ku Klux Klan watch, and for the safety of prisoners held hostage in the Middle East, including David Dodge, president of American University in Beirut. Petitions celebrated the beginnings of the national domestic Episcopal emphasis, Jubilee Ministry, and a judge's positive ruling on Haitian refugees. Special prayers protested national budget cuts that damage "only the poor," and the scandal-mongering tone evident in much of the news media.

1981—

The **Companion Conference** (theme: *The Way of the Cross*) focused on changing attitudes within the Society. Helen White was the Conference chairwoman. Former C-in-C Alice Lewitin had compiled a scrapbook of humor titled *Memories–Echoes of Adelynrood,* that focused on Companions who had belonged to SCHC more than 40 years. "Remember when EMM contemplated owning a car? And when she would break the tension in a meeting by displaying her blue satin garters? When she advised Companions and Probationers to 'never never take yourself too seriously'?" Former C-in-C Virginia Huntington shared the recollection that, when her name was suggested for that office, EMM had said: "Oh no, she won't do, she's a poet." Some years later, at the same suggestion, EMM had said, "Oh, she'll be wonderful! She's a poet."[25] Frank Griswold (now Presiding Bishop) was the retreat leader, Mary Morrison the Bible Study leader. Companion-in-Charge Turnbull's Opening Paper was based on the hymn: "*When I Survey the Wondrous Cross.*"

Income for 1980 had been $201,178, and expenditures $200,970. In 1981, 482 Companions had paid dues, with 295 pledg-

---

25 *Annual Report 1981*, 7.

ing. The *Centennial Committee* had made no final decisions; the proposed book *Well-Tuned Hearts* would be scaled back to the stories of ten Companions, one for each decade—perhaps reflecting a concern that there would not be enough human-interest material for a longer volume.

There was a tribute to Bob Mars, resident Superintendent of *Grounds and Buildings*, and a report from the *Ad Hoc Committee on Worship*. A Florence Risley Fund (to bring non-Companions to Adelynrood) was established; there were workshops on journaling and Jungian psychology. The *Outreach Committee* began bringing nursing home patients, halfway-house residents, and inner city street people to Adelynrood for hospitality. An updated organization chart was appended; membership had risen to 700 Companions.[26]

> A Fall *Companions Along the Way* (Vol. 8 #1) reported the growing popularity of "praying the Risley Round," the legacy from Florence Risley who "deepened our sense of oneness with each other." She had initiated the practice of praying for the entire Society, two Companions per day, starting from last names beginning with A and running to Z. All Companions could thus be prayed for by name, within a year. "This has proved to many to be a real blessing in the doing."

The *Annual Report* observed that the membership of the Society was growing older, "five nonagenarians having been in residence all summer: Ann Mundelein from South Dakota, who entered Companionship in 1913, Mary Edgerly who entered in 1918, Virginia Huntington and Alice Brooks entering in the 1930s, and Evelyn Wood, entering in 1940. The 90th birthday of Companion Sophie Brown was celebrated at Adelynrood, also honoring her "beloved violin called Peter" with which she had accompanied hymns and the Adelynrood Grace in the dining room for many years, from 1961-76. Along with her civic achievements as legislator and county commissioner, she had presented many summer-conference papers on topics of Christian Unity and Social Justice at Adelynrood (where she built the cottage named New Bemerton). She continued to live

---

26 Ibid, 43, 108.

with her devoted Companion Marion Rollins.

IP topics that year urged prayers in support of a nuclear freeze, for disarmament and peace, for Ho Chi Minh, for the Pearl Buck Foundation, for Job Training Partnerships and for Border Refugee programs in Central America. Petitions were offered for the opening of shelters for the homeless, as well as for the "Greenham Common" women in England who were protesting against nuclear proliferation, and for TV advertising to promote helping the homeless and jobless. Special prayers urged reversing "our immoral immigration and naturalization policy in El Salvador," and supporting the protest against nuclear testing in the Marshall Islands in the Pacific Ocean. A prayer asked support for the establishment of migrant-worker services that could move with them from crop to crop, and for the support of the work by St. Margaret's Sisters in poverty-ridden Haiti.

> The new occupation called Home Health Aides (supervised by the local visiting nurse) was described in the **Spring 1981** *Companions Along the Way* by Companion Jane Schutt, as an example of the creative volunteer roles in local communities that Companions enjoyed. Its special assistance enabled elderly people to remain in their own homes, and offered rich friendships in return for that ministry. The bulk of the issue consisted of extensive news and reports from various individual Chapters.

1982—

Companion Conference again focused on Social Justice, the theme this time *The Cross in the Market Place,* Frances Young chairing. In the printed **Annual Report,** the Companion-in- Charge of Probationers pointed out that "numbers in a chapter" were not the only sign of health. Small chapters complaining about lack of growth were advised to take on only what you can "successfully nurture"—and should the national C-in-C-of-P role be enlarged to include an assistant?[27] Planners for the Centennial celebration sadly

---

27 *Annual Report* 1982, 21.

concluded that it would be too expensive to transport the whole conference to Emily Morgan's ancestral home (and former hospitality house) Putnam Elms, valuable as visiting this ancestral site might be; they would have to settle for a Festival Eucharist on that day conducted by the Presiding Bishop. Lee Beaty was still working on the proposed book [never completed].

The *Finance Committee* offered a detailed 6-page report with no deficit for the past year, thanks to bequests. The Society was able to purchase its own copy machine for Adelynrood, thanks to an anonymous donor. And 512 Companions were paying dues (the highest ever). Of that, 301 Companions were pledging, the average pledge about $87. There were reports on investments, and Spring Conference plans. Topics of discussion were *The Church in Revolution, Women in Leadership, The Church and the New Right, Electronic Media*, and *the Rev. Jerry Falwell*, evangelist.

A **Fall** *Companions Along the Way* (Vol.9 #1) announced that a library of tapes from summer conferences or retreats was now available to rent or borrow on winter-loan, among them the conference "In The Beginning," led by Companion Madeleine L'Engle, and "The Cross in the Marketplace," led by Gordon Cosby. It also announced that the Vida Scudder Award, from The Episcopal Church Publishing Company, had been presented to Companion Marion Kelleran "for being on the cutting edge of social issues", and that Companion Cynthia Wedel was honored by the Presiding Bishop for being "the focal point of ecumenical work" for the Episcopal Church. The Spring Conference topic was announced: "Into the World: Evangelism in the Anglican Tradition," to be led by the Rev. Terence Kelshaw of the Maria Assumpta Academy, Petersham, Mass.

IP Petitions included petitions for civil rights workers in Alabama, for farm workers, wood workers and soup kitchens, for the work with alienated drug-addled youth of Fr. Bruce Ritter at Covenant House (NYC), for the Rev. Gordon Cosby and the Church of Our Savior in Washington, DC, for the Vietnam Memorial in Washington, DC, and for a new Woman in Crisis Center in Concord, MA. There were thanksgivings for the special contributions of such great

Jewish thinkers and writers as Hannah Arendt and Martin Buber, and for the new magazine *Sojourners*.

1983—

The **Companion Conference** theme was *"Make Us Glad...obedience,"* in Helen Turnbull's last year as C-in-C. A report was presented on by-laws revision, the first major updating since the Task Force changes in 1975. There was an eight-page Treasurer's Report, reporting that 516 Companions were paying dues. The *Centennial Committee* had to report that the Presiding Bishop would not be able to celebrate at the anniversary observance, but that plans for the Festal Eucharist would proceed with Bp. Daniel Corrigan [husband of Companion Elizabeth] as celebrant. The pilgrimage to EMM's Putnam Elms home would take place the day before conference opened, with Companions who were able to attend paying their own way. There would be a centennial poem written by Elizabeth Randall-Mills; chapter histories were being assembled for a centennial volume, and an art show was being planned. A major Social Justice Conference with a "big name" to attract attendance was also in planning.[28] Once again there was a discussion about low Companion attendance at Social Justice conferences, centering on the need for prominent public figures as magnet, and balancing that with presenters who demanded limits on the number of attendees. The title from Vida Scudder's autobiography *On Journey* was chosen for the Centennial observance. It alone seemed to summarize and rededicate Companions' sense of urgency about revitalizing a social justice component.

In the *Annual Report*, the Opening Paper by the Companion-in-Charge contained a cultural (and Companionly) reflection of an ethos prevalent in 1980s Episcopal mentality: she confessed her own "reluctance to pray aloud with others, even Companions! Yet when I ask if they *want* me to pray, the response is: 'oh please do'!

---

28 *Annual Report* 43-44.

May God forgive my reticence!" Concerned that the present Society was overly absorbed in its own organization and structure, Turnbull had asked advice from Bp. Bayne. His reassurance was: "Helen, everything needs structure, backbone, to keep it from disintegrating!"

Sister Teresa Corcoran's newly published biography, *Vida Scudder,* was saluted, especially her emphasis on Scudder's "spiritual & social Christianity." That combination should be the intimate union of "catholic faith at its fullest, and social radicalism at its boldest." Corcoran had quoted one of VDS' many unstinting appraisals of the contemporary Christian scene: "The Anglican Church has lost sight of its ideal." Followers of Christ have now become, in theory as so often in practice, champions of the "established rights of the well-to-do" rather than "champions of liberty and the poor."... "We [Companions] must not live for ourselves."[29]

The **Annual Report** named a list of one-day program events, occasionally adding the number of those attending: *"In Christ there is no East or West,"* 23 people; Group Bible Study *"Our Ecumencial Bond,"* 16; *"Hosea, Prophet of God's Judgment and Compassion,"* 39; *"Potpourri—resource day for those 50 and above,"* with only 3 registered, thus cancelled; *"The Challenge of the World Council of Churches Assembly,"* 22 participants, presented by the Rev. Daisuke Kitagawa, about listening to what the "Third World" is saying to U.S. and Western European Churches.[30]

Two- or three-day conferences included: *Our Dreams, Vehicles of Incarnation*—50 participants, *Christians & Jews: Plea for a New Relationship; A Peaceful Interlude* (no structure, just reading and sharing books); *Choices and the Inner Journey; the Altar Guild Conference; the Healing Conference; Singing our way into the 21st c.,* 32 attending; *Intensive Journal Workshop* led by Dr. Ira Progoff, 49 participants; *Living the Truth,* led by Bp. Burgess, 60 attending.

IP petitions included prayer for the Episcopal Medical Mis-

29 *Annual Report* 1983, 18, 16, Corcoran, *Scudder,*
30 Ibid., 82.

sion to Honduras, Diocese of Mississippi; for the Monroe Valley Unemployment Committee, for the Rev. Clarence Mitchell's JOBS program for Black inner city youths (Philadelphia), for Amnesty International, and for abused children and single mothers who are coping. Special thanksgivings were offered for an Absalom Jones Feast Day (the first African American Episcopal clergyman ordained deacon in 1795, priest 1802, in Philadelphia) finally added to the church calendar of *Lesser Feasts and Fasts*, also for the Food Stamp program, and for Henri Nouwen's devotion to Latin American peace efforts.

A **Winter** *Companions Along the Way* (vol.10 #2) announced a change in the SCHC paid staff. Eleanor Spinney had completed 4 years as Program Developer, having enlarged the hospitality outreach programs that brought people to Adelynrood from nursing homes, halfway houses and local community groups. The bulk of this issue was filled with Chapter news reports: from Hartford, New Haven CT, Philadelphia, Ann Arbor, New York, Sewanee, New Hampshire-Vermont, Boston, Washington DC area, California, Texas, Buffalo, and Virginia-North Carolina. New Companions welcomed as bringing new life to the New Haven Chapter were Marie Clark, a lay reader and student in EFM, Judith Conley who was working with the elderly at St. Paul's Church, New Haven, and Alinda Stanley, a business woman in charge of the Logos Bookstore and mother of two young daughters (wife of the Rev. E. Bevan Stanley, "recently appointed curate at Christ Church, New Haven").

A **Spring** *Companions Along the Way* (vol. 10 #3) began with C-in-C Margaret Ann Young's editorial entreaty about "financial realities…evergrowing costs and relatively static income." It ended with encouraging Companions to make a "thanksgiving Birthday gift" in honor of the Centennial observance. *CAW* also contained a preview of the upcoming **Companion Conference** from Pat Gaukler, chair: The Rev. Frank Griswold would present the retreat. There were reports by the chairs of the Theme Committees: Grace Henley for *Christian Mission*, Iris Cully (reporting on many ecumenical gatherings in local communities) for *Christian Unity*, and Alice Skalnik for the *Social Justice* Committee. Her report filled a page, reporting Companion involvement in and support of *The Hunger Networker*, the *Virginia Child Protection News*, Church World Service projects in Central America, and *Amnesty International*.

A poetic exhortation by Assistant C-in-C Nan Clarkson anticipated the Bicentennial Observance by noting that someone had dubbed SCHC "the St. Theresas of the Episcopal world." She cautioned "<u>simplicity</u>! lest undue pride [from such high praise] embroider our confession." Then, asking "How do we honor Emily, Adelyn, and all the rest?" she suggested that a birthday gift "sent to the Treasurer...would blow out all the candles on the cake, and honor *new* life, as we have the old."

1984—

The SCHC Centennial Celebration chose Vida Scudder's autobiographic phrase *On Journey* to sum up the Society's first century in active terms. The formal bulletin, cover and program, appears on the next page. Janet Morgan and Nan Clarkson prepared the written report on that observance for the **1984** *Annual Report*. They described the group pilgrimage to EMM's ancestral home in Connecticut, Putnam Elms, and Lee Beaty's biographical account

of four Companions: Grace Crosby, Deaconess Judy Clark, Georgiana Sibley, and Helena Dudley.

Companion Conference, chaired by Patricia Gaukler, took the theme *OUR CALL, OUR JOURNEY*. The Opening Paper (summarized) by C-in-C Margaret Ann Young, titled *"With Gladness and Singleness of Heart,"* asked: what do we see God accomplishing through our Society? As Companions tell their experiences supporting labor unions, peace, and China missionaries [surprisingly, no mention of the predominant domestic issue, race], we may envision our web of intercessions as a kind of "trampoline." During our first 22 years, we had no By-Laws—really, we had minimal organization *per se*. EMM and VDS had seen their *"real work"* as elsewhere, not at Adelynrood where the crucial focus was retreat, prayer, and recharging one's inner life. Perhaps we can say that God has used the Society as a personal call to discipleship, dedicated to simplicity of life, and a life of intercession and thanksgiving. After SCHC concern over working conditions in factories, next came the China missionary chapter—and the development of community at Adelynrood and in chapters. Who could have guessed? The Society was not planned—it grew.

And the serendipity of "life in the SCHC," the unexpected, rich gifts from God to us all. From its beginning, SCHC has offered women leadership positions, when the church was not ready...Companions have learned to fit themselves for work in which they were previously untrained: preparing papers on "topics we must learn from scratch," conference planning, learning legislative byways, challenging vast corporate interests...including the church itself, through women now becoming priests. She too commented on Episcopal reticence toward speaking openly of spirituality, even at Adelynrood. However, Companions seem able to make a "rapid plunge into discussing prayer and things that matter most, whenever we meet...*this is the most central vignette of Companion accomplishment"* (emphasis added). Recently a young priest in her parish had commented: "we need desperately to recover the biblical sense of Holiness." And that IS the particular gift of the Society to the world, and the church, as we "continue to strive to be servants of love in a troubled world."[31]

The focus of her **Annual Report** was on Chapters' ministry of hospitality: she recommended flexible meeting times and days, not turning into "blessed sororities," and understanding the meaning of vocation: "We don't have to *like* every Probationer—it's who God calls, not who <u>we</u> call." If a Companion is ill and can't ever come to a meeting, try meeting around her bed!

---

31 *Annual Report 1984*, 10-12.

The 1982-1983 financial deficits had been nearly $15,000; Eleanor Spinney was leaving the paid Program position, to be succeeded by Companion Betty Sawyer; Margaret Tyson was appointed Chair of the *Long-range Financial Planning Committee*. In March '84, Nan Clarkson had been appointed Assistant C-in-C. Revised *Manuals* would be a gift to all Companions in honor of the 100th anniversary **Companion Conference**. A Memorial honored Companion Elizabeth Goudge, the well-loved British novelist. The Buffalo Chapter, eight years old in 1984, had been founded in 1972 when the Utica Chapter dissolved. A first conference on the topic of *women* was announced, its title: "Give Words to our Experience as Women in the Body of Christ," Companion Betty Sawyer leading. The *Finance Committee* voted that annual dues be raised to $30, and that Adelynrood charges for 1985 be raised to $30 per day, $15 each for room and board.[32]

Also, July 6-8, 1984, brought a major conference on race, *Roots of Prejudice*, led by Professor Charles Willie (sociologist at Harvard) and Brother Tom Shaw (SSJE). Panel participants included Companions Barbara Brown, Ethel Colt, and Eleanor Spinney along with the Rev. Ed Rodman and the Rev. Barbara Harris.

A resolution reaffirming <u>"no corporate stands"</u> again freed Companions from any implication that SCHC as a Society supported or endorsed any political platform or other organization. When participating in other organizations, Companions should refrain from being identified as such. This policy covered 763 Companions (the number on the Society roll). Committees were listed in full at the end of the Report.

> *Companions Along the Way* in **October, 1984**, highlighted the summer's major occasion with several pages of photographs, and a long list of special thanks for <u>*centennial contributions from Companions*</u>: needlepointed sacramental stoles for chapel use worked by four Companions, poetry anthologies, a prayer collection, an art exhibit, chapter histories, a centennial poem by Elizabeth Randall-Mills, a thematic history of the Society *To Bind Together*, by Miriam Chrisman, a Centennial Cookbook,

---

32 Ibid, 65.

SCHC tote bags, a bulletin for the Festival Eucharist especially designed by Mary Steigner, a musical setting of the SCHC Companion Prayer, a catalogue of Adelynrood art objects, photograph albums, a Centennial logo, scrapbooks, documents of historical import, a Putnam Elms booklet, and "calligraphy everywhere, thanks to El Spinney."

Companion Evening, orchestrated by Marjorie Dower, recouped 100 years through song, dance and story. It began with Companions in Isadora Duncan-style floating scarves, then a 'Twenties Charleston performed by Jill Bigwood, and an elegant "Valentino" tango by Rowena Thompson. A Barbershop Quintet harmonized on "O Chapel Cap, sweet Chapel cap, like down upon my head you sat" (to the German carol *O Christmas Tree, O Christmas Tree*). And the evening's end was "Centennial lyrics" written to the song "Kiss the Days Goodbye," from the Broadway musical *Chorus Line*.

IP Petitions prayed for good food crops all over the globe, especially crops other than poppies that would be turned into heroin. There were petitions for the Jackson, Mississippi, shelter for homeless children, for "Bobby and Ethel Kennedy's son working to reject oil subsidies and assist the poor through lower gas prices," for the work of Habitat for Humanity, for India to overcome its ethnic hatreds, and that Guatemala turn away from its military government. There were special thanksgivings for ecumenical groups, for the anniversary celebrations of the SCHC, and for the unsung work and countless intercessory prayers of Companions over the past century.

The theme announced for the **1985 Companion Conference**, intended to evoke revitalized Companion commitment and vigor, was *On the Road: The Next 100 Years*. The evolution of the Society and its retreat house summer programs had demonstrated that this quintessentially Anglican women's association could be viable in the complex 20th c. Rooted by Founders EMM and VDS in the distinctive protestantized blending of Catholic order and ritual, and dedicated to passionate involvement in social justice concerns, this Society's hybrid structure proved a worthy vehicle for 20th c. women's quest for holiness, sending them into the world in peace and

battle. Somehow SCHC, an Americanized and continually modernizing offspring of Church of England monasticism, was a living "via
media" witness to and beyond the Episcopal church. Meanwhile,
the *IP* well of prayers continues building, as year succeeds to year.

(clockwise from top) A map of the grounds, circa 2000;
the chapel with garden in foreground; the Great Cross.

Epilogue

History written within a quarter century of its happening is not very historical, so here is my impressionistic summary of events and emphases since the 1984 centennial.

C-in-C Margaret Ann Young died very suddenly in 1985 and was succeeded by her Asst. C-in-C Nan Clarkson. After Nan came Betty Sawyer 1990-1994, then Joan Melvin, 1994-1998, and Roberta Walmsley, 1998-2002. This winter completes the four-year term of Pat Gaukler, 2002-2006, and the newly elected C-in-C is Jeanette Renouf from Arizona, one of the newest and most geographically distant chapters. Each of these dynamic Companions turned out to be the hand of God for her times. It will be fascinating to review their distinctive gifts to the Society one day in the future.

Focusing on Chapters, in 2005-06, we see that the huge Boston chapter accomplished one of the 1974 Task Force recommendations: dividing itself by 3: a Charles River Chapter, a Parker River Chapter, and a Boston Chapter *per se*. This reorganization allows closer bonds within the chapters, and encourages the multiplying of those bonds. The Florida Chapter has seemingly come to the end of its cycle, due to geographic distances and loss of membership through death, but Companions there continue with the Society through the Far and Near Chapter.

Since 2000, the venerable house Adelynrood enjoys a winterized, modernized, climate-controlled addition called St. Clare, vastly expanding and modernizing the business maintenance of the Society. [Adjusting to the temperature change as one moves between the two locations on a steamy August day often summons new dimensions of spiritual fortitude.] A skilled professional managerial staff was hired in 1996. This excellent team has initiated contemporary processes of registering for conferences, managing the kitchen-food dimension, cleaning and caring for the house, and maintaining the buildings and grounds. They make it possible for the old building to continue welcoming diverse outside groups who want to rent the house, while the new St. Clare wing allows gatherings in spring and fall that were formerly out of the question. Having a place where Society committees can meet during the winter means that year-round planning and development of the Society's programs is done "on site." This increased availability of the retreat center deepens the connection among Companions, between them and the Society, and with Adelynrood's physical ministry.

The organizational structure itself was again re-designed in the late 1990s, and new long-range planning is underway about finances, program and membership formation—sponsoring new Companions.

The difficulty of attracting large numbers of Companions to Social Justice conferences continues to be a concern, though the number and quantity of retreats is up, the library is constantly updated, the amount of work to keep the house beautiful and functioning done by dedicated volunteers, enormous. Grounds and garden-committee Companions have completed (in the early 2000s) an excellent landscaping design and done extensive trimming and planting.

Thanks to C-in-C Pat Gaulker's shouldering a massive financial undertaking, the dues structure has been brought into a more realistic proportion of the Society's basic expenses. This corporate assumption of fiscal responsibility is gradually reducing a huge deficit that followed the building of St Clare. A campaign to awaken Companions to their responsibility for financial commitment is underway, and continued vigilance about finances is maintained. A Financial Oversight Committee is bringing contemporary stewardship and money-management practices to bear on our assets, including the initiation of an annual fund drive under the leadership of former C-in-C Roberta Walmsley.

Meanwhile, the most moving of all Companion traditions continues seamlessly. I refer to the service of Memorials, which honors the lives of those Companions who have entered "the Paradise Chapter" during the previous year. An afternoon and evening in the chapel are set aside for Memorials. Companions who knew them, their lives and gifts, write these brief biographies and tributes, read aloud with hymns and prayers interspersed. On Companion Day, the procession of Companions (traditionally dressed in white, "if convenient") halts at various "stations" around the grounds that also honor earlier generations of Companions. In fact, these ritualized customs revere our antiquity (125 years as this is written), freshly inscribing it on Companion hearts and souls each succeeding year.

In summary, this organizational unfolding offers a cautionary account. Through its first century, the vitality nurturing the Society was the life of prayer and service envisioned in 1884 by an outgoing, generous-hearted Emily Morgan. In mid-20th century, the ever-present specter of resistance to change was still determining the Society's structure in earnest attempt to preserve Adelynrood "the way she left it" in 1937. The 1974 upheaval was crucial in upending this near-strangulation of custom and practices, and succeeding revitalization was well underway by 1984. It took the centennial focus on Emily's and Vida's legacy to open the Companionship in redefining its vocation. Barbara Crafton, leading an Adelynrood retreat in July 2006, embraced the affect of the Society and its 'mother house' in her aphorism, "All Love gardens the world." The Founders would have welcomed that catholic benediction.

Author's Notes

Thoughts about the IP (Intercession Paper)

The central thread of this SCHC organizational history is the *Intercession Paper* that arrives monthly in each Companion's mailbox. (Some Companions in 2005 may choose to read it electronically, but the majority embrace the portability of its customary design.) The *IP* is deceptively simple-looking, a 3 1/2"x 6" printed pamphlet of about sixteen pages. It may in fact be the most significant product of Emily Morgan's organizational genius, yet its beginning was almost casual. In the Society's first year, 1884, it was a single handwritten sheet of paper circulated among the initial eight Companions, naming a few "objects of intercession" and personal concerns: "hardness of heart," "blind prejudice," the poor, "the sick in cities," the deaf or dumb, and children in hospitals. After the Society's fifth year, an annual *IP* grouped petitions from individual Companions under five topics (quoted literally): *Deepening spiritual life, Personal troubles, The sick, Temporal and spiritual blessings,* and

The church with its different branches of Episcopal work. In 1897, the *IP* expanded to six pages and was sent out monthly with the petitions grouped by the above five themes.

A year later, in 1899, each month was assigned its own theme, e.g. March, prayers for "the tempted," September, thanksgivings only, and November, prayers for those who were dying. [That year, a quintessentially Victorian petition prayed that the American drive toward "commercialization" would not "destroy the chivalry of our nation."] By 1916, the *IP* theme *Reconciliation of Classes* began to gather its petitions out of those in the more general category *Missions,* the July *IP* theme. Until that time, *Missions* pages had encompassed the larger work of the church beyond parish boundaries. During the late 1920s, each *IP Missions* page carried a large number of prayers for the church that included missionaries and missions, as well as petitions concerning social justice. Petitions about social-class inequities began taking up more and more space: in 1930, the April *IP* contained three pages of separate petitions under the theme *Reconciliation of Classes for Social Justice.* Perhaps because of this increasing volume, the *IP* theme *Reconciliation of Classes* was changed that year to the more inclusive theme, *Social Justice.* [Interestingly, from 1928 to 1942 the number of and detailed legislative information in *Social Justice* petitions was remarkable. That section was often the longest in the monthly pamphlet.]

From the remainder of the 1940s into the early 1960s, the *IP* petitions focused less on external and national issues, and more on spiritual, internal SCHC and church issues. In the mid-1960s, as daily newscasts reported more racial violence, Companions once again submitted large numbers of individual *Social Justice* petitions. That focus of prayers, race and desegregation, did not decline noticeably until the 1980s, though environmental topics also began to appear under that theme. In 2005, for reasons of cost, the *IP* attempted to confine each "theme" section to two pages. Sundays, devoted to *Thanksgivings*, and Saturdays, devoted to *Needs Personal and General,* were granted more leeway. The final four pages are set aside for SCHC organizational information, including Administrative Companions and staff, names of Companions received as Probationers and/or admitted, withdrawals, deaths, announcements of the month's chapter-meetings, and Companion address changes (mailing address, telephone, and e-mail).

The symbolic and spiritual meanings conveyed through this humble monthly medium, however, have continued to bear major Companionly weight. Occasionally a Companion even writes an IP thanksgiving that specifically names her joy over receiving and praying the IP. Probationers often report that the larger, invisible Society suddenly becomes actual when they begin to read and pray the IP. Even if they did not know personally the Companion named in a petition, the act of shared praying begins to weave the numinous web of "community."

Over the years, the number of IP pages has expanded and contracted; noticeable shifts in vocabulary can denote a given era. Whatever its variations in form, this printed prayer agenda of the Society has become much more than a tangible link among dispersed and busy Companions: it has come to seem the very cement of Companionship—filled with Companions' ideals, frustrations, spiritual and physical miseries, and potentially world-changing aspirations. These prayers often defy the way the world is at any given point in order to claim what it may become through God's power (epigraph, Chapter 1).

The IP also serves as a laboratory for Companion consciousness-development, fostering the exploration and definition of issues being put into words. Basically, it is the link that personalizes and makes the Companionship 'real.' This humble monthly brochure is, in fact, the corporate conscience and consciousness of the Society. Emily Morgan, who originated it and personally produced it for the first eighteen years, was amazingly prescient—or, as she might have said, providentially led to establish this concrete component of Companionship.

Probation: the process of recognizing, cultivating, and incorporating new members into the Companionship.

As early as 1906, EMM closed her *Annual Letter to Companions* with plain words capturing the prophetic essence of Companions' vow: "It is not enough for us to be Churchwomen just fulfilling the yearly round of church observance...there must be an increasing fulfillment in ourselves, a more steady reaching-out to grasp an ever-wider conception of truth."[1] Never has the profound depth of spiritual Companionship been expressed more simply. With that as goal, recognizing among acquaintances or friends those women who may be "companions [whom] God has already made"[2] is the charge to all Companions—the calling of or inviting new lives and gifts into the Society. How women first become aware of the Society of the Companions of the Holy Cross, and discern a vocation to it, was and remains both a mysterious and a pragmatic matter. From its beginning, the Society has expanded more or less underground, like tubers in a garden, via personal relationships that recognize a shared hunger for the spiritual in everyday life. In its first years, those responding to the Society[3] were invited to visit in a local chapter, and officially invited into Companionship by Miss Morgan.

As the Society expanded, a "definite consciousness of vocation" began to be defined. Vida Scudder, the first Companion-in-Charge of Probationers, wrote many philosophical and theological statements about the SCHC system of calling of Probationers and the period of probation. In 1937, for instance, she pointed out that some women who could write insightfully about the soul, or about justice and unity, might be "quite unsuited to the Companionship." Similarly, many deeply committed Christian women "would not find their needs met by the Society." To her, the distinctive and essential

---

1 Scudder ed., *Letters of EMM*, 93.

2 Betty Jacobson, C-in-C of Probationers, prayer at Admissions Service rehearsal, Adelynrood, 1997.

3 As of 1977, any woman who is a communicant of the Episcopal Church or any church in communion with it is considered eligible, upon fulfillment of the current guidelines...who feels a call to Companionship, Intercession and Thanksgiving, dedicated to Social Justice, Christian Unity, and Christian Mission.

commitments were: "consecration to the Way of the Cross, to Simplicity of Life, and to Thanksgiving; steadfastness in the secret work of healing, through intercession, [various] social disorders... that rend the human family," and the pledge to grow into the disciplined Companionship that unites the Society.[4]

Scudder named the true understanding of probation as the "happy privilege of accompany[ing] a pilgrim mind" into Companionship. That process permitted Sponsors to "throw off the false reserve in Episcopal culture about personal religion"—inhibiting open spiritual conversation. To assist this growing friendship, the would-be explorer and Sponsor discuss a prescribed reading list—updated from time to time to incorporate the language of and issues in contemporary Christian theology and ethics. They discuss the Companionship path provided in the monthly *Intercession Papers*. The visitor is formally welcomed into the probation process after her written application, supported by written endorsements of two Sponsors and the chapter AC-in-C, is accepted. Then the Probationer and Sponsors spend up to two years of prayer, conversation, and discernment. Their exchanges cover the Society's aims, purpose, and practices, plus the commitment to support the Society physically and financially. Sponsors are most often the person (and chapter) who first acquainted the newcomer with the Society. Scudder charged Sponsors to "quicken and Christianize [the Probationer's] social imagination." At the same time, the probation process itself actually puts the chapter "on probation:" it must be the setting where Probationers see and experience the "love of justice [that] is really born at the Altar." And most of all, the primary aim of this initiating into Companionship process must include EMM's lifelong emphasis on "practicing the difficult art of fellowship."

As EMM expressed it, each woman joining the Society "makes a *profession* of intercessory prayer, in a world where disbelief in

---

4 Vida Scudder, *A Letter to Companions: the Responsibility of Sponsors*, Oct 1937, privately printed pamphlet.

God and prayer dominates popular thought."[5] VDS amplified that "profession" [verbal and sacramental commitment] to include "the secret, creative forces of thought and desire...vibrating through a common spiritual ether in which we all have our being." Explicitly, she believed that "God...demands, but I dare say also *needs*, our co-operation on the spiritual as well as the material plane. The Cross-bearer of the universe does not act *for* us as He passes in our midst, but in [and through] us."[6]

The questing Probationer is encouraged to share her doubts, interests, and concerns with a Sponsor. The sponsoring Companion or Companions are her fellow travelers in study, praying, and retreat, nourishing the newcomer's experience that is <u>her</u> gift to the Society. The Probationer and Sponsors each write a letter to the C-in-C of Probationers at 6-month intervals, reporting issues and questions about the Society and the Companionship. At the end of this process, by mutual agreement among the Probationer, Sponsors, and the C-in-C of Probationers, the new Companion is ready to ask for "the Questions." She writes out her "answers" [understandings of the aims and purposes of the SCHC] to the official "questions" and sends them to the C-in-C-of-Probationers. These signal the Probationer's commitment to full Companionship, and she is welcomed in a formal Admission liturgy, either at Adelynrood or in a church near her home chapter.[7]

"The Questions" were never intended as a test to be passed or failed, but rather an overview of the Probationer's journey into Companionship. She summarizes her experience thus far with Companions, the chapter, and the Society, her developing understandings of intercession and thanksgiving, and her responses to the Reading List and Miss Morgan's *Letters*. At the Admission service, the new Companion, standing between her Sponsors, is admitted by the AC-in-C who asks: "Will you seek to serve God day by

---

5 *EMM Annual Letter 1938*, quoted in SCHC *Annual Report* 1938, 14.

6 Scudder, *On Journey*, 384-386 (italics added).

7 *Op.cit*, #4, unpaginated pamphlet.

day in thanksgiving, in the ministry of intercession and in simplicity of life?" Her ritual answer is: "I will, by the grace of God."[8]

---

8 *SCHC Manual*, 7th edition 1984, 29.

Sources

All footnote references to SCHC documents are in Adelynrood archives.

Allchin, A.M., *The Silent Rebellion: Anglican Religious Communities.* London: SCM Press, 1958.

Avila, Eric, *The Age of White Flight: Fear and Fantasy in Suburban Los Angeles.* Berkeley, CA: University of California Press, 2004.

Bartlett, Alice M., "Picture of Miss Morgan as She Appeared to her Contemporaries." Byfield, MA: SCHC Pamphlet, 1957.

Braden, Anne, *The Wall Between.* Knoxville, TN: University of Tennessee Press, [1958] 1999.

Canaday, Margot, "Building a Straight State: Sexuality and Social Citizenship under the GI BILL." *Journal of American History* 90 #3, 935-957 (December 2003).

Carden, Ron, "The Bolshevik Bishop, William Montgomery Brown's Path to Heresy, 1906-20." *Anglican & Episcopal History LXXII #2*, 197-228 (2003).

Carter, Paul A., *The Spiritual Crisis of Gilded Age, 1865-95.* DeKalb, IL: Northern Illinois University Press, 1971.

Corcoran, Teresa, *Vida Dutton Scudder.* Boston: G. K. Hall & Co., 1982.

Chrisman, Miriam U., *To Bind Together: A Short History of the SCHC.* Byfield, MA: SCHC, 1984.

Dailey, Jane, "Sex, Segregation and the Sacred after *Brown v Board of Education.*" *Journal of American History* 91#1 (June 2004).

DeMille, G.E., "The Catholic Movement in the American Episcopal Church." *WHO'S WHO IN AMERICA,* 2nd ed. Philadelphia, 1950.

Donovan, Mary S., *A Different Call.* Wilton, CT: Morehouse, 1986.

Freedman, Estelle B., "Separatism Revisited: Women's Institutions, Social Reform, and the Career of Miriam Van Waters. Chapter 8, *U.S. History as Women's History: New Feminist Essays,* ed. Linda K. Kerber *et al.* Chapel Hill: University of North Carolina Press, 1995.

Gillespie, Joanna B., *Women Speak of God, Congregations and Change*. Valley Forge, PA: Trinity Press International, 1995.

—"Sarah Patton Boyle's Desegregated Heart," in *Beyond Image and Convention*, Coryell, Swain, Treadway, and Turner eds. Columbia, MO: University of Missouri Press, 158-183, 1998.

— Oral History of Mary Morrison. Austin, TX: EWHP Archives of the Episcopal Church, 1996,

—"What We Taught." *Anglican and Episcopal Historical Magazine* LVI #1, 45-86 (March 1987).

Goudge, Elizabeth, ed., *A Diary of Prayer*. New York: Coward McCann, 1966.

Graham, Gael, *"Flaunting the Freak Flag"* in *Journal of American History* 91#2, 544-543 (September 2004).

Halberstam, David, *The Children*. NY: Random House, 1998.

Hall, Jacquelyn Dowd, "Women Writers, the 'Southern front,' and the Dialectical Imagination." *Journal of Southern History* LXIX#1, 4-38 (February 2003).

Heeney, Brian, *The Women's Movement in the Church of England 1850-1930*. Oxford, England: Clarendon Press, 1988.

Higham, John. *Writing American History*. Bloomington, IN: Indiana University Press, 1977.

Hobson, Fred, *But Now I See: White Southern Racial Conversion Narratives*. Baton Rouge, LA: Louisiana State University Press, 1999.

Hymnal 1940 Companion, The. Church Pension Fund, New York, New York, 1949.

Journal of American History, 91 #1, entire issue (June 2004).

K'Meyer, Tracy Elaine, *Interracialism and Christian Community in the Postwar South: The Story of Koininia Farm*. Charlottesville: University of Virginia Press, 1997.

Lantzer, Jason, "Hoosier Episcopalians, Women's Ordination and the 1979 Book of Common Prayer." 229-254, *Anglican & Episcopal History LXXII #2 (2003)*.

Lasch, Christopher, *Narcissism: The Culture of American Life in an Age of Diminishing Expectations*. New York: W. W. Norton [1979] 1991.

Lattin, Don, "Following our Bliss," Review, the Rev. Robert Cromey. *The Living Church* (February 8, 2003).

Lears, T.J. Jackson, *No Place of Grace: Anti-Modernism and the Transformation of American Culture 1880-1920*. Chicago: University of Chicago Press [1981], 1994.

Lynn, Susan, *Progressive Women in Conservative Times: Racial Justice, Peace and Feminism, 1945-1960*. New Brunswick, NJ: Rutgers University Press, 1992.

Markwell, Bernard Kent, *The Anglican Left: Radical Social Reformers in the Church of England and Protestant Episcopal Church 1846-1954*. New York: Carlson Publishing, 1991.

Marsh, Charles, *God's Long Summer: Stories of Faith and Civil Rights, 1964*. Princeton, NJ: Princeton University Press, 1997.

Martin, the Rev. Steele W., "Social Justice and Spirituality." *The Witness*, December, 1986.

McNamara, JoAnn, *Sisters in Arms*. Cambridge, MA: Harvard University Press, 1996.

McWhorter, Diane, *Carry Me Home*. New York: Simon & Schuster, 2001.

Morgan, Emily Malbone, *Adelyn's Story*. Byfield, MA: SCHC, 1915.

—*Letters to her Companions*, V.D. Scudder, ed., Byfield, MA: SCHC, 1944.

— *Memories*. Byfield, MA: SCHC, 1887.

Morgan, Ted, "REDS: McCarthyism in 20th c. America." *New York Review of Books* 21-23 (February 12, 2004).

Murk-Jansen, Saskia, *Brides in the Desert: The Spirituality of the Beguines*. Maryknoll, NY: Orbis Books, 1998.

Myrdal, Gunnar, *An American Dilemma*. New York: Harper & Row, 1944.

Neale, John Mason, *Ayton Priory: The Reformed Monastery* [novel], London, 1843.

Robert Bellah, *et al.*, *Habits Of The Heart*. Berkeley, CA: University of California Press, 1973.

Rose, Anne C., *Voices of the Market Place 1830-1860*. New York: Twayne Publishers, 1995.

Rosen, Charles. "Culture on the Market," *New York Review of Books*. (November 6, 2003).

Roth, Claudia Pierrepont, Essay, *New Yorker.* (February 8, 2002).

Rothauge, Arlin J., *Life Cycle in Congregations: A Natural Process.* Washington, DC: Alban Institute, 1996.

Saarinen, Martin F., *Life Cycle of a Congregation.* Washington, DC: Alban Institute, 1986.

Schulman, Bruce J., *The Seventies: Great Shift In American Culture, Society, and Politics.* New York: Da Capo Press, 2001.

Schultz, Rima, "'To Realize the Joy of Dedication and Vocation in the Grace Conferred in our Order:' Deaconesses in Twentieth-Century Chicago." *Anglican and Episcopal History* LXXIII#3 (September 2004).

Scudder, Vida Dutton, *Inward Light* #34, 10-13 (Spring 1949).

—*The Church and The Hour: Reflections of a Socialist Churchwoman,* Boston: E P Dutton, 1917.

—*House of Holiness.* Byfield, MA, 1964. SCHC *(pamphlet from On Journey).*

—*On Journey,* New York: E.P. Dutton, 1937.

Select Index, Letters to Her Companions. Byfield, MA: SCHC, 1952.

Shattuck, Gardiner H., Jr., *Episcopalians And Race: Civil War To Civil Rights.* Lexington, KY: University Press of Kentucky, 2000.

Shepherd, Massey, *The Oxford American Prayer Book Commentary.* New York: Oxford University Press, 1959.

Simpson, James B. and Edward M. Story, *Stars in His Crown: the History of the Community of St. John Baptist.* Seabright, NJ: Plowshares Press, 1976.

Sister Mary Hilary, *Ten Decades of Praise: The Community of St. Mary 1865-1965.* Racine, Wisconsin: De Koven Foundation, 1965.

Smith, Lillian, *Killers of the Dream.* New York: W.W. Norton, 1949.

Strouse, Jean, *Morgan, American Financier.* New York: Random House, 1999.

Prophetic Visions of our Founders, The, Part 1: Emily Malbone Morgan, by Emily Sophie Brown; Part 2: Vida Dutton Scudder, by Winifred Hulbert. Byfield MA: SCHC, 1955.

Vicinus, Martha, *Independent Women: Work and Community for Single Women, 1850-1920.* Chicago: University of Chicago Press, 1985.

Williams, Peter W., "American Church History: The Gospel of Wealth and the Gospel of Art from the Gilded Age to the Depression." *Anglican & Episcopal History* LXXV#2, 170-223 (June 2006).

Wink, Walter, *Engaging the Powers: Discernment and Resistance in a World of Domination.* Minneapolis, MN: Augsburg Fortress Press, 1992.

Woodham-Smith, Cecil, *Florence Nightingale.* New York: McGraw Hill, 1951.

Yates, Nigel, *The Oxford Movement and Anglican Ritualism.* London: Historical Association, 1983.

Index of Companion Names

Abbott, Rita – 213
Ackerman, Isabelle – 220
Acock, Lucy – 213, 245, 253
Aldrich, Peg – xvii
Allen, Emily – 163
Barlow, Alpha W. – 76
Barron, Mary Grey – 76
Bartlett, Alice – 161, 215
Beaty, Lee – 194, 209, 215, 247, 253, 258, 262
Bigwood, Jill – 265
Bishop, Josephine – 245
Booth, Jeannette – 71, 107, 109
Boyd, Doris – 213
Bremer, Althea -106
Brooks, Alice – 189, 256
Brooks, Josephine – 103
Brown, Barbara – 264
Brown, Carolyn Sophia – 37
Brown, Emily Sophie – 76, 194, 256
Brown, Nina – 135
Bull, Mary – 166
Burgess, Esther – 156, 164, 181, 199
Cameron, Evelyn – 65
Capen, Julia -139
Carver, Estelle – 149
Case, Adelaide T. – 77, 78, 96, 107
Chaplin, Dora – 107, 151
Charles, Joanna, – 21
Clark, Judy – 101
Clark, Marie – 261
Clarkson, Elisabeth (Nan) – 18, 66, 211, 231, 245, 261, 262, 264, 267
Cockrell, Susanna – 230, 238, 243-7, 250
Colt, Ethel – 179, 213, 216
Conley, Judy – 261
Converse, Florence – 37 n.14, 65, 67, 183, 246
Cook, Elizabeth C. – 92, 135
Craighill, Marian – 101, 149
Crite, Annamae – 88, 152, 196
Cross, Mary – xxi
Davis, Hilda – 113, 116, 139, 245
Davison, Peg – 244-5
Dower, Marjorie – 265
Dudley, Helena, – 67
Edgerly, Mary – 252, 256
Evans, Mary O. – 129
Falck, Elizabeth – 165, 209
Foster, Elima – 110
Gaukler, Patricia – xvii, 261
Gibson, Martha Jane – 84, 110, 116, 129, 187
Gillespy, Deaconess Jane – 88, 93, 158
Gilson, Dorothy – 164, 166
Goudge, Elizabeth – 189, 264
Gropp, Donna B. – 101, 106
Guild, Dorothy – 238, 242
Gwin, Elizabeth B. – 109
Hall, Gladys – 109
Hamilton, Grace – 184
Hastings, Harriet – 3, 4, 12, 135
Hawkins, Michelle – 178, 179, 207, 213, 214, 216, 220, 222

Heers, Helen – 245
Henley, Grace – 261
Hepburn, Frances – 215
Hoff, Phebe – 245
Howard, Adelyn – 1, 2, 4, 104, 135
Howe, Priscilla – 245, 253
Hulbert, Winifred – 64, 67, 70
Hull, Mona – 251
Hunter, Carman – 132, 198
Huntington, Virginia – 119, 131, 133, 136-7, 140, 142-7, 150-160, 192, 212-3, 231, 255-6
Hurd, Emilie – 16, 38, 43,135, 188, 254
Innan, Roberta – xvi
January, Josephine – 213
Jenkins, Ruth – 163
Jewett, Myra – 251
Keating, Elizabeth – 213
Kehl, Gloria – 206
Kellemen, Harriet – 213
Keller, Clare – xvii
Kelleran, Marion – 258
L'Engle, Madeleine – 219, 258
L'Hommedieu, Marie – 129
Lansing, Elisabeth – 154
Leonard, Ruth – 207, 216, 224
Lewitin, Alice – 162, 179, 198, 201, 203, 210, 212-3, 216, 218-221, 229, 234, 240-1, 245, 255
Lichtenberger, Florence -141
Lindley, Grace – 89, 96, 101, 135
Lloyd, Elisabeth – 134, 184
Lowell, Ann S. – xvi
Ludwig, Martha – 199
Martin, Priscilla – xxii, 219, 243
Mason, Eleanor -96, 158
Melvin, Joan – xvii
Merigold, Kay – 216
Micks, Marianne – 206, 239
Mithoefer, Fi – 248-9
Morgan, Emily (EMM) – see Topical Index
Morgan, Janet Barton – 109, 209, 213, 225, 251, 262
Morrison, Mary – 110, 131, 195, 224, 243, 255
Morse, Gwendolen – 76
Morton, Rebecca – 92
Mundelein, Ann – 256
Neide, Edith – 245
Nielsen, Nicki – 245
Paradise, Alma – 245
Phisterer, Isabel – 216, 245
Pifer, Isabel – 64, 184, 193, 213
Pillsbury, Dorothy – 246
Pinder, Viola – 177, 204-6
Porter, Violet – 196
Potter, Mary – xxv, 95
Putnam, H, – 135
Randall-Mills, Elizabeth – 207, 259, 264
Rynbergen, Henderika – 93
Risley, Florence – 96, 106, 187, 225, 246, 256

Index of Companion Names *continued*

Roberts, Ethel C. – 213
Rollins, Marion – 17, 159, 164-5, 194, 200, 256, 220
Rose, Caroline – 215-216
Rucker, Aileen, 245
Russell, Joan – 241, 245, 254
Russell, Keyo, – 245
Sawyer, Betty – 263
Schutt, Jane – 123, 149, 257
Schwarz, Amelia – xxv
Sharkey, Connie – 156
Shoemaker, Helen – 103, 157
Sibley, Georgiana – 91, 167, 189, 262
Simkhovitch, Mary – 164
Simson, Mimi – 251
Skalnik, Alice – 261
Spinney, Eleanor – 254, 261, 263, 264
Stanley, Alinda – 261
Starr, Ellen – 67
Steigner, Mary – xvii
Sydnor, Fran – 245
Thompson, Rowena – 208, 213, 216, 223, 245, 265
Titus, Irma – 210
Torrey, Jan – 166
Townsend, Leslie – 129
Tracy, Clara G, – 76
Turnbull, Helen – 113, 140, 220, 230, 250,

253, 255, 259
Tyson, Margaret – 133, 184, 263
Van Waters, Miriam – 100, 133
Vester, Bertha Spafford – 109
Walberg, Elsa – 216, 222, 238, 243
Walmsley, Roberta – xvii
Waterman, Margaret – 37, 37 n.14
Weckel, Laurie – xxii
Wedel, Cynthia – 100, 101, 107, 134, 138, 202, 203, 209, 244, 251, 258
Weidenhammer, Lillian – 164
Wells, Victoria – 238, 250
Weske, Dorothy – 76
White, Grace E, – 76
White, Helen – 255
Whittier, Kay – 245
Wickenden, Elsie – 76
Wiley, Polly – 190, 213, 245
Williams, Angela – 219
Wilson, Doris – 158
Wilson, Ruth Mary – 136
Woolverton, Maggie – xviii
Worrell, Dorothy – 159, 246
Wylie, Bea – 188
Young, Frances M. – 78, 139, 150, 190, 245, 257
Young, Margaret Ann – 186, 229, 242, 246, 261-2, 267

Chronological Index

Adelynrood: construction, including chapel shortly before **WWI** – xxv
Beguine movement in Europe, early **Middle Ages** – 6, 7
C-in-C during "caretaker" period, **1941-54** – 75
Cs-in-C, terms of: EMM **1884-1937**; Emilie Hurd **1937-41**; Elizabeth Cook **1941-45**; Grace Lindley **1945-51**; Jeannette Booth **1951-55**; Virginia Huntington **1955-1963**; Marion Rollins **1963-69**; Alice Lewitin **1969-75**; Susanna Cockrell **1976-79**; Helen Turnbull **1979-83**; Margaret Ann Young **1983-85**; Elisabeth Clarkson **1985-90**; Betty Sawyer **1990-1994**; Joan Melvin **1994-98**; Roberta Walmsley **1998-2002**; Patricia Gaukler **2002-2006**; Jeanette Renouf **2006-**
Companions listed before 1890: **1884**: Mary Adams, Lena Barber, Elizabeth Gould, Harriet Hastings, Adelyn Howard, Florence Humphries, Marie Johnson, Susan Johnson, Sarah Legate, Annie Plumb, Harriet Putnam; **1885**: Gertrude Emery; **1886**: Melissa Bryant, Anna Cameron, Rebecca Cameron, Jean Hyde; **1889**: Vida Scudder; **1890**: Caroline Fellowes, Eleanor Prince, Charlotte Tracy; in Paradise list with entry in **1887**: Minnie Anderson, Hetty Buck, Frances Jones, Lettie Smith, Lucy Smith, Mary Upson, Rosa Watson, Caroline Whitney
Companion Conferences: **1936** – 24, 31; **1937** – 29; **1938** – 33-4; **1939** – 37; **1940** – 37; **1941** – 39; **1942** – 77; **1943** – 73; **1944** – 84; **1945** – 85; **1946** – 89; **1947** – 92; **1948** – 96; **1949** – 101; **1950** – 103; **1952** – 110; **1953** – 112; **1954** – 114; **1955** – 68; **1957** – 136; **1958** – 139; **1959** – 142; **1960** – 147; **1961** – 150; **1962** – 154; **1963** – 158; **1964** – 164; **1965** – 182; **1966** – 186; **1968** – 171, 194; **1969** – 200; **1970** – 177, 203; **1971** – 206; **1972** – 209; **1973** – 221; **1974** – 217, 240; **1975** – 240; **1976** – 242; **1977** – 244; **1978** -175, 247; **1980** – 253; **1981** – 255; **1982** – 257; **1983** – 259; **1984** – 260; **1985** – 255;
Culture of Art as field of benevolence in early 20th c. – xiii
Depression **1937** – xii
Landmark changes in US society **1973** – 176-7
Newsletter (SCHC) sometimes called *Companions Along the Way*: **1947** – 93, 94; **1949** – 99; **1950** – 102; **1951** – 107; **1952** – 109; **1954** – 114; **1955** – 128; **1962** – 155; **1965** – 183; **1968** – 194; **1969** – 199; **1978** – 247; **1979** – 250; **1981** – 256, 257
Post **Civil War** period – 3
Rise of counter-modernism, **1870s** (art, religious architecture) – 7, 8
WWII – 77; Conscientious Objectors – 103; prisoners-of-war – 84; post-WWII, Marshall Plan for rebuilding Europe, 92

Topical Index

AA (Alcoholics Anonymous) – 157, 194, 110
Abortion – 176, 206
Addams, Jane, of Hull House, Chicago – 57
Adelynrood Chapel, rearrangement – 199
Adelynrood, remaining closed, 1974 – 173; alterations after 1974 – 246; dedication – 7, n.17; design and construction – xxv, 3; discussion of uses – 154
Adult Education – 107, 155, 185, 188, 189, 196
Air Pollution concerns – 197, 212, 242
Alcoholism – 89, 113; threat to family – 128
Alternate Life Style – 179
American Church Institute for Negroes – 82
American cross-cultural ignorance – 166
American Indians – 105, 113
American Individualism, impacting religion – 17; in SCHC – 10
American Occupation of Japan – 109
Americanization of Church of England Practices – 10-13
Anglican Fellowship of Prayer – 160, 190
Anglo Catholicism (American) – 5, 8 -11,17; Gothic church architecture – 10; "high church" – 71; Bishops Horatio Potter, William C. Doane – 9; Mulhenberg – 9; Morgan Dix – 13; establishing first sisterhood with Anne Ayres, 9; break-off Reformed Episcopal Church – 13; "lay sisters" – 13
Anglo Catholicism (English) – 6
Anti-military protests, Vietnam War draft – 173, 188
Anti-modernism, T. J. Jackson Lears – 11
Anti-Semitism – 110
Archives Committee established – 251
Associate Companions, proposed membership category – 19
Atomic Control – 94
Atomic Scientists at Los Alamos – 126
Back to the land movement, hippies – 178, 206
Beatniks – 166
Beguine movement in medieval church – 3
Black bishop, first diocesan, Burgess (MA) – 156
Black churches, burning of – 129
Black Congresswoman, Shirley Chisholm – 200
Black Consciousness – 204
Black priest celebrating Eucharist at Adelynrood – 81
Black Retreat leaders – 112
Black Supreme Court judge – 188
Black teachers losing jobs – 132
Black Voter Registration Drive – 152
Boyle, Sarah Patton, writer on desegregation – 121, 124, 155, 157-8, 164, 167, 189
Braden, Carl and Ann – 126
Change, in "white certainty"- 196; to see as positive – 198
Chapters, SCHC – 4, 109
Characteristics of US post-civil-war period – 3

China missionaries/ Companions – xxx, 107, 139
Christian education, new Seabury Series Curriculum – 75; revitalization of Adult Education – 107
Christians and Jews in Israel – 137
Christians historically responsible for anti-Semitism – 82
Church League for Industrial Democracy (CLID) – 20, 52
Churchmanship high, low, broad, "but all catholic" – 11
Civil Religion – 178
Civil Rights, consciousness – 92; kneel-ins – 147; church bombing in Birmingham – 156; JFK, MLK Jr. – 145; legislation – 146; march, Selma to Montgomery – 181; bus boycott in Alabama – 130; workers murdered – 161; 1963 March on Washington – 159
Class consciousness – 53
Committee (Temporary) on Furnishings & Decoration – 24
Committee on Artistic Planning, principles established – 78
Communes – 179
Community Action Programs (War on Poverty) – 109, 198
Community of St. John Baptist – 6
Community of St. Mary – 6
Community, print as binding link – 22
Companion Paper, Lee Beaty, on Little Gidding/Nicholas Ferrar – 209-10
Conference format, educating for change – 124
Consensus Historiography, modifying to Social History – 123
Corcoran, Sr. Teresa, author of biography *Vida Scudder* – 260
Corporate Public Stands – 201, 259
Corporate Stands issue – 66-7, 91, 204
Crite, Allan Rohan, painter, *Stations of the Cross* – 151
Critical stance toward Episcopal Church – 16, 22
Cross as symbol, identity – 8, 13
Cultural (external) society) and national change – 173
Culture of art, Della Robbia imports – xiv
Cycle of organizational evolutionary stages – 41, 43
Desegregation, growing awareness of – 120; of US Military, 1948 – 95; of schools, public facilities – 1954; Supreme Court decision – 102, 103, 114; Boston schools – 163; Little Rock AR – 140; sit-ins, kneel-ins – 141
Detroit Industrial Mission – 135, 156, 174, 184

Director of Religious Education (women's church career) – 96; retreats for – 111; role – 186

Displaced (by WW II) persons – 92, 98

Divorce – 153

Donovan, Mary Sudman – 2

Education for Ministry (Sewanee Adult Education program) – 154

Election procedure for SCHC, 1941 (first) – 22

Emergency Prayer Chain – 222, 241

Environment, Alaska pipeline – 205

Environmentalism – 148

Episcopal "denominational idolatry" – 244

Episcopal Church Women, national reorganization – 126; organizations – 57; Triennial, 150

Episcopal Society for Cultural and Racial Unity [ESCRU] – 146, 150, 153, 163, 167, 175, 191, 198

Failure of white Christians regarding race – 196

Feminism – 11

Feminist ideas, influence – 18

Finances – xiv, xv, xvii, xxiv,12, 15, 32, 35-9, 42, 47, 53, 66, 76, 97, 107, 112, 124, 130, 145, 159, 167, 168, 171, 172, 179, 180, 181, 208, 211, 214, 216-18, 221, 231, 235, 236, 248, 250, 252, 254, 258, 261, 264, 270, 271, 277

Finances, alarm about – 179; attitudes toward money – 231; deficit – 32, 33, 38, 93, 100, 190, 195, 208, 211, 220, 221, 246, 251, 252, 258, 264, 271; guidelines for financial goals – 217; Ruth Mary Wilson bequest – 137; socially responsible investments – 217, 252

Franciscans – xxv

Freedom Rides – 152

Gandhi, non-violence – 121

Gardner, Isabella Stewart – xiv, 7, 12

General Convention, Special Program – 191

Generation gap – 183, 200, 207

Gilded Age – xiv, 1

Gothic church – architecture and design, 16; design as late 18th century standard -16

Governor Dummer Academy – xxix

Group Dynamics movement, adult education – 201, 203

Haiti – 152, 193, 255

Healing Conference – 190

Healing service – 92, 111

Hippies – 206

Holiness, personal – emphasis on, 11; EMM emphasis, 20

Hospitality Fund, named for Emilie Hurd – 105

Hospitality houses of EMM – 4, 6 n.14

Housing, improved, for all races – 107; for poor black, 141

Howard, Adelyn, source of retreat house name – 7

Human Rights emphasis – 166

Human sexuality, conference topic – 248

Huntington, VS against corporate stands – 144, 146

Hydrogen Bomb test – 108

Hymnal 1940 (Episcopal) – 141

Immigrants, Mexican, "wetbacks" – 126

Industrial Mission in Boston, Detroit – 135, 184

Inner City work – 135, 140, 148, 184-5, 203, 242, 247

Institutional interracial charter, YWCA, first – 88

Intercession Paper (*IP*), 13, 22, 24; 1937 – 32; intercessory prayer as ground of action – 69; small number of submissions – 136; standards for written petitions – 34

Intercessory praying – 20; broadening horizons in petitions – 74

Interfaith organizations – 84

James, William, philosopher of religion – 7

Jane Addams of Hull House, at Adelynrood – 57

Japanese Christian rebuilding after WWII – 133, 155; reconstruction – 196

Japanese-American evacuees – 81, 83, 86, 87

Jews persecuted in Europe – 82; as refugees – 88, 100

Juvenile delinquency – 147

Kennedy, John F., death – 156

Kerner Report on violence in cities – 193

King, ML Jr. – 192; receiving Peace Prize – 161

Kitagawa, the Rev. Daisuke – 165, 166, 196

"Knowledge of conditions" (Companions' study) – 54

Korean War – 102

Label "Paradise Chapter," first appearance of – 89

Labor Movement – 140

Labor organizations, AFL-CIO – 127

Labor peace – 88, 108

Labor, United Farm Workers – 206

League of Women Voters – 122, 140

Liberia, first "colored Bishop" – 85

Liturgical Renewal – 190; *Prayer Book* and *Hymnal* changes – 174

Liturgy, Trial Prayer Book Revisions – 194

Lynching, condemnation of – 21, 38, 92, 116; of Emmet Till – 122; declared a crime – 141

Marriage, prayer for – 105; inter-racial – 198

Memorials, published in *Annual Reports* – 133

Migrants and sharecroppers, working conditions – 81; migrant labor – 110

Ministry in Higher Education – 196

Mission, World Conference, Edinburgh – 146

Moonwalk – 153

Morgan, Emily M., as leader of SCHC – 30; as Lady Abbess – 32; attitude toward change – xxvii, xxix; childhood faith – 37; family background – 7; genealogy – 5 n.13; 1937 death – 15, 17; determination to engage in "real life" – 68; history as authentication – 20; institution of whisper lunches – 38; 100; 108; monologue from 1920 Annual Letter – xxi-xxx; her 'religious order' – 11; on simplicity – xxix; organizational dream – 25; public relations – 23; resistance to church partisanship – 21; thanksgivings for – 27-28, 36, 39, 84, 95, 108, 184; understanding of Society – xxix, xxx; traditions established by – 142,143; vision of – 135

Morgan, J. P. assumed to be kin – 9; financier and Episcopal churchman – 15

NAACP – 129, 159; and lynching a crime, 21

Narcotics – 108

Negroes excluded from white parishes – 80

Nightingale, Florence – 11

Order of the Holy Cross (male) – 6; the Rev. James Otis Sargent Huntington – 10

Organization, stages of development – 17-23

Ossifying of custom at Adelynrood – 170

Other Religions, study of – 160

Oxford Movement (Buchmanites) – xxiv, 18

Paradise Chapter – 89

Peace Corps – 150

Peace organizations – 199

Peace talks, post WWII – 85

Pearl Harbor, attack on – 80

Planned Parenthood – 95

Prayer Book Revision – 174, 215

Prayer caps, women's white net, for chapel – 130

Prayer Groups, proliferating – 201

Print, the tangible medium of community – 23, 275

Probation, SCHC membership formation – 23, 58-60, 61, 276-9

Psychological focus, emergence in larger culture – 119

Public schools, desegregation of – 152

Race, in church politics – 13; in society – 48; MLK Jr. – 160; racial hate a sin – 160; white moderates' prayer – 149; Freedom Rides – 151; Companions' quest for "prophetic" stance on – 132; Conference, Roots Of Prejudice – 264

Race prejudice in South Africa, Palestine, America – 97; attitudes toward – 105, 110

Race Rioters – 187

Racial injustice, petitions – 73, 82, 83-84

Racial integration – 201

Refugees, Palestinians in camps – 110

Religious orders, "bridge" role for Episcopal Church – 22

Religious orders for women – 10, 86, 94

Religious parties or "camps" – 177

Renewal, blocks to – 218-9

Repeal of Poll Tax – 81

Retreat Movement – 182

Retreats – 18, 24; for wives of clergy – 111;

retreat leaders – 32; 53, 56-58; 101

Roosevelt, Franklin Delano, death – 86; wife Eleanor's leadership – 99, 155

Rynbergen, Henderika, tribute to C-in-C Lindley – 145

Sacramentalism – 10, 13, 16, 19; in first election process – 22-23, 44, 53, 60

Same sex relations – 179

SCHC, as organizational form for women's religious quest – 3; attitude toward organizational change – 35; attitude toward "rules" – 233; call for renewal – 208; 1984 Centennial Celebration – 262; Centennial planning – 250, 253; change in demographics – 147; changing attitude toward Missions – 119; Chapters, emphasis on Chapters – 211; "Sister Chapters" – 223; Companion Day – 147; 1940s-1950s Code of silence about – 90; Companions' quest for "prophetic" stance – 132; comparison with other intercessory organizations – 33; dining room arrangement – 233-4; 1894-1914 early years – 1-13; exclusiveness accusation – 244; first election procedures in 1941 – 40; Guidelines for offices – 161; in-house changes after 1974 – 244-245; modernizing "hospitality" – 248; modernizing rituals – 230; official SCHC prayer – 62; organizational trajectory – 229; policy for Companion-task expenses post-1974 internal dynamics – 233; self-centered 'in-look' – 106; Social Justice conferences, poor enrollment – 130; version of Corporate Life as in "organization man" – 127; views of leadership – 234; Liberia, first "colored Bishop" – 85; views of 1974 Adelynrood closure – 231

School of Religion – 154, 159, 163

Scottsboro boys [poor black illiterate laborers] – 20; victims of racism – 36

Scripture, contemporary Phillips' translation – 74

Scudder, Vida Dutton, (VDS), active in Companionship, 1889-1954 – 4, 48, 96, 101, 135, 137, 142, 143, 146, 181; in CLID (Church League for Industrial Democracy) – 36, 56; determination to be "real" – 68; editing EMM Letters as theology of Companionship – 60; "House of Holiness" (pamphlet) – 10, 53; her Franciscan liturgy – 114, 116; importance in the larger church – 20; life overview – 47-71; professional life, 47- 60; originating process of Probation – 7; 1944 major paper on race – 84; 98; Memorial – 65; 97; 101; paper Per Crucem Gaudium – 62; ten thanksgivings for her life, 114; ed. *Letters to Her Companions, 1944* – 85; Retirement as C-in-C of Probationers – 77; 90th birthday remembrances – 108

Seabury Series – 75, 98, 103, 126, 188, 196

Secretary of Labor, first woman, Frances Perkins – 87

Settlement houses, initiating – 9

Sharecroppers – 186

Sheila-ism – 178

Sisterhoods – 11, 13, 16, 18; patterns of – 44; Women's orders – 5, 149; All Saints – 146

Sisters of St. Margaret – 3, 106, 157; Haiti mission, 125, 187-9, 257

Sisters of St Mary – 13, n40

Slums as emblem of injustice – 15

Smith, Lillian, white Southern writer on race – 99n, 121, 189

Social class privilege – 13, 19

Social Gospel – 48, 63; applied to inner city mission work – 164

Social Justice awareness – 9, 14, 20, 24, 48, 63; issues in – 54, 70; Mississippi Delta Negroes – 190

Social Justice Petitions – 82-5, 107, 110, 113, 115, 159, 208, 212, 214, 217, 241, 243, 274

Social Problems, focus of Companion Study – 33; racial, cultural difference – 114; unrest – 158, 185, 203

Socialism (Christian) – xxxii; 20, 53

South Vietnam – 130

Sputnik – 148

St. Catherine of Siena – 7, 12, 52, 56, 117

St. Francis – xxix, 37, 52, 55; Hymn of (said antiphonally from Adelynrood porches) – 21; Scudder's study of – 117

Stress on "natural" – 179

Suburbs, development after WW II – 105; topic for Spring Conference – 161

Summer Calendar – 144

Taize, post WWII interfaith pilgrimage center – 146, 148, 153, 183, 185

Task Force I – 180, 216, 235; Task Force II – 180, 214; 1974 Recommendations – 180, 222-3

The "me" decade – 178

Theme Committee functions – xxix, 28, 172

Third Order religious associations – 53

Thurman, Howard (The Rev.), chaplain at Howard University – 182, 201, 113

Twing, Mary Abbot Emery, 1880s Episcopal Church women's organizer – 2

Underhill, Evelyn, British laywoman mystic and retreat leader – 2, 140

United Nations – 85, 86; prayers for – 127

United Thank Offering – 127

Urban Industrial Mission – 174

Urban Poverty Programs – 187

Urban Renewal – 201

Vietnam – 202, 206, 207, 246, 253, 258

Vocation, definitions of SCHC – 69

Voter Registration drive – 133, 152, 167, 182, 184

Voting Rights Act of 1973 – 177

War on Poverty – 181

White Christians fear of desegregation – 126

White Episcopal Church culture – 121

William James' 1902 *Varieties of Religious Experience* – 4

Windham House – 95

Wink, Walter (epigraph) – 1

Women as Ivy League (Princeton) undergraduates – 197

Women, as institution builders – 12

Women, caricatured – 200

Women's movement, emerging – 234

Women's ordination – 173, 174, 180, 216

Women's organizations in the Episcopal Church – 57

Women's quest for authority in religious writing – xiv